(Continued)

WRITING SUPERHEROES

CONTEMPORARY CHILDHOOD,
POPULAR CULTURE, AND
CLASSROOM LITERACY

▼ ▼ ▼

Anne Haas Dyson

Teachers College, Columbia University
New York and London

Based on project supported by the Spencer Foundation and by the Educational Research and Development Center Program (R117G10036) as administered by the Office of Educational Research and Improvement, U.S. Department of Education. The findings and opinions expressed in this report do not reflect the position or policies of the Spencer Foundation, the Office of Educational Research and Improvement, or the U.S. Department of Education.

Published by Teachers College Press, 1234 Amsterdam Avenue, New York, N.Y. 10027

Library of Congress Cataloging-in-Publication Data

Dyson, Anne Haas.
    Writing superheroes : contemporary childhood, popular culture, and classroom literacy / Anne Haas Dyson.
        p.   cm. — (Language and literacy series)
    Includes bibliographical references and index.
    ISBN 0-8077-3640-6 (cloth : alk. paper). — ISBN 0-8077-3639-2 (pbk. : alk. paper)
    1. English language—composition and exercises—Study and teaching (Primary)—Social aspects—United States—Case studies. 2. Child development—United States—Case studies. 3. Popular culture—United States—Case studies. 4. Multicultural education—United States—Case studies. I. Title. II. Series: Language and literacy series (New York, N.Y.)
    LB1529.U6D87   1997
    372.62'3—dc21   97-1488

ISBN 0-8077-3639-2 (paper)
ISBN 0-8077-3640-6 (cloth)

Printed on acid-free paper

Manufactured in the United States of America

04 03 02 01 00   8 7 6 5 4 3 2

For Kristin, Louise, Mary Lee "Margaret,"
and all the teachers who have shared their classrooms
with me and us.

Contents

▼ ▼ ▼

Preface

▼ ▼ ▼

I come from ancestors whose brains evolved so far beyond those of all their relatives that speech was the result, and with this in hand they became the masters of the earth, God's image, self-aware, able to remember generations back and to think generations ahead, able to write things like, "in the beginning was the word."... But this kind of talk is embarrassing; it is the way children talk before they've looked around....

L. Thomas, *The Fragile Species,* 1992, pp. 24–25

One Sunday when I was 5, almost 6, I sat in the front of the church just listening to the angels sing. I turned to my big brother sitting beside me in the pew. "I don't know why people don't believe in God," I whispered. "All they have to do is go to church and they can hear the angels sing."

"Those aren't angels." My brother whispered back. "Those are people. Turn around and look." He pointed to the back of the church and gestured upward.

"You're not supposed to turn around in church," I countered. But it was too late. The seeds of doubt were sown.

Later, when the last of the faithful were headed back from the communion rail, my brother whispered again. "There's your angels," he said. "Turn around and look where they go."

So, with one eye on my mother, I did. And there, backward and upward, was a loft. With people in it. Singing. No angels. Just people.

Truth is harder to come by than you think it is, my brother was telling me. There are no obvious angels. Break the rules. Turn around and look.

In this book, the setting is not the church, but the school; the cultural substance is not the supernatural, but the superhero, among other figures of popular culture; and the phenomenon of interest is not childhood spirituality, but childhood literacy. Nonetheless, the book's basic narrative line is captured in that childhood memory: children turning around and looking, situating themselves among humankind. The featured children are learning to compose stories and, in the process, to imagine—and to reimagine—the roles each other might take, and the words they might speak, in an ever-expanding world.

Acknowledgments
▼ ▼ ▼

My own turning around in a wider world has been greatly assisted by family members, friends, colleagues, and students. Here I thank just a few of the people who have given needed nudges and much appreciated support.

To begin, I thank the gracious faculty and staff at the East Bay school site, where I was able to study comfortably and happily over a five-year period. The enthusiasm of Kristin, the courageous teacher featured in this book, kept me enthused, as did, of course, her engaging young students (especially my focal students Sammy and Tina—two grand storytellers who are themselves marvelous stories).

Even when I was young, I was not particularly "with-it" about popular culture, so I am especially grateful to my smart, young, with-it (and very fun) research assistants, without whom a project this complex would have been impossible. Elizabeth Scarboro and Wanda Brooks were my first assistants. They took control of the daily grind of photocopying, organizing, and analyzing children's products; they also began the enormous task of watching, analyzing, and summarizing all the child-referenced popular media programs. Along with studying superheroes and femme fatales, they did extensive literature searches on the popular media and, also, on children's play patterns in integrated schools. As Wanda and, then, Elizabeth moved on to other endeavors, Gwen Larsen and, then, Sheila Shea took over the work, joined for a time by Michael Ford. Gwen and Sheila helped me extend into new areas of scholarship, especially children's folklore and folk stories. They also visited video game arcades, surfed the net for media character info., did battle with the reference list, and tamed all the figures. Margaret Ganahl, secretary-par-excellence in the Language, Literacy, and Culture office, provided much valued production assistance.

From the Spencer Foundation (and Rebecca Barr in particular), I gained critical support for rethinking writing development and its link to sociocultural diversity and childhood identity. (I thank Liz and Herb Simons and Mary K. Healy for helping me seek that support.) Additional financial support came from the U.S. Department of Education, through the National Center for the Study of Writing and Literacy, and from the Faculty Grants Program of the University of California at Berkeley.

Finally, I wish to thank the many others who have helped me venture further out into childhood and literacy. Colleagues have provided unexpected and much appreciated messages of support and encouragement—among others, Michael Apple, JoBeth Allen, Barbara Comber, Allan Luke, Marty Nystrand, Ellen Seiter, Carole Edelsky, and my longtime teacher, colleague, and good friend Celia Genishi. My mother, Athleen Haas, my siblings, Mary, Ruthie (and Peter), Joanne, and, of course, my big brother David, have all had a part to play too. And then there are the many, many fine students who have graced my life at Berkeley; to paraphrase Lena, one of the children herein, were it not for my students, always urging me on, I probably *would* be watching *Barney* (Leach, 1988).

Introduction
▼ ▼ ▼

On the Trail of the Superheroes

[A] new breed of developmental theory . . . will be motivated by the question of how to create a new generation that can prevent the world from dissolving into chaos and destroying itself. I think its central technical concern will be how to create in the young an appreciation of the fact that many worlds are possible, that meaning and reality are created and not discovered, that negotiation is the art of constructing new meanings by which individuals can regulate their relations with each other. . . .

J. Bruner, *Actual Minds, Possible Worlds,* 1986, p. 149

W ith these words, Bruner envisions children as potential superheroes, whose given mission is to save the world from itself. These are superheroes of a special kind, whose force is found, not in the sword, but in the word. And they are the sort of heroes needed to sustain a democracy, people whose transforming gifts bespeak the power of articulated ideas (Greene, 1988; Meier, 1995).

These words seem a bit melodramatic. Certainly small children, vulnerable youngsters, cannot assume responsibility for the world's disarray (although children have long served as symbols of adult hopes and fears [Steedman, 1992]). Still, strong statements are useful for shaking up taken-for-granted ways of thinking, a fact not lost on the child characters who people the literacy drama to be shared herein.

In truth, these children were sometimes superheroes, in two senses. In their creation of imaginary worlds on paper and playground, the children often imagined themselves heroes with powers rooted in accidents of nature or science. Their actions were responses to impending physical doom—most often,

1

the destruction of the world by evil others. But in their own social worlds, children sometimes became superheroes of another sort, ones with powers rooted in social circumstance. Their actions were responses to verbal constraints—they were not intent on saving the adult world, but on engaging in child imagined ones.

Consider, for example, the following classroom scene:

> The boys in Tina's second grade class have been writing stories about ninjas and X-Men (Lee, 1963) to perform in their classroom Author's Theater. Tina and her best friend Holly (both working-class girls of color) have been begging for a role in these stories—for a part to play—with no luck at all. Once in a while, their peer Sammy includes a girl to be rescued but then he picks Melissa or Sarah, both white middle class girls. Seldom is *any* girl chosen to be a tough superhero, a person who saves others, despite the presence of strong women, including women of color, in the X-Men comics and cartoons.
>
> Tina has had it. She and Holly decide to write their own X-Men story for a classroom performance. "And no boys," she says firmly to Holly, "'cause the boys doesn't let us play."

So began one critical event in the unfolding literacy drama in Tina's urban classroom. In this drama, many of her peers used popular cultural symbols—like the media superhero—to achieve a sense of personhood and social belonging, of control and agency in a shared world. In making use of these symbols, children could assume identities within stories that revealed dominant ideological assumptions about relations between people—between boys and girls, adults and children, between people of varied heritages, physical demeanors, and societal powers. These stories reflected the immediate values and interests of some children—but distorted those of others.

Thus, children sometimes became superheroes of another sort, able to take on powerful cultural storylines (Bruner, 1993; Lavie, Narayan, & Rosaldo, 1993). They campaigned for space in seemingly closed stories; they questioned taken-for-granted story characters, plots, and themes. Their powers were limited, however. Change in social and community relations could come only through the complex negotiations that might follow their actions—if the requested space, the voiced questions, and the child superheroes themselves were acknowledged.

The complex plot of the classroom drama to be presented herein came from the interplay among individual child writers, their social companions, and the wider classroom community. These were not young children turned into themselves, engaged in private explorations and creations of written meaning; these were children turned outward, engaged in public performances and text discussions. In their actions and reactions, they made visible to me, the adult observer, the social and ideological possibilities and constraints of child composing as a mediational tool, as a means for learning to "regulate their relations with each other." In this book, I examine the link between learning to compose and learning to be a community participant, and to do so I focus on the social and ideological processes undergirding children's use of media symbols—especially the superhero—as material for constructing textual and social worlds.

THE ADVENTURE BEGINS

The fact that I would compose a book featuring superheroes came as a surprise to me. This project began in the spring of 1993, during an informal visit to an East San Francisco Bay school, a school serving children from different racial and socioeconomic groups and one in which I had been involved since 1989 (for previous project, see Dyson, 1993). A young teacher, Kristin, who was new in the school, had invited me to drop by her room. Just before I did so, I stopped off in a first grade, where I overheard two young boys discussing media characters. They were clearly talking about superhero characters engaged in varied karate moves. But when I asked who exactly these superheroes were, the boys denied their own conversation: They had been talking, they said, about ocean creatures, you know, like dolphins.

After all, "why would anyone want to talk about fighting ninjas in school?" asked one boy.

"Yeah," said the other.

In their classroom, talk and writing about such figures were part of the children's peer-governed or unofficial social world; they were not welcome in the official teacher-governed one. This material, so central to many children's social and imaginative lives, is ideologically unsettling to many adults. As the "ocean discussants" suggested, these stories contain much physical aggression, often embedded in gender-stereotyped plots. For adults concerned about a world on the brink of chaos, these stories hardly seem good child fare.

In addition, as "cultural capital" (Bourdieu, 1973) in the knowledge economy of school, this material is of low value. Professed knowledge of certain symbolic substance—the stuff of school-introduced Greek myths, for example, relative to the stuff of Saturday morning cartoons—may position children within stereotypical class relations, which, in this country are interwoven with those of race (Bakhtin, 1981; Bourdieu, 1984; Buckingham, 1993; Levine, 1988; Willis, 1990). The ocean discussants were proper young men: They certainly did not discuss crude matters like fighting ninjas (at least not in front of teacher-like adults).

Nonetheless, superhero material was strikingly visible in Kristin's second grade room. She had a daily "free writing time," and the openness of that period was one reason why commercial culture became so visible. She also had an optional practice called "Author's Theater," in which children could choose classmates to act out their stories. This practice encouraged the children to bring their peer play life into the official school world and, thus, to also bring the superheroes and other popular media figures. Like many people, young and old, the children appropriated commercial culture as play material, as material for exploring social roles and social identities (e.g., Fisherkeller, 1995; Jenkins, 1992; Moss, 1989).

The charged nature of those media stories—their centrality to children's unofficial social lives, their clear ideological links to societal stereotypes, and their problematic relation to the official school world—made them compelling research material: The children's use of such stories provided an access to the social and ideological dynamics of school literacy learning, including how child composers used cultural material to orient themselves to each other within the institution of school. Thus, I began to observe Kristin's second grade classroom, paying close attention to children's use of media stories. Kristin returned to the school for the children' s third grade year, and so did I, continuing my observations.

To make sense of these observations, I drew on the dialogic vision of language developed by Bakhtin (1981, 1986). In this view, learning to use language involves learning to interact with others in particular social situations and, at the same time, learning to be, so to speak, within the dominant ideologies or "truths" about human relationships; that is, it involves learning about the words available in certain situations to a boy or girl, to a person of a particular age, ethnicity, race, class, religion, and so on.

Thus, our texts are formed at the intersection of a social relationship between ourselves as composers and our addressees and an ideological one between our own psyches (or inner meanings) and the words, the cultural signs, available to us. In Figure 1, the social relationship mediated by the text is represented by the horizontal axis, the ideological one by the vertical axis. The arrows suggest selves who move in sociocultural space, positioned in relationships with diverse others, with different aspects of their own identity foregrounded or muted, with different possibilities for speaking.

Composers, then, are not so much meaning makers as meaning negotiators, who adopt, resist, or stretch available words. For example, in Kristin's class, Sammy was the most consistent composer of superhero tales; by learning to exploit a familiar storyline, a lonely child could affiliate with the boys, few of whom could resist being a tough good guy. But the boys' available words, reflecting dominant ideologies about gender, were resisted by Tina, the classroom's most consistent social activist. She responded to her marginality in their texts by reworking an all-too-familiar storyline. On the edges of media tales were children like Melissa and Sarah; as the literacy drama evolved, they responded by distancing themselves from the unruly players of superhero texts.

[margin annotation: dialogic view of language.]

Figure 1. *Composing as a dialogic process: Its horizontal and vertical dimensions.*

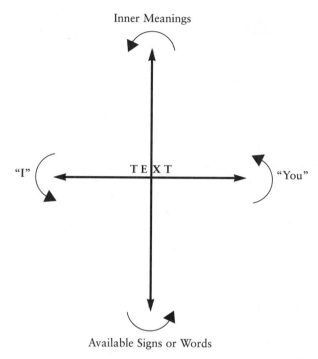

Inner Meanings

"I"   TEXT   "You"

Available Signs or Words

In Kristin's classroom, the Author's Theater functioned as a kind of public forum. In that forum, authors presented their texts and, in so doing, the ideological echoes of those texts could become immediate social voices who "talked back" (hooks, 1990). Moreover, that forum had official rules about respectful listening, an enforced public pressure for fairness, and an instructional focus on composing, which emphasized that texts were crafted and could be crafted differently. Thus, deliberateness about authorial choices potentially could become linked to deliberateness—thoughtfulness—about the classroom community in formation.

As classroom observer, I documented the interplay between individual children's writing processes and products and their participation as social players and community members in their classroom. Along with the children themselves, I learned of their common desires for adventure and action, security and place, power and love. Whatever their particular and collective differences, they could work toward common visions of what was good, be it in a story or a real world. Since this was a human, not a superhuman world, the children did not achieve a "happy-ever-after" ending—human superheroes, unlike some of the commercial variety, are complex, contradictory, and subject to the demands of the moment.

PURPOSE OF THE BOOK

In this book, I intend, first, to add to our understandings of child literacy in a way consistent with a "new breed of developmental theory," to return to Bruner's words. In this new sort of theory, children are not featured only as individual inventors of pre-existent knowledge systems (cf., Piaget & Inhelder, 1969), nor only as novices in adult-guided activities (cf., psychologists inspired by Vygotsky [1962, 1978], e.g., Brown & Palinscar, 1982). Rather, they are active contributors to evolving communities that both draw on and influence larger cultural systems (see also, Corsaro & Miller, 1992; Ochs, 1992).

Moreover, this new breed is not an attempt to provide a reified or detached account of children's development, of "natural" evolution. It is a "motivated" account by adults who hope to have some influence on the developmental projects children adopt. The present motivated account is grounded in the challenges of the historical moment: Ours is an ever-smaller world of ever-increasing sociocultural diversity, a world requiring a developed appreciation of the fragility of human life and of the possibility of reinventing, rewriting, ways of living together.

Thus, through analytic narratives of the literacy actions and reactions of Sammy, Tina, and their peers, I situate child writing within the social and ideological complexity of children's lives and contemporary times. I hope to contribute to and extend sociocultural visions, which portray learning to write as learning to use the medium to participate in cultural life in socially appropriate ways (e.g., Heath, 1983; Moll & Whitmore, 1993; Rogoff, 1990). I illustrate that children's ways of writing are shaped, not only by their interaction in adult-guided worlds, but also by their social goals and ideological positioning in peer-governed ones. Moreover, social identification and social conflicts, not only social interactions, make salient new kinds of writing choices, newly imagined ways of depicting human relationships.

Interwoven with this theoretical intention is a second and pedagogical one: to illustrate how classroom diversity is a potential classroom resource for individual and collective growth. Given this goal, gender, race, class, and other constructed categories must be presented as more than "variables" that may make literacy development problematic (cf., Knapp & Associates, 1995; Needels & Knapp, 1994). They must be constructed as potentially critical aspects of children's sense of, and expression of, self and other.

In forming imagined worlds on both paper and playground, children reveal their sense of the social world; their unfolding stories reflect deeply embedded cultural storylines about human relations (Gilbert, 1994). To become conscious of these ideological assumptions, children, like adults, benefit from the dialogic response of those for whom the world works differently (Greene, 1988, 1993; Perry & Fraser, 1993). Such dialogues themselves benefit from the potential of texts to hold imagined worlds still for joint reconsideration, for reimagination (Freire, 1970).

In Kristin's classroom, these social dialogues occurred intermixed with much social fun—a quality often missing from discussions of diversity and urban schooling. It was the joy of imagining worlds of pleasure and power and, moreover, of performing those worlds that kept the community in formation and individual members engaged. Energized by the desire for inclusion, child superheroes initiated (and a teacher superhero guided) explorations of social fairness—of access to power and pleasure—and, indeed, of the very nature of power and pleasure; at the same time, they experienced the possibilities and the responsibilities of writers.

Finally, an intention both theoretical and pedagogical: I hope this close examination of children's media use will both complement and complicate discussions of children and the popular media. Many adults worry about children's engagement with the popular media's images of power and pleasure, with its depictions of human relations. Discussions of the reasons for these concerns, of their sources in our consumer culture, and possible public remedies are found elsewhere (e.g., Kline, 1993; Levin & Carlsson-Paige, 1994). In most such discussions, children are constructed as victims of current commercial media and potential threats to the future social order. (For rich discussions of adult views of children, see Thorne, 1987; Wallace, 1995; Zelizner, 1985).

And yet, the commercial media are central to contemporary childhood. The media—not adult storytellers (or readers)—provide most U.S. children with their common story material. Thus, herein, I aim to contribute to discussions of contemporary culture by portraying ways in which young children, like their older counterparts (e.g., Fisherkeller, 1995; Jenkins, 1992; Willis, 1990), are active interpreters of the media, who "reconstruct its meanings according to more immediate [social] interests" (Jenkins, 1992, p. 35). Indeed, sometimes children themselves are superheroes who overcome the ideological constraints of media offerings, not to save imagined others, but to live more equitably and/or more harmoniously with real others. Moreover, I aim to argue that educators may both foster and influence these interpretive processes if school curricula are "permeable" (Dyson, 1993)—not impervious—to children's playful appropriations and critical examinations of diverse cultural material. Teachers and, more broadly, communities do have a responsibility to make judgments about, and provide the young access to, valuable cultural products—but they also have a responsibility to attend to those cultural materials children themselves find accessible and meaningful. To fail to do so is to risk reinforcing societal divisions of gender and of socioeconomic class.

PLAN OF THE BOOK

In Chapter 1, I present the conceptual tools—the theoretical lenses—used to shape this analytic study of the social and ideological dynamics of child composing. I present as well a discussion of the methodological tools—the procedures and techniques of interpretive research through which I gained access to the study's rough material, the children's talk and texts, their actions and interactions in and around stories.

In Chapter 2, I set the stage for, and introduce the main characters of, the literacy drama to be presented herein. I first provide a brief tour of the school playground, pointing out the forms of child play (and configurations of child players) visible there. Then, along with the child players, I enter Kristin's classroom; I describe the language arts activities available there, especially the composing period, with its community forum of text, drama, and talk. (The conventions used in the presentation of these transcripts are presented in Table A1 in Appendix A.) Finally, I formally introduce the two focal children—Sammy and Tina; these children were my primary access to, and reference points within, the evolving literacy drama.

Beginning with Chapter 3, I present the drama itself, detailing the interplay between the dynamics of children's classroom lives and the changing nature of their authorial decisions. Chapters 3 through 6 feature children appropriating media superhero stories and, in so doing, constructing and reconstructing their relations as boys and girls, as people of different races and classes, in and out of stories. Chapter 7 features children exploring, not superheroes, but boyfriends and girlfriends. The children's sensitivity to these stories, which could situate them within gender *and* race relations, illustrates both the potential revelatory power of the text and its capacity for silence, for circumvention. (Publishing information and descriptions of all media stories appropriated by the children are included in Appendix B.) Finally, in Chapter 8, I explore the pedagogical implications of this project about childhood identities, ideology, and learning to write. In so doing, I draw on the dialogues of a teacher study group in which both Kristin and I participated (Dyson, 1997). The group grappled with the complexities of permeable curricula, including their own ambivalent feelings about children's cultural materials.

Kristin's means of responding to such material—her pedagogical practices of open-ended composing, public performing, and community discussions—may not yield the same sorts of dynamics in other classrooms populated with different configurations of children. The qualities and consequences of any particular *pedagogical* practice depend on how, as *sociocultural* practice, it engages children's sense of purpose, their linguistic and experiential resources, their motivated grappling with text features and forms (Comber, personal communication; Dyson, 1993; Heath, 1983; Jacob & Jordan, 1993). The practices presented herein, then, are not models but illustrations of children engaged in both learning to write and learning to participate in a complex community of differences, a community in which they were sometimes superheroes.

ON LIMITS AND STRENGTHS

The children featured in this book could have given rise to other empirical but motivated accounts of childhood. For example, the children might have emerged as victims of a society that tolerates poverty, that is uncomfortable with difference (e.g., Children's Defense Fund, 1994; Polakow, 1993). The vision constructed herein is rooted in a way of working that aims to situate children center stage in the world as they see it (Geertz, 1973). Such a way of working has its limits, particularly since ours is not a society that pays close attention to the views of children.

And yet, when observed inside their own fields of action, *child* strengths emerge—strengths born of ordinary human inventiveness and of common-place empathy. Moreover, when that creativity and that social sensitivity are given supervised play in a public forum, they may reveal a new childhood strength—a growing consciousness, deliberateness, about the social conse-quences of words (Bakhtin, 1981; Volosinov, 1973; Vygotsky, 1962, 1978).

These strengths are all needed in a world that, unfortunately, lacks obvi-ous angels, a world where good guys and bad ones can be hard to discern. In the words of another author worried about a world in disarray, this one an educator, Deborah Meier:

> We cannot assume everyone will react the same way to the theory of evo-lution, the "discovery" of America, the Gulf War, or the value of "life-style" choices [nor, I would add, to X-Men (Lee, 1963) or Power Rangers (Saban, 1994)]. Differences make things complicated. But dealing with the compli-cated is what training for good citizenship is all about. . . . [Public schools] could provide an exciting opportunity to use our often forgotten power to create imaginary worlds, share theories, and act out possibilities. This time not just on the playground but in all the varied public arenas in which we meet with our fellow citizens (1995, p. 7).

These powers, these strengths, are all in evidence in the chapters ahead. They are used by young children who are not unidimensional cartoon char-acters, found on a television tube. They are complex, contradictory human ones, found in classroom scenes. Their literacy drama is presented herein in the interest of fostering other such dramas, in other classrooms, where super-heroes of a human sort are waiting for their cue.

▾ 1 ▾

▾

Studying Children's Social and Textual Lives: Appropriated and Disputed Heroes

> It is about the other that all the stories have been composed, all the books
> have been written, all the tears have been shed . . . so that my own memory
> of objects, of the world, and of life could also become an artistic memory.
>
> M. Bakhtin, *Art and Answerability*, 1990, pp. 111–112

Paddy Clarke, the 10-year-old hero of Roddy Doyle's (1993) novel of the same name, wanted to minister to lepers. He'd read a story about Father Damien, the nineteenth-century Belgian missionary who had made lepers his particular cause. Paddy rounded up the neighborhood boys to be his lepers, and he, of course, was Father Damien. "Our Father who art in heaven," he prayed, as each boy "wobbled a bit" (p. 52). And the lepers were properly grateful.

But when Paddy told his parents he had a vocation, they did not react as he expected.

"'Good boy,'" said his mother to him, dry-eyed.

"'[You've been] encouraging this rubbish,'" said his father to his mother, with anger in *his* eyes (pp. 52–53).

And Paddy Clarke's own vision of a good life, appropriated from a loved text, was disrupted.

In the current book, the child characters also are envisioning possible lives by appropriating figures from other people's stories. And, like Paddy Clarke, sometimes their envisionments meet with unexpected responses from flesh-and-blood others. Their appropriated heroes more often come from the media, rather than from written texts, and their peers are sometimes disruptive, rather than cooperative. But the social and ideological processes they experience are, like Paddy Clarke's, illustrative of the dependence of "selves" on "others."

As individuals, Bakhtin explained, we have unique points of view. But, as we look around in a world of diverse others, we experience our own perspective, our own particular place in the world, in dialogue with others—most importantly, flesh-and-blood others—who see us against the landscape behind our backs. Thus, as Bakhtin notes, others are the central figures, or heroes, of our life drama. (Of course, those heroes are sometimes elliptic, like Paddy's parents, who seemingly deemed him unready for whatever was behind his back.)

As story composers, we also imagine "others." Our own lives are always in process; we do not remember their beginning, nor will we remember their end. To experience coherence, to make some holistic sense of the "chaos of events," we use the "ordering ability of language" (Holquist, 1990, p. 84). From remembered voices, we fashion heroes for a world removed from the flux of existence. But these textual others are also offerings to real others: Like Paddy, we reach out to our social companions with our stories, and we wait to see what they make of both the stories and us.

Consider, for another example, the conversation below between Tina and her good friend Holly. They have been talking over the latest story in the classroom grapevine. The heroes—more appropriately, the antiheroes—of that story are Thomas and Aloyse, who have just been suspended for hitting Monique. This story is a way for the girls to try to make sense of being "girls" and, also, to make sense of each other.

> *(Holly states the moral of the classroom story.)*
> HOLLY: You're not supposed to slap girls, 'cause girls are not that strong, like boys.
> TINA: HUH! The yellow girls are. Like you. You just don't know. You can use your strength. But you just don't know you can. I used it before.
> *(Tina is African American; Holly is mixed race—African American and European American—"yellow," in Tina's terms.)*
> HOLLY: I can beat up Aloyse. You saw me beat up Aloy—You saw me slap Aloyse twice.
> TINA: You saw me beat that boy up. Right here.
> *(Tina points to the upper part of her arm, bent at the elbow.)*
> That's your strength. Right there....

HOLLY: I know. I slapped Lawrence.
 TINA: I slapped him and air punched him.
        (Tina acts out her swift moves.)
HOLLY: I slapped him five times and punched him six times.
 TINA: You must really <u>like</u> him. If you punch him and slap him,
        that means you like him.
HOLLY: I <u>hate</u> him! *(distressed)* I was just joking.

The story the children told was, at first glance, a simple one—a story in which boys abuse their superior strength and hit a girl, and suffer the justifiable consequences. But as the story reverberated in the relationship between the real-time girls, that simple story—that coherent text—slipped away. Its words were, in fact, unfinished, open to interpretation and reinterpretation as the two children struggled with their own desires to be seen by each other as both tough and female, desires complicated by ideologies of gender, strength, love, and, in less explicit ways, race and class.[1] "*You* saw *me*" being tough, say the girls to each other before Holly denies her own tale: A serious punch—in contrast to an airpunch—may become a teasing "love tap" in children's cultures.

In this book, I explore how children's composed stories were shaped at one and the same time by their social goals, their need for social belonging, and by their ideological positioning, their need to define a place for themselves in a society crisscrossed with difference. Tina and her peers used crafted words to form textual worlds they hoped would appeal to their friends. But those words could slip away from them, when other community members interpreted them differently. This engagement in social negotiation—sometimes social conflict—mediated by slippery words supported children's more deliberate construction of both textual and social worlds. And sometimes, in the midst of such struggles, children became, in *my* eyes as author, superheroes, with the power to transform the usual storyline.

In the following sections, I discuss key theoretical concepts and methodological tools that shaped the dialogic drama to come. First I consider theoretical constructs related to children's use of social play, popular culture, and text itself. I then explain the interpretive methodology used to gain access to the children's words and worlds.

WRITING AS PLAY WITH GIVEN WORDS: A FRAMEWORK FOR STUDYING SUPERHEROES

Like Paddy, Tina, and Holly, children spend much intellectual and social energy trying to figure out how to position themselves among others in the world. Should they, or should they not, identify with a Father Damien? a victimized girl? a tough boy? They answer such questions, not by turning inward to listen to some inner voice, but by turning outward, by listening to, and appropriating, the voices around them. Language, then, is not a transparent medium, a window to the soul, but, rather, a medium through which the self is constructed.

In the following, I first consider how children's play with available voices, whether on playground or paper, fosters a sense of social identity and belonging. Second, I consider the particular nature of the popular media, including superhero stories, as play material. Third, I discuss the potential contribution of writing to children's consciousness of the social and ideological tensions of play with given words. Deliberately participating in such struggles links learning to be an author with learning to be a community member.

Social Identity and Social Play

The essence of play is the creation of imaginary situations (Franklin, 1983; Vygotsky, 1978).[2] In this play, children are "free" from the constraints of concrete objects, real actions, and, indeed, from their own voices. They infuse their own intentions—their own meanings—into those objects and actions. Their voices both declare and deny themselves. "I am the mommy," says a young child and, despite herself, acts accordingly. In such ways, children begin to make conscious, willful choices, to rise above, as it were, situational constraints.

But, Vygotsky observed, the freedom of play is "illusory" (1978, p. 103). Children rise above situational constraints and subject themselves to cultural meanings. Thus, their make-believe play, whether on playground or paper, reveals their knowledge of "classes of individuals and their relations, of categories and types of goals, of the possible actions and sequences of actions that can be employed to accomplish these goals" (Garvey, 1990, p. 81).

Such taken-for-granted knowledge allows children to negotiate a shared world, in which each player has a clear identity, a place among others. For example, to enact family scenes—or, for that matter, X-Men ones—children must deliberately act on their understandings of the requirements of such a role. Child players must agree that babies need mothers, the desired need suitors, and, of course, good guys need bad guys.

In this way, child players may resolve the ambiguity and lability of everyday experience in the articulation of more unified selves, defined in opposition to unified "others" (James, 1993; Scott, 1988; Walkerdine, 1990). The "us" and the "them" so constructed have social ramifications both in and out of stories. Inside their stories, child players may become highly stereotyped characters: Babies, as Garvey (1990, p. 87) notes, "do not (cannot) say 'Goo Goo.'" And outside the stories, children may have to negotiate their own rights to be those characters.

The right to appropriate "pretend" identities in social play hinges on children's "real" ones, so to speak. As Bakhtin explained, language is a "living ideological thing" precisely because it does not come from dictionaries but from other people in other situations (Bakhtin, 1981, p. 293); words "taste" of these situations and of the version of social reality—the ideology—implicit in those situations. In these versions, not anyone can be somebody's mommy, an X-man's teammate, or a victim-in-distress worth saving.

Thus, social enactment of stories involves complex negotiations of identity, which themselves raise issues of inclusion and exclusion. "We already have all the parts," the children in the story might say to an outsider wanting to play too. Through such rejections, children may protect their fragile story space from disruption (Corsaro, 1985). But they may also ward off others who do not fit their visions of who can and cannot play certain roles.

Still, play is about desire and pleasure—about possible roles in possible worlds. Play creates a space between child intentions and physical reality and, in this space, children do not always follow blueprints for cultural action. They improvise and, in fact, sometimes deliberately violate expectations for certain words and acts just for the joy of it (Franklin, 1983; Garvey, 1990; Opie & Opie, 1959). Moreover, speech itself exists in a space between children's present time emotions and images—their meanings—and the words others have given them, their linguistic reality, as it were (Bakhtin, 1981). This in-between space can be a place in which willful, contemporary children can infuse new possibilities into old words and worlds. But such ideological transformations are inseparable from social ones, as seen when children—like Paddy and Holly—find that their desires and pleasures meet unexpected responses from others.

Popular Culture and Unpopular Play

For both children and adults, media stories may provide images and events that fuel imagination and interaction (e.g., the "trekkie" fan clubs, inspired by the television series *Star Trek* [Jenkins, 1992]). Indeed, much of common or popular culture is produced in the social use of commercial culture (Willis, 1990). Young children seem especially drawn to media stories that tap into themes already deeply embedded in "the immortal . . . dramas of children's folk culture": "chase–escape, attack–defend, escape–capture" (Palmer, 1986; Sutton-Smith, 1995, p. 281).[3] Superhero stories in particular allow children to feel powerful in a (pretend) danger-filled world.

The media scholar Stephen Kline (1993) traces contemporary superheroes back to the characters featured in nineteenth-century action–adventure stories for children, stories that marked our society's turn from moralistic to more entertaining literature for the young. These stories contain the mythic elements of powerful men—cowboys, pioneers, soldiers, policemen—triumphing against evil, armed with moral righteousness, as well as with human strength and technological tools.

As Kline notes, many recent superheroes in comics and cartoons have been influenced by science fiction and, more generally, by our society's emphasis on technology. Both good and bad guys have bodily and technological powers rooted in alien worlds. The human motivation for the conflicts between good and evil often is not clear: those possessed of the power to blow the world to smithereens seem inevitably to plan to use that power; those possessing the superhuman capacity to thwart their efforts inevitably do so.

Parents, educators, and others concerned with such stories often cite their blatant links to toy marketing, their repetitive story lines, their gender and race stereotypes, and, most especially, their violence (for an especially coherent, incisive critique, see Levin & Carlsson-Paige, 1994). Although some recent superhero teams do include women and people of color, most superheroes are "Aryan type[s]"; in their account of the toy industry, Stern & Schoenhaus (1990, p. 179) quote a television producer, who explained that "you have very little time to tell your story, and you don't have time to get bogged down. You can't deal with a short, dark character as the hero without taking more time to set it up."

There is also concern that superheroes, unlike the powerful heroes of Greek mythology, tend to display neither human vulnerabilities nor human powers; muscles, machines, and magic are the secret of keeping catastrophe at bay— and of marketing associated action toys to small boys (Anderson, 1984; Carlsson-Paige & Levin, 1991; Charren, Szulc, & Tchaicha, 1995; Kline, 1993). Commercial marketing strategists emphasize physical action and technological dazzle when targeting boys, unlike the physical beauty and soft feelings usually emphasized when targeting girls. Moreover, argues Kline, there are few "points of contact with reality and with the social dilemmas associated with the child's experience" (1993, p. 135).

And yet, in their playful enactment, these stories do have "points of contact with ... the social dilemmas associated with the child's experience." After all, children often play stereotypical roles, gender and racial divisions are common on school playgrounds (even when not specifically organized by adults), and physical aggression run amuck accounts for many a small body seen unhappily "benched" during playtime—or, like Thomas and Aloyse, suspended from school altogether (Finkelstein & Haskins, 1983; Opie & Opie, 1959; Opie, 1993; Thorne, 1993). (And, it should be noted, the "quality," school-promoted literary stories are also subject to ideological critiques, especially those involving stereotyping [Apple, 1993; Gilbert, 1989; Kohl, 1994; Luke, 1994; Sims, 1982]).

Further, commercial culture often does become semiotic material for making sense of social experience. Since commercial culture is not reified, not set apart for study in schools or museums, it is widely available and widely appropriated for what Willis (1990, p. 21) calls a "grounded aesthetics"—a creative process through which the meanings provided by commercial culture are not reproduced but reworked. In this process, meanings are "selected, re-selected, highlighted, and recomposed" to make some statement about individuals' views of themselves and their social worlds (Willis, 1990, p. 21).

Given this process, contemporary cultural studies, like dialogic literacy theory, emphasize that the meaning of any symbol is not in the form itself but emergent in the social field in which the symbol is incorporated and within which it resonates (Hall, 1981; Storey, 1993). Similarly, theories of contemporary selves emphasize that identities themselves are fluid, shifting as their semiotic offerings mediate relations with diverse others in the course of everyday life (Bakhtin, 1981; Lemert, 1993; Roasaldo,1989; Williams, 1991).

For Kristin's children, the media did provide potential semiotic material for a "grounded aesthetics." The children appropriated elements of media source material for social affiliation and social play in the unofficial or child-controlled spheres of school. Moreover, the ideological assumptions of appropriated stories generated social resistance, from those denied access to certain "fun" roles, and social distancing, from those who viewed such fun as disreputable, especially in the official school world.[4] The fluidity of children's identities—their desire to both defy and conform to dominant images, evident in Tina's airpunches and Holly's "joking"—could potentially fuel the reworking of these stories.

However, in their play in the unofficial peer world, the children's understandings about human actions and relations, about the nature of power and love, were more implicit than explicit. Indeed, in such play, most children's ideological assumptions are "written"—made visible—primarily in their words and actions as they engage in activities, not discursively recorded or explicitly critiqued (Corsaro, 1992).

Moreover, school age children prefer to play with "others" viewed as like themselves; thus, in multiracial schools, their play tends to be segregated by gender and, especially as they grow older, by race as well (Boulton & Smith, 1993; Finkelstein & Haskins, 1983; Fishbein, 1992).[5] Among similar others, social spats and quarrels occur—but ideologically informed conflicts are less likely. Indeed, commercial culture is useful precisely because there is no need to detail the pleasures of being a certain character; these are well-known and generally agreed on by regular playmates.

In Kristin's class, learning to deliberately manipulate textual material—composed words or symbols—in order to deliberately assert, resist, or rework both ideological "truths" and social relations was fueled by the *interplay* of unofficial and official worlds and, more particularly, by the organizational structures and literacy events of the classroom composing time. In this permeable but official context, the children were more apt to interact with others who experienced the social world quite differently—and they were also more apt to receive guidance on the possibilities of constructing textual worlds quite differently.

The Interplay of Textual and Social Spaces

For the most part, students of children's literacy development have not stressed the fluidity of cultural symbols or human identities, offering instead more stable, more fixed, and, in some cases, more dualistic (e.g., "mainstream" and "nonmainstream") visions of both. However, influenced by Vygotsky (1962, 1978, 1987), those working from sociocultural perspectives *have* stressed the inextricable link between children's literacy learning and their participation in community activities.

Vygotsky, like Bakhtin, emphasized that children's consciousness is appropriated from, and exists only in response to, a social world. It is from others that children acquire the oral signs—and other symbolic forms—that they use to interact with and about the world. The gaps between child and adult understandings of those appropriated signs become interactive spaces in which common meanings for signs are negotiated—and membership in a community of sign-users gained. Children, as Vygotsky said, "grow into the intellectual life of those around them" (1978, p. 88).

This process is even more complicated—or, more accurately, more abstract—in learning to write. In Vygotsky's view, child speakers appropriate words that name an experience physically shared with others, signs that later become a means for inner thought, for "inner speech." But child writers must grapple with that newly emergent inner speech, those words saturated with shared experience; to participate in a writing activity (e.g., to compose a letter, a report, an essay or story), they must reflect on and consciously choose signs that will help them organize and articulate their inner thoughts. The spontaneous activity of speaking must become the more "volitional" (Vygotsky, 1987, p. 204), more deliberate act of rendering meaning through societal signs and, most especially, through written words.

From this point of view, then, the process of becoming literate involves learning to deliberately manipulate language—specifically, the letters and words of the written system—in order to participate in culturally valued literacy events (e.g., Dyson, 1989b; Gutierrez, 1993; Heath, 1983; Moll & Whitmore, 1993; Wertsch, 1991). Through involvement in literacy activities with others—and through their own efforts to participate in such activities, children learn who reads or writes what, to whom, when, why, how, and, of course, for what reason. Adults and more expert others "loan" children their own consciousness about language and language use (Bruner, 1986, p. 175); they thus negotiate the developmental gap, helping children to choose, encode, and reflect on their written choices. In pedagogical discussions of writing, there are many visions of children as "apprentice" journalists, novel writers, and researchers in classroom "learning communities," getting guidance from adults and from each other as well (e.g., Graves, 1983; Rogoff, 1994).

From a Bakhtinian point of view, though, children's written language learning is not only enacted through helpful relationships; part of children's developmental challenge is to learn to manipulate relationships, to achieve particular responses from others, through the written medium. Among those most amenable to children's manipulations are, in fact other children (Corsaro & Miller, 1992; Daiute, 1993; Dyson, 1989b). Children's responses to each others' symbolic acts imbue those acts with social meaning, and it is the sense of a functional goal—of participating in some social communion—that organizes and drives the symbolic process.

Moreover, from this perspective, communities—and the words their members use to mediate their relationships—are much more contested, much more conflicted sites for language use. In addition to *developmental gaps* between children and more knowledgeable others, and *interactional gaps* between composers and their addressees, there are also *ideological gaps* between community members—gaps that reveal larger fault lines in societal power (i.e., in control over symbols and their interpretation). Children struggle to use written signs to bring order to their own inner thoughts and simultaneously to reach out to addressed others. But their signs are themselves symbols of societal order—they are public signs, drenched in community experience, not just the child's social experience.

As Volosinov, a colleague of Bakhtin, explained, communities sharing words are socially divided—they encompass different "social interests" (1973, p. 93). Thus, social struggle is implicit in language use. Volosinov, influenced by Marx, was referring to class struggles, but these same processes reveal many different kinds of social struggles, including those linked to religion, race, ethnicity, and gender (Clark & Holquist, 1984). For example, in this chapter's opening vignette, Paddy's declared vocation—and his choice of Father Damien as an appropriated hero, a valued cultural symbol—positioned him in an immediate social situation that itself reflected and refracted a larger societal one, one in which religious truths and spiritual callings could not be taken for granted.

Related fates awaited Sammy, with his penchant for physically aggressive male superheroes, and Tina, who sometimes longed to be a tough "bad guy." Their chosen heroes reflected the interests and values of some members of the classroom community—and refracted those of others. Thus, in reaching out to particular others, children *chose* their words from those available to them, from those *given;* and the ideological content of those words positioned them in a contested world. (Figure 1 in the Introduction graphically depicts these social and ideological dimensions of language use.)

In the observed classroom, the laborious process of making speech visible in and for the company of others supported child reflection on and planning of imagined worlds. Moreover, enacting those worlds in public dramas allowed children to crawl into the spaces of those stories, to examine them from the inside by playing and replaying them (Paley, 1980; Palmer, 1986; Rosen & Rosen, 1974; Wagner, 1991). And public discussions of text allowed children to hold those worlds still so that they could be jointly reconsidered, and jointly re-examined (Freire, 1970). The children interactively experienced a textual space—a space in between their desires and their realities, their own viewpoints and those of others, and a space where words could simultaneously create coherence and disruption.

Thus, to meld Vygotskian and Bakhtinian concepts, in Kristin's "free" writing activities, the act of writing was interconnected with—became a means of more deliberately enacting—social play.[6] With the guidance of their teacher, the children reflectively engaged in what they were already doing in that play: making decisions about named characters, their described qualities and actions, based, in part, on their social sensitivities and cultural knowledge. In the public forum, social and ideological "gaps" could potentially become matters of authorial choice and critical literacy in a more "open and inclusive community" (Edelsky, 1991; Freire, 1970; Green, 1993, p. 194; Greene, 1988).

Certainly writing events are not the only sorts of social activities through which children might be guided to more deliberate use of words or other "organized material [symbolic] expression," to use Volosinov's definition of consciousness (1973, p. 84; John-Steiner, 1985; Watson-Gegeo, 1992). But in our society such events constitute a major source of such reflection—or so they should or could. In organizing speech on paper for flesh-and-blood others, children may more "deliberately structure the web of meaning" (Vygotsky, 1962, p. 100). And, when their stories, filled with imagined others, are presented to those outside their usual social circles, those new addressees may startle them with unanticipated responses.

Thus, in a complex community of differences, child composers' more differentiated understanding of their social worlds may be dialogically related to their more differentiated understanding of their textual worlds. Indeed, Bakhtin (1981) argued that becoming alive to the socioideological complexity of language use was critical to becoming a responsible, a responsive, composer and, potentially, a more playful composer too, able to use a diversity of social voices, of perspectives, in articulating one's "own" ideas.

As author of this chapter, I am providing (or so I hope) a diversity of social voices—those of "real" and "imagined" children, of present and past scholars—to try to bring forth my "own" notion of what a dialogic perspective on literacy learning entails. In the book as a whole, I describe how flesh-and-blood children appropriated imagined media figures, among other "popular" others;

through these means, I hope to illustrate the social and ideological processes—processes like affiliating with others, resisting them, or negotiating with them—which undergirded the link between literacy learning and community membership in an urban classroom.

The observed children were young and complex, their social needs and sensitivities changing over time and across situations. They were not "mastering" how to be a community participant, any more than they were "mastering" how to write. But collectively they were entering a more complex social and cultural dialogue. The interplay between individual and collective social and textual actions—and the exploits of particular child heroes and sometime superheroes—comprise the narrative stuff of the literacy drama to come.

MEANS FOR CONSTRUCTING A LITERACY DRAMA: SITE, DATA, AND INTERPRETIVE TOOLS

To construct this literacy drama about children and their composing of stories and social lives, I used interpretive methodology as conceptualized, in particular, by Geertz (1973, 1983, 1988). He has studied the role of symbols and symbol-making in collective life. He asks why certain symbolic materials and rituals matter—how they "color" the way in which people make sense of their daily lives. To find answers, he pays attention to the mundane details of particular lives, trying to "locate in the tenor of [a symbol's setting] the sources of [its] spell" (1983, p. 120).

Geertz studies "exotic" locations—Balinese corners and Moroccan pastures, not local schoolhouses and playgrounds. He has tried, in the main, to convey the "imaginative universe" of people called "Balinese" or "Moroccan" (Geertz, 1973); he writes about *a* culture, not about "border zones ... in motion" (Rosaldo, 1989, p. 27), zones that might be formed around borders of age, gender, race, ethnicity, and class, among other possible differences. His focus is on a community's shared meanings for traditional symbols, not on contemporary symbols whose meaning pointedly is not shared.

However, a focus on diversity, on communities whose shared meanings must be negotiated, whose plurality must be attended to, is necessary to understand the experiences of many children in our society's schools. Like this project's site, big city schools in particular are increasingly "high poverty" (i.e., more than half of a school's families qualify for the federal school lunch program) and increasingly "segregated" (i.e., most of a school's students are children of color [Orfield, 1993]). The project school is unusual, though, in that it also serves a substantial percentage of white, predominantly middle-class students.

As Geertz notes, one can "study different things in different places" (1973, p. 23); and, given its diverse population, the project school was an ideal place in which to newly examine the link between community participation and literacy learning. Unlike studies in more homogeneous communities (e.g., Rogoff, 1994), the children in this school made visible what may remain invisible (but not absent) in less diverse rooms: the processes linking learning to use a symbol system and negotiating one's social and ideological place in both the local community and, more broadly, in the society sustained by that system.

Project Site and Participants

I first began working in the project school in 1989, drawn by the striking diversity of its children as well as the strength of another of its teachers (see Dyson, 1993). I entered that school already interested in the interplay between children's social lives and their literacy learning (e.g., Dyson, 1984, 1985, 1989b). But, in this school, studying child literacy in the context of child social relationships brought into the viewing frame interrelated issues of gender, race, class, and culture. It was a school in which there were sharp contrasts in children's backgrounds and, moreover, one in which there were clear connections between race and class.

The school then served children from two neighborhoods. The school building is in a predominantly European American, working- and middle-class community, which stretches to the northeast and borders the campus of a prestigious university. But the school's children came in the main from a poorer neighborhood, predominantly African American, which stretches to the southwest and to the borders of the next municipality. During the school year in which this project began, 45% of the children were identified on parental enrollment forms as African American, 31% as White, 13% as Mixed, and then there were small percentages of children from many different racial and ethnic heritages, among them Chinese, Korean, Mexican, and Native American. Approximately 59% of the children qualified for the federal school lunch program.

The school's service area, encompassing the neighborhood children and bussing in those from the poorer section of town, reflected the school district's attempt to integrate the schools. The plan dated back to the late sixties, when the district was one of the first in the country to attempt racial integration. The schools for the youngest children (kindergarten to third grade) were in middle-class neighborhoods, and the children from poorer, predominantly minority neighborhoods were bused in. The pattern reversed itself for the older elementary school children (fourth to sixth grade).

The plan did not work as envisioned, because of the flight of more affluent White parents to private schools (especially as their children grew older). As detailed in a study of parent–teacher relationships at the project school site (Conrad, 1994), distrust existed between parents from the differing neighborhoods, as well as between parents and teachers. Kristin, the classroom teacher, felt this social division permeated her classroom experience. In her words, taken from her comments to the teacher study group:

> The strange thing about [my school] is that you have this huge differ-ence between the kids, because some of the kids are bused in and some of the kids are neighborhood kids. And you have the really powerful ... parents [who closely monitor your curriculum] and then you have the parents you don't see at all.... The African-American kids took the bus together, went home together, [and] their parents knew each other. And the White kids were the same way. They had slumber par-ties together. And the mixing just didn't happen on any real level, and it was hard to work with.

Kristin herself was a young teacher, in her late twenties. She earned her teaching credential at the University of California in San Diego, whose cre-dential program emphasizes learning to teach in diverse, urban communities; and she also had a Masters from the University of California in Berkeley, which is where I first met her. Her first teaching experiences, with 11- to 12-year-olds from diverse backgrounds, strengthened her interest in the power of the creative arts, especially poetics and drama, to engage students in learning about their present selves and their collective cultural heritages.

I was not surprised, then, that Kristin had started an Author's Theater as part of her daily composing time. I was surprised, however, by the preva-lence of popular culture. Kristin, as her young students knew, did not even own a television—but she was interested in what they were interested in, as, of course, was I.

Kristin became the teacher of the 28 children in her second grade in March of the school year and, then, kept her class through their third grade year. I began observing shortly after she had arrived and also returned in the third grade. Tables A2 and A3 give the totals by sex and ethnicity of the composite makeup of Kristin's second and third grade classes, respectively. Pseudonyms and demo-graphic information for each child can be found in Table A4. Although I came to know all the children, I required guides into and through the social com-plexities of their classroom lives, and I found such guides in Sammy and Tina.

In his advice book for ethnographers-to-be, Agar observes, with the utmost common sense, that "inarticulate people who have poor recall and who don't get around the community much, would be poor choices [as guides or infor-mants] to work with. It's good to remember, too, you're looking for a teacher with whom you have a rapport" (1980, p. 89). Sammy and Tina, both African American, were articulate people, who got around the classroom community quite a bit, and who were comfortable with me following them around.

For both, popular "others" from commercial culture were central to their ways of participating in the social and literate activity of the daily composing time. Sammy was the most prolific writer of superhero stories; moreover, he was explicit about his use of these stories for social affiliation. On the other hand, Tina persistently sought inclusion in such stories; as in her conversation with Holly, she was explicit about the ideological basis of her social resistance (although, of course, she did not use words like "ideological basis"; she used words like "fair" and "you *can* [do that, be that, write that]").

Throughout the project, these children, along with Holly in the second grade, and Lena in the third, were key players in the classroom drama evolving through and around media figures. And, since each interacted with many children in the class, they were my access—and also my reference points—for the wider classroom drama. By tracing the "social history of [their] imagination[s]," as reflected in their actions as writers, social players, and community members, I aimed to gain insight into the concrete particulars of the theoretical abstractions about dialogue, diversity, and development (Geertz, 1983, p. 98).

Data Collection

To probe the dialogic nature of child writing amid human diversity, I focused on the actions and reactions of Sammy and Tina to each other, to their social companions, and, more broadly, to the evolving community. The individual cases, then, were understood as not only embedded within a classroom context, but also as intertextually linked to the evolving case of the classroom community as a whole. "Both children and contexts change," as Gaskins, Miller, and Corsaro explain (1992, p. 13), "reconstituting one another as children grow older." Thus collected data included that gathered within the case boundaries of individuals (e.g., composing events) and, also, within those of the classroom community as a whole (e.g., Author's Theater events).

This classroom community, as earlier noted, was not so much selected as stumbled on. The project began during informal school visits in April of the children's second grade year and then became a formal occasion for systematic data collection through June. After a summer and fall of watching cartoons and videos, reading comics and superhero trading cards, and seeking out the haunts of comic book fans—a crash course, immersion-style, in the stuff occupying so many children's imaginations—I returned to the school in December of the children's third grade year and, once again, stayed through June.

During the periods of classroom observation, I gathered data from one to five times weekly, for a total of 2 to 5 hours per week; the exact number was dependent on what might be called narrative contingency. For each child, I aimed to follow the social history of a written text from its beginnings until its eventual presentation to the class; to do so, I observed on consecutive "free" writing days. During each observation, I made handwritten notes and, also, audiotaped the focal child's composing event; each event included all child talk and other nonverbal action during the production of a text on 1 day. The audiotapes were transcribed after each day's observation and annotated, using the observation notes.

Sometimes the demands of my teaching schedule or unexpected changes in Kristin's schedule interfered with such observational contingency. In that event, Kristin provided information from her own perspective on the child's activity. I alternated between observing Sammy and Tina; Tina, though, missed school frequently, and, in her absences, I followed Holly (in the second grade) and Lena (in the third).

To trace the interplay between individuals' actions as writers, peers, and community members, I gathered varied types of data from the class as a whole. I audiotaped all observed Author's Theater events (each event involved a child author's presentation and, then, a class discussion of that text). I followed the children out onto the playground and made notes about who played what with whom during recess. I collected *all* children's written products produced during the composing period throughout the project (124 in the second grade, 302 in the third), in order to know who wrote about what. And, as the project progressed, I talked informally with children about their attraction to media figures and, also, about whether or not their parents allowed them to watch certain cartoons. I talked extensively with Kristin as well; she confirmed and extended my own information through regular discussions with both parents and children.

Finally, with the help of research assistants, I examined the commercial media programs referred to by the children, focusing especially on the roles of male and female characters. All media productions that figure in prominent ways in the literacy drama to come were watched by at least three people (i.e., by me and two assistants). In the second grade, the children's popular media stories focused on ninjas (both the human and mutant turtle varieties) but, in time, those ninjas were overtaken by X-Men, superheroes with mutant powers found in comic books, videotapes and games, trading cards, and, most accessible of all, Saturday morning cartoons. In the third grade, we had to watch new productions: Some boys (including Sammy) became interested in the Power Rangers (among other new shows), and a number of girls began to write about movies featuring romance—among them were films marketed primarily to adults (e.g., *Jungle Fever* [Lee, 1991]) as well as those marketed to children (e.g., *Aladdin* [Musker & Clements, 1992]).

"We're doing *research*," my assistants would tell the curious as they huddled in my closet-office to watch *Biker Mice* (Unger, 1994), *Three Ninjas* (Chang & Turteltaub, 1992), or some other unusual academic fare. There was reason to explain themselves, since we are judged by what we confess or declare to watch. In fact, at least one of the children wondered about my own media tastes.

Lena, new to the third grade, asked me one day if I watched a certain show she liked. I did not, I told her. Later, on that same day, I sat silently beside Lena, Sammy, Aloyse, and Lettrice for about 30 minutes as they planned a playful story—one in which every child in the class was going to have a role, even if it was only to be a roll. (Classmates were designated as royalty, servants, food, and furniture.) As the group play was coming to an end, Lena brought me quite unexpectedly into the fun.

"You watch *Barney*, huh?" she said to me. She found this quite funny and laughed hard. She said it again, louder, to the other children: "Anne watches *Barney*."

I suppose a quiet woman with an unconditional smile could indeed be one who watches *Barney* (Leach, 1988), a preschool program known for its unconditionally loving lead character, a dinosaur (which is just what a middle-aged woman could feel like, watching children). Interestingly, though, the other children seemed as startled as I was by the comment; and Sammy and Liliana told this new girl that she wasn't supposed to talk about me. I felt defended.

This incident, I think, suggests both the delicacy of my situation and also my dependence on the good will and kindness of the child heroes of my drama, especially Sammy, Tina, and their friends. Young children, of course, are used to being watched, and children of color have mainly White women, like me, for teachers. But this project focused particularly on issues of diversity, on conflicts with ideological roots. I did not want to be a "Big Anne," analogous to Corsaro's (1985) "Big Bill," who played along with the children. I wanted to be just as I felt, a curious, rather ignorant but very non-threatening person, who wished to witness their goings on. (In this, I did share relational goals with Corsaro.)

To establish a place for myself, I relied on being regularly present, unobtrusive, quiet, and too "busy" to help children with their work, but never too busy to smile, acknowledge their presence, and say "hi." I also relied on the legitimacy conferred on me by Tina and Sammy, two children too involved with their peers to let me interfere with their doings, but pleased nonetheless with my interest.

To maintain this relationship between nonthreatening adult and child informant, I did not formally interview the children about their friends, their teachers, or their writing. I depended on my observations, on their increasingly frequent side-comments to me, and also on occasional quiet conversations when they found themselves without a child companion and engaged in some nontaxing activity, like recopying an old written draft or coloring in a drawing. (Coloring can be a rocking-on-the-front-porch activity, a calming activity that gives rise to comfortable conversation.)

On these occasions, as will be evident, both Tina and Sammy commented explicitly on their ongoing relations with others and, when relevant, on matters of gender and race. On these occasions too, I was sometimes reminded of the potential impertinence of questions that do not grow directly out of a child-initiated conversation with a "friend"; even more impertinent are questions that deny the researcher's own identity and own relationship with the "informant."

For example, one day Tina told me about how angry she was at her friend Makeda, which led to comments on her own size (too tiny to be scary to Makeda or anyone else), which led to talk about her "all Black" daddy (who was small like her), her "mulatto" mother, whose own mother was Cherokee and Black but who had a White father. All Tina knew about that White grandpa was that "he loved to eat salami—no baloney. Baloney, baloney. He died before I was born." (This was some conversation.) I then asked her, before I thought what I was doing, if most of her friends were Black. (I had only seen her play with African-American children.) She said they were. But then she thought again. "I got White and Black friends. You're one of 'em." I knew that.

Data Analysis

In data collection, the holistic experience of being in Kristin's classroom became fragmented—it became typed records of children's words and actions, written remains of composing events, and descriptive summaries of the media productions themselves. In data analysis, coherence needed to be restored: Consistencies in children's actions and reactions needed to be identified and named, narrative movement needed to be plotted in the individual and class data, and key incidents needed to be found that could bring together these different strands of data and reveal the links between textual and social action. Moreover, in this "searching for a coherency," it was important not to "hid[e] the contradictions and instability," the messiness, of human experience (Wolf, 1992, p. 129).

To construct a coherent interpretation of the social and ideological dynamics of the children's composing, I needed to develop a set of categories, a kind of analytic vocabulary for naming and describing the children's actions and reactions. I analyzed the content and interactional structure of the child talk accompanying and surrounding their writing. Through this inductive analysis, I developed a vocabulary for discussing the kinds of social goals evident in the children's interactions and, also, the ways in which written texts served those goals (see Table A5).

Among the children's *goals* were affiliating with others, resisting others, distancing oneself from them, or, more equitably, negotiating with them. These goals were evident in official composing time events, those organized and governed by the teacher. Nonetheless, they emanated from the child-controlled unofficial world underneath and accompanying the official one, a social world that "provides [children] with a sphere of autonomy" (King, 1987, p. 149). Indeed, because the children's writing actions were organized and guided by both the official and unofficial world, the free writing period was a prime site for the display of children's negotiated identities as students and as peers (Dyson, 1993).

At first, however, many children made minimal use of writing itself to accomplish their social goals. The *function* of their texts was primarily to serve as a prop for (or, more accurately, as a "ticket" to) the theater; texts were largely invisible—children stood up and pretended to read texts that were not actually written. The children relied on oral language—and sometimes drawing in their writing books—to represent their stories and to enter into the classroom social life.[7] Over time, though, their texts became more important—they began to serve as representations of valued characters and actions, as reinforcers of their authority, their right to say how the world is, and as dialogic mediators between themselves and others, as ways of anticipating and responding to others' reactions to their stories.

I also studied the nature and content of talk during the Author's Theater events themselves, paying attention to teacher and child response to presented texts. This response included talk about textual decisions (e.g., a perceived need for more "action" or "details") and ideological and even moral ones (e.g., an objection to the lack of action for girls, to the lack of details about the reasons for characters' fights). Initially, children's own responses to peers' texts related primarily to the text's function as a ticket to play—children expressed the fun they had in playing a certain role or, conversely, complained about social exclusion, about being denied a ticket (Dyson, 1994, 1995). But, in time, their responses also focused explicitly on the text's function as represented world, as a coherent embodiment or reflection of valued characters and actions. Moreover, their responses to community discussions could be revealed not only orally but also in writing: ways of developing texts (e.g., the characters included, specifications of characters' qualities and of plot actions) could be dialogically linked to those discussions.

In addition to studying child talk, I studied the nature of the texts themselves. With the help of project assistants, I analyzed how children organized and marked human relations and the ways in which gender and/or race figured into those relations. Among such relations were parents and children; spouses and lovers; friends or peers; good guys and bad guys; and perpetrators, victims, and rescuers. Varied actions energized those relations, including nurturing, romancing, rescuing, and joint or oppositional physical forcing. For the focal children in particular, I studied the relationship between media source material and actualized child product: Children could appropriate human relations as depicted in the source material, or they could invert or in some way transform those relations.[8] Finally, analyses of gender and sociocultural patterns in children's use of media-based texts served to substantiate or qualify patterns in media use identified through observation. (Descriptive statistics on the children's products are given in Table A6.)

In sum, from case study analysis of the writing and talking of particular children and broader analyses of the data from the class as a whole, I traced the interplay between individual children's actions as constructors of stories and their participation as social actors and community members in the class as a whole. I aimed:

- to identify the kinds of social goals that energized children's appropriation of cultural source material;
- to identify the ways in which written texts served those goals;
- to reveal changes over time in how focal children appropriated cultural material through composing to participate in and help construct a classroom community of and for a diversity of children;
- to illustrate how the interplay of social, ideological, and authorial processes undergirded those changes.

The children's actions and interactions to achieve their goals constitute "social processes"; the texts' reflections of some children's ideological assumptions and their distortions of others (as evidenced by child objections, for example) are "ideological processes." And, in the intersection of social processes like affiliation and negotiation with ideological ones of reflection and refraction could emerge "authorial processes," conscious decision making about the portrayal of human relations and human experience, that is, about the construction of stories.

To make clear this dialogic vision of child composing, I offer in this book my own constructed narrative about children's appropriation of cultural material—especially the superhero—to participate in and transform the local culture of a classroom. The child heroes of this narrative are energized by the desire to play and by complex issues of inclusion and exclusion; and the resulting plot line is dialogic, as competing visions conflict, coexist, and interweave.

If I had different sorts of skills—and the academic world different sorts of forums—this narrative would no doubt be clearest in visual, perhaps animated, form. In this visual story, children like Paddy, Holly, and Tina would be playing underneath a nighttime sky filled with a kaleidoscope of constellations. Those constellations would depict cultural "stars" found in society's stories, male and female stars of different ethnic heritages and born of diverse media. As the stars shift, so too would the particular ecology of playing children, who organize themselves with reference to those stars. It is the social and ideological dynamics of these playing children—and the ways in which those dynamics are wound up with learning to write—that I aim to capture in the drama to come.

▼ 2 ▼
▼

Orientation: The Children, the Teacher, and the Shifting Social Ground

[The "intelligentsia"] were astonished and horrified that children possessed such an extensive underworld culture of their own. . . . On the BBC's book programme . . . the chairman, Nigel Gosling, said helplessly, "A lot of the rhymes are very stupid indeed. 'Horse, pig, dog, goat, You stink, I don't'—well, I don't think anybody could say that was very witty, clever, nor is it poetic." He had forgotten (or had never known) the necessity for punchy, defensive weaponry in the playground. . . . Children's rhymes and games satisfy the requirements of children.

I. Opie, *The People on the Playground*, 1993, p. 12

In the unofficial world of childhood—whether enacted in the cracks of the official curriculum through exchanged glances, asides, and the occasional snack, or in the more open expanse of the playground—children declare themselves as members of the society of children. And these declarations sometimes strike adults as rowdy, "punchy," and a bit vulgar as well. In Sutton-Smith's words (1990, p. 6), there are "the wild eyes of monsters, the loud verbal barracking of baseball players, the screaming of those escaping from an 'IT' figure. There are stylizations of language, paralinguistics, and behavioral gestures, as are characteristic of play forms as well as verbal art forms" (Bauman, 1977; Sutton-Smith, 1989).

These symbols children use in their own social worlds, however, are complexly interrelated with those of adults. Their stories, songs, and clapping rhymes are sometimes revitalized discards from the adult world, be they after-school TV sitcom reruns or rhymes with medieval roots. Tina and Makeda, for example, played a clapping game to the beat of the old Macy's rhyme—but unlike the rhyme preserved for adults (Abrahams, 1969; Opie & Opie, 1985) and the one written for children (Cole, 1989), their version featured vernacular grammar and played with concerns about big kids who might beat up little ones on their way to school: "I don't want to go to school no more no more/ There's a big fat kid at the door door door/ He grabbed me by the collar/ And made me pay a dollar/ I don't want to go to school no more no more."[1]

Children also use material that has been deliberately manipulated by adults to appeal to their ideological conservatism. As noted in the previous chapter, commercial marketers of media for children tend to exploit stereotypes in their images of good guys and bad ones—not to mention their wasp-waisted beauties. Children may aim, for example, to be the muscled boy, the silken-haired girl, and thereby become "unique" and "popular" by conforming most closely to the cultural categories of male and female (James, 1993). Such symbols of "toughness" and "beauty" may become complexly interwoven not only with gender relations but also with race and ethnicity (Schofield, 1989). And, as children grow older, these identities may become intertwined as well with children's orientations toward school, as academic resistance or academic credentials become class-based markers of gender identity (for discussions, see Connell, 1994; Connell, Ashenden, Kessler, & Dowsett, 1982; Willis, 1977).

Some, like Sutton-Smith (1990, p. 7), see children's free play with the symbolic and social stuff of childhood as, in effect, the equivalent of children's right to free speech, especially on the playground:

> If it be contested that this is a matter for their own private and home time, it can be pointed out that with smaller families and less street play, many of the political opportunities and skills once taken for granted as being acquired in children's free play are not so readily available. The schools now remain one of the few places in which access to other children is in sufficient numbers for playmate choices in age and disposition to be available.

Still, it is not so easy to be "free" to choose one's symbols and social companions. Human experience is more fragile, more complex than the usual narrative line might suggest. Take, for example, second-grade Sammy—small, new in school, physically awkward, who found it hard to break into the social circles of tough good guys and bad guys on the playground. Or consider Lynn—who described herself as not "girly," because she would much rather play superheroes with the boys than jump rope or do gymnastics with the girls. Or imagine Tina, who did not do the boys' games on the playground— but who gave detailed accounts of her superhero play at home with her sister and cousins; in *her* play, Tina (unlike Lynn) played *female* members of the powerful team of mutant human superheroes named *X-Men* (Lee, 1963).

Indeed, the popular media themselves sometimes offer more complex, more contradictory images of human relations than might be assumed from playground superhero play (Douglas, 1994). The "X-Men" team includes women "as strong as men," as Sammy said; they can take on any bad guy—but they look drop-dead beautiful as they do so. April, of the mutant turtle stories (Dawson, Fields, & Chan, 1990), is a smart news reporter—and a real "babe" who, unfortunately, needs rescuing by the turtles-cum-ninjas.

In Kristin's room, the children's symbolic material re-emerged in the adult-governed sphere of composing time, and then the potential contradictions within the original media stories and between the children's experienced and imagined worlds seemed to become salient to them. This saliency was not the result of Kristin informing her children that their playful material and their written stories were not "'very witty, clever, nor . . . poetic,'" to return to Opie's exasperated adult. It resulted, in part at least, from the permeability of the composing period, the way in which it allowed the children's symbolic ways of meeting their "requirements" for social belonging and social fun—their symbolic material—to emerge and, at the same time, the way in which it subjected those symbols to new requirements.

These requirements included creating written texts that were clear and engaging—communicatively competent, as it were. But, of course, what is "clear" and "engaging" is a matter of interpretation. Thus, when the social ground under the children's media-inspired stories shifted—when new participants joined in the meaning-making activity—the complexity of human identities and human experience emerged. That complexity was collectively enacted in the interactions between official community members who often occupied different unofficial corners.

In the following sections, I provide readers with a first look at those unofficial corners, locating Sammy and Tina out on the playground. Then I enter the classroom and, at the same time, move to the official world of Kristin's composing period. I describe the nature of the composing events and, more particularly, the Author's Theater events observed in the beginning of the project, highlighting both Kristin's agenda and the children's early responses. Finally, I bring Sammy and Tina center stage, and more fully introduce these two children, whose actions and interactions will anchor the bulk of the drama to come.

UNOFFICIAL GROUNDS

The "big kids'" playground—no kindergartners or preschoolers allowed—was nestled between two structures: the two-story school building on one end of the city block and the one-story preschool bungalows on the other end. In between those structures, tall fences with locked gates separated the lively children from the somewhat tired-looking wooden homes that surrounded it. To get onto the playground, I had to first enter the school's front door and then (like the children) walk-run down a long corridor, skip down a few concrete steps, and push open the heavy metal doors that separated the loud schoolyard noises from the quieter ones of the school proper.

On the other end of the doors, I usually took a quick scan of the playground scene, hoping especially to see the often-absent Tina somewhere amid the throngs. If she was there, she would not be in the kickball or the basketball areas, which filled the black asphalt that stretched in front of those metal doors. Nor would she be on the grass-covered field to the left of the kickball space, where games of tag (where one person chases many) regularly gave way to games of good guys and bad guys (where teams chased each other about, engaging in mock battles). Those spaces were usually dominated, but not exclusively filled, by boys.

If Tina was there, she would be over near that part of the playground covered with bark chips: the part with the wooden climbing structure, where she seldom played, and with the child chest-high metal bars, which were a favorite. She and her friends would lean their bodies against those bars and swirl around and around, heads bent, legs scrunched. Sometimes Tina and Makeda (both tiny girls) would straddle Lettrice and Rhonda (two bigger girls) and they'd go around together. "Look Anne! One hand!" one would say, and I'd cover my eyes and pray for their small heads. Other favored activities were jump rope, with two swingers holding the rope, and clapping and chanting routines (like the Macy's chant and the McDonald's rhyme: "Big Mac, Filet of Fish, Quarter Pounder French Fries . . . ").

Although the gymnastic equipment and the jumping ropes were used by all the girls (and, on occasion, by the boys), the groups of playing girls were usually racially divided. When Tina complained one day that she had nobody to play with, she went one-by-one through all of the African-American girls (who were absent or playing with Makeda, whom she was mad at that day). She did include Liliana, however, in her litany. Liliana was officially "White," but she considered herself "White-looking" and "Mixed" because her grandfather was from Colombia; she usually played with the girls of color, singing the same songs from the radio and using some of the same nonstandard features (e.g., multiple negation and regularized third person singular verbs ["it don't make no difference . . . "]).

Although Tina and her friends played mainly with other girls, on the inside, in the unofficial sphere of the classroom, they interacted with other children, especially neighborhood boys. This observed relationship between housing patterns, race, and social companions was made explicit one day, when Tina and Victor asked Rhonda, who had just moved, about her new friends.

> *(Rhonda has just told Tina and Victor that, after dinner, she goes to bed.)*
> VICTOR: You don't go outside with your friends?
> RHONDA: Huh?
> VICTOR: You got any friends around there?
> RHONDA: My aunt usually be out there. It's all <u>White</u> kids. Ain't no Black people there, except me.
> TINA: If you was still living where you used to be living, then I woulda come over your house everyday.

Of course, wherever one lives and whoever one's neighbors, it can be hard for newcomers to a school to make friends. And this is why, early in the project, Sammy was not to be found in the usual spaces dominated by boys. He was to be found hanging on the side of the playground or inside the classroom, complaining to Kristin that no one would play with him. And by "no one" he meant the multiethnic group of boys (sometimes joined by Lynn) who played superhero games—especially X-Men—on the grassy expanse. And he complained in particular about Seth, a major classroom figure.

Not only were Seth and his "sidekick" Jonathan the only two middle-class boys—which class was evident in their dress, possessions, and reported experiences—but a relative of Seth's was a local celebrity well known to the children. Moreover, Seth had a major role in organizing the superhero games. He was able to name needed characters and unneeded ones—despite the fact that he was not allowed to watch the superhero cartoons. (He had learned about the characters and their roles, he said, from studying a video and super-hero cards [a variant on baseball cards, sold in comics stores].) Sammy, on the other hand, was a new kid, seemingly just learning the locally popular cartoon fare, less knowledgeable about possible roles, and without strong allies.

All of the children, whatever their gender, sociocultural background, or individual style, shared with Sammy a desire for social belonging and social fun. And that child (and human) agenda re-entered the classroom each day, along with the children, as the recess bell rang and the children followed Kristin back through the metal doors, up the steps, and down the long corridor to the classroom.

OFFICIAL GROUNDS

Inside Kristin's large room, the children entered a space filled, not with asphalt, grass, and play equipment, but with desks, blackboards, and study equipment—books, paper, marking tools. Still, the unofficial world did not disappear. It reworked itself, becoming quieter in volume, more constrained in movement, and, whenever possible, spreading into the official world, bringing new intentions, new social meanings, and new ideological complexities.

Tina and her friends, for example, could no longer swing on the bars—but a few bars of a popular song could be quietly intoned as they made their way to their desks. Jump rope was out of the question, but a game of mommy and baby could fit in almost anywhere. "Babies" could talk baby talk and mothers could fuss while writing folders were passed out and pencils sharpened. Moreover, if they were real discrete about it, babies could almost sit on mommies' laps during writing time class meetings and lessons, which were held on the large gray carpet at the front of the room.

For Sammy, the unofficial life became at least potentially more attainable.[2] Superheroes were not chasing each other madly about but, rather, transformed back into small boys who, not surprisingly, often discussed their favorite superhero team. It was possible, now and then, to join a conversation with "Oh yeah, I saw that too." Moreover, after any opening class meetings, when the children were to find a place to sit and write, it was always possible to find a seat by someone. The desks, after all, were bunched together in clusters of four. Sitting by Seth was near impossible, since Seth and Jonathan always sat together (unless it was a day for teacher-engineered seating). But Patrick often chose to sit by Sammy, so Sammy would not be alone.[3]

For both Tina and Sammy, though, the official writing curriculum itself—the composing and performing of stories—became a central site for unofficial work, that is, for establishing and managing social connections. Their participation in the official activities of composing time shaped their sense of writing's functional possibilities for unofficial work; that sense in turn shaped their ways of participating, of using the written medium (Dyson, 1989a, b).[4] Moreover, this interplay of unofficial and official agendas generated social and ideological processes that contributed to the community of the whole.

To illustrate the beginnings of this interplay, I turn to the official composing time, explaining Kristin's official planned activities and illustrating the early enactment of Author's Theater. Kristin's teaching activities did not comprise a curricular "method" that led to a particular child "result." Rather, they were, to use Vygotskian terms, both "the tool and the result": Initially conceived as a means for teaching children to write, the activities were themselves reconceived and reworked in response to the writing children (Newman & Holzman, 1993; Vygotsky, 1978, p. 65).

The Planned Composing Time

When Kristin took over this classroom in the spring of the school year, she initiated a daily writing time and, as an optional activity during that time, an Author's Theater. In this practice, similar to one used by teachers of both young (e.g., Paley, 1980) and older (e.g., Dixon & Stratta, 1986) students, the children chose classmates to act out (i.e., play out) their written stories.

Stories and the performing arts, however, occurred throughout the day in Kristin's class. During the early morning reading period, the children could choose from varied literature selections, and sometimes, right before the midmorning recess or the midday break for lunch, they dramatized the poems and poetic prose that Kristin would read to them. Both fiction and nonfiction books were regular staples of the social studies and science units, as were imagining the worlds of scientists, political leaders, and (in math) problem-solving people. The emerging dominance of popular culture in the official composing time (the time between recess and lunch) did not have to do with the absence of school-introduced literature but with the permeability of the official world itself.[5]

Kristin's instructional goal was to encourage and improve her children's writing. Although the children wrote on many teacher-assigned topics and in varied genres throughout the day, during the composing period, the children were to choose their own writing topic; in fact, some class periods began with whole class discussions of possible sources for story ideas. After any such opening class meetings (which generally were about 15 minutes), the children spent about 45 minutes freely writing, as it were. And then they gathered on the rug to see who had "finished" a piece and was ready to share.

The children had two choices for sharing: Author's Chair (Hansen & Graves, 1983), for those who preferred to just read their pieces, and Author's Theater, for those who wished to "film" them, as Victor put it. Whatever the chosen means for presenting one's work, Kristin assumed that the children's ways of writing these stories would change because of the interactional guidance provided by classmates and by herself as teacher. In Author's Theater in particular, she imagined that children would work to write in ways that would yield more elaborate and more pleasing play (i.e., the texts would become more complete and complex story representations).

The Enacted Public Forum

From the beginning of the project, the Author's Theater was a very popular activity. That activity did provide Kristin with the desired opportunities to highlight texts and authorial decision making, but it also provided the children with opportunities to engage in social fun. In the second grade, the text quality most discussed was "action," a word introduced by Kristin; but a story without action (without anything for the actors to do) was boring and no "fun," a word introduced by the children.

Early on, then, Kristin called attention to the text's representational function, that is, to the information it offered about characters and actions. And, also early on, the children exploited the text's function as a ticket to play. Both these functions were evident in the first recorded Author's Theater events; and (with the benefit of hindsight) evident too were the interactional and ideological dynamics that would yield the text's function as dialogic mediator. The first two of these early events are presented in the following.

Johnetta's "Three Little Pigs"

The very first event featured Johnetta's presentation, which was based on a brief text about "The Three Pigs." A presentation based on folk stories was not common in this class. Still, Johnetta's event illustrates the children's clear focus on social fun and Kristin's consistent focus on authorial decision making about content.

In her event, Johnetta chose actors primarily from her pool of regular companions. Makeda, Holly, and Ricky were the pigs; Rhonda was the mother pig; Penny (an instructional assistant) was the wolf; and Tina was the wolf's mother.[6] As Johnetta called her actors to the front of the rug, grumblings of "you promised" could be heard among the audience members. Johnetta, however, was firm in her choices. After all of the actors were called, Kristin reminded them to listen to the author and to follow her text. Johnetta then began to read or, rather, tell a story about the pigs, a story more elaborate than her brief written version; that version was as follows:

Once upon a time
there were 3 pigs
and the wolf tried and tried but
he couldn't catch
them. Instead the pigs ate the wolf.

Johnetta's elaboration was supported by the actors, who knew the basic story and thus asked for clarifications and elaborations of their roles and actions.

JOHNETTA: This story is called The Three Little Pigs. (*looking at her paper and reading*) "Once upon a time there were 3 little pigs—"

RICKY: (*interrupting her*) Johnetta, do we build our houses?

JOHNETTA: "The mother wolf sent the 3 little pigs off."

GENERAL OUTCRY: "MOTHER WOLF!!!"

JOHNETTA: Mother pig. (*a pause as Johnetta apparently regroups*) . . . "And they build their houses."

RICKY: With what?

JOHNETTA: "with straw—"

> *(General confusion among "the pigs" about which per-*
> *son is which pig.)*
> JOHNETTA: Makeda's the first pig, Holly's the second pig, Ricky's
>   the third pig.
> RICKY: I use bricks.

As the story continues, the wolf attempts to catch the pigs but fails and, instead, the pigs collectively catch the wolf and eat him. The mother wolf goes to the funeral and "cried and cried." As she does so, the little pigs spontaneously begin teasing her in a singsongy chant, "Nah: nah, nah: nah, nah: Nah: nah, nah: nah, nah."

After the event, Kristin asks for comments and questions, and she reminds them to talk "about the writing," not about "'Why did you choose me? Why didn't you choose me?'" Despite this admonition to focus on the writing, most of the remarks come from the actors, who comment on their feelings, especially on how much fun they had.

> TINA: When I went to the funeral [as the Mother Wolf], and the
>   pigs were teasing me, I felt like eating them.
>   . . .
> MAKEDA: I liked the story—when we ate the wolf, and the mama was
>   coming to the funeral, and we was laughing.
>   *(Kristin then focuses their attention on the text, asking if that*
>   *teasing and laughing is in the writing.)*
> MAKEDA: No.
> JOHNETTA: But that was fine with me.
>   *(Kristin asks Johnetta if the performance [including the*
>   *improvisations] gave her any ideas about things she could*
>   *add to her written story.)*
> JOHNETTA: Yeah. Like I could say . . . "The mother wolf told the um
>   the um kid wolf to go find some pigs to cook'em, but he
>   couldn't."

In her role as teacher, Kristin did not highlight the difference between the author's oral improvisation and her or his reading of a set text, a decision that contributed to the potential inclusiveness of Author's Theater events. (She did not emphasize this until the following year, when all children were relying primarily on a basic written text.) Kristin felt that the children's story composing would benefit in any case from the experience and, moreover, that some kind of involvement in the writing period was important. Further, the children who engaged in this improvising (including Tina and Sammy) gave every indication that they knew that writing was the more valued channel during composing time. Like Johnetta, the children seemed to figure that, even if nothing at all was written, if one's writing was held close to one's chest, one's eyes kept on one's paper, and one made remarks like "Oh. I lost my place," even a near-empty page could be discretely handled.[7, 8]

Kristin *did,* however, highlight the difference between actors' improvisations and author's "readings." In these improvisations, these elaborations, was potential information that the author might want to insert. The actors also focused on their own elaborations—their own playful inventions, which signaled their involvement in and ownership of the story. "We was laughing, having a good time," said Holly, a triumphant pig. "I felt like eating the pigs," said Tina, the grieving and hassled Mama Wolf. Thus, as authors, children had to negotiate their stories with their actors—and in this way the social enactment of Author's Theater contributed to the emergence of writing's function as a dialogic mediator. This negotiating was especially likely when children used familiar cultural texts, like folk stories or, more commonly, commercial productions.

Although not evident in Johnetta's event, audience members too could be responsive others with whom authors must contend. They could react as appreciative fellow players, who enjoyed the acting and, especially, the humor of improvisations. Moreover, as suggested in the following event, they could also react as excluded players, objecting that they "never got to play." When an enacted story refracted the classroom community so that the issue of access to a story world became tied to sociocultural identity (not just personal affront), ideological issues began to emerge.

Kevin's Battling Superheroes

The second event featured Kevin's presentation of battling superheroes: the teenage mutant ninja turtles and the X-Men. Kevin first chose his X-Men: Jonathan (Wolverine) and Radha (Cyclops). Next, he named three of the ninja turtles: Seth (Donatello), Lawrence (Raphael), and Nyeme (Michaelangelo, the "party dude," as Johnetta pointed out). Finally, he chose Ricky to be Splinter (the master of the turtles) and the very pleased Sammy to be another turtle (Leonardo).[9]

> *(When Kevin had finished calling his actors and was raising his paper to read, Holly spoke up clearly and directly.)*
> HOLLY: We need girls.
> JOHNETTA: Somebody's gotta be April [the ninja's "babe"].
> HOLLY: And Storm [a female X-man].
> *(Kevin was not so direct in his reply. He did not say what "we" or "I" did or did not need. He referred to the authority of the written text to reinforce his decisions—another function of texts.)*

KEVIN: It don't have any girls in it.
(Kristin then asked the children to make their bodies and minds "peaceful," so that they could listen well. Finally, Kevin began.)
(reading) "X-Men Meets the Turtles. Once upon a time there wa: —were 4 baby turtles. Their names were Donatello, Michaelangelo, Raphael, and Leonardo. Wolverine didn't like them. But he did like their master Splinter."
(Jonathan puts his hand on Ricky's neck.)
And this is where they're fighting *(shows his picture of the battling superheroes and reads the conversational blurbs).* "WOW!" "AHHHHH" "OUCH!"

KRISTIN: Do you have some narrative that goes along with it and tells [the actors] what to do? Can you make some up?

KEVIN: Well, I didn't have time to finish it so it says "to be continued."
(Kevin exploits the text's function as memory support; unlike Johnetta, he does not stray from what is written.)
(After the performance is over, Seth and then Radha comment on their lack of anything to do.)

KRISTIN: Remember what happened the other day, when somebody said, "These are the people in my class," and they just stood there. What did we say about that?

LASHANDA: [No] action.

KRISTIN: We asked about adding action. We said that if you had an essay ... if you had something that didn't have action in it, you should share it in Author's Chair. In Author's Theater, we have all the action. Well, Kevin had action in his. But what happened? Jonathan?

JONATHAN: I think it was a really good play, because I liked my part. And—like—it was sort of like telling about the thing, and then you could—like—tell about all of 'em, and then you could get moving and do the story.

KRISTIN: OK, so you're saying it was a good beginning for the play, right?

SETH: It was coming to more action ... but in the beginning it wasn't long enough.... But it was going to have lots of action in it.

JONATHAN: But it wouldn't really be good to have action in the beginning. So it's like peace, a little action, more and more and more.

KRISTIN: "Peace." What do you mean by that?

JONATHAN: They aren't really fighting anyone.
 RICKY: I liked my part ... Jonathan had to be one of the ninja tur-
          tles, and um Jonathan was the only one—he only liked <u>me</u>.
          (Kristin asks Ricky and then the class if there are any
          thoughts about how characters or plot could be developed.
          There is general agreement that Kevin needs more action.
          However, as is the pattern, Kevin will just begin another
          story—one with more action; he will not return to this one.)

Throughout this event, Kristin maintained her focus on teaching the children to write, introducing the conceptual tools and the vocabulary used by authors (e.g., character development, plot, action). Moreover, the interactional dimension of writing is evident in both Kristin's and children's talk about the representational content of text. If someone is to have a good story—and if one's affiliated peers are to have a good time, then a text will need to have sufficient action. That action may come in a certain place in a story, it may modulate in intensity, but it must come.

The ideological dimension is barely audible, but it is there. It is being enacted in the resistant voices of Holly and Johnetta, who both know the stories and want female roles. And it is these girls—and Tina too—who, as second graders, will continue to raise issues about female access to the pleasurable worlds of superheroes. They will act first in the corners of the official free writing time, pressuring the boys for entry; and, then, Tina and Holly will bring their own superhero tales to the public stage. Their desire to be included (a desire linked to the text's function as a ticket to play) will lead to community consideration of ideological assumptions and, moreover, individual play with textual possibilities (a play itself linked to the text's representational function).

Superheroes as Mediators

Commercial productions, and the superhero stories in particular, were key mediators of the evolving classroom drama. Stories based on common culture were just that—common. Both audience members and actors knew of the universe of possibilities in these stories.[10] Moreover, the superhero stories in particular, with their teams of good guys and bad guys, involved many more children than did more "original" stories. For example, in an event that followed Kevin's, Seth presented his own good guy—bad guy adventure—a story featuring his invented superhero, "Super Dog," who was on the trail of diamond robbers. No one questioned Seth's chosen male actors, who, in any case, numbered only three.

Further, if I move back the narrative lens here and consider who does and who does not write these officially framed media stories, an ideologically more complex drama begins to unfold. In this drama, human relations are not only displayed in the representational stuff of media-based stories, but they are also displayed in the sociocultural configuration of their authors. In the second grade, as the described events suggest, media-based stories were written mainly by boys; girls were much more apt to write about their experiences and relations at home and at school. However, in the third grade, working-class girls of color, unlike their female peers, also drew relatively often on the popular media, and working class boys of color did so almost exclusively. (See Table A6.)

These product differentiations were the tracings on paper of the social actions of the children themselves, as they arranged and rearranged themselves in the interplay of official and unofficial worlds. Their stories served as a means of displayed affiliation, of webs of connection, often undergirded by the interplay of gender, race, and class. But, in the public forum, the stories also generated ideological processes of value reflection and distortion and, thereby, new sorts of social processes. Among these processes were resisting by the excluded, distancing by the seemingly unimpressed, and, perhaps most important, negotiating among children who, after all, were without exception desirous of being powerful, respected members of a classroom community in which composing was a key medium for participation.

This is a complex literacy drama, one that weaves in and out of unofficial corners and official stages. A focus on Sammy and Tina will provide a narrative path through this shifting social ground. In the final section of this chapter, then, I formally introduce these two heroes and guides.

SAMMY AND TINA: CROSSING GROUNDS

Sammy and Tina were each singularly complex people, with distinctive histories as classroom members. Their selves emerged in the patterns and variations of their responses to the shifting social milieu.

Out on the playground, the children's paths seldom crossed: Sammy sought entry to the places for competitive, tough play—the team games of superheroes and of sports; Tina usually was found engaged in athletic but less competitive events, like the hanging bars. But on the underside of the inside-classroom-life, Sammy and Tina did engage at times in the same unofficial events. And in these events, it was Tina who seemed the more socially assured child, one who knew "when to hold 'em" and "when to fold 'em," as the country song goes. Listen, for example, to the following unofficial child talk during an official composing event.

> *(Michael and Kevin are trading boasts about which fighting "moves" they can make on the "Streetfighters" video game. Tina hears their talk and intervenes.)*

TINA: What are you doing, [talking about the video game] "Streetfighter"?
          (Michael thinks Tina is asking about their written stories, rather than their talk.)
MICHAEL: No, we doing X-Men.
TINA: It's "Streetfighters," 'cause I got the [video] game.
MICHAEL: You can't beat me in it.
TINA: I got the game. I know what you guys are talking about.
MICHAEL: So. You can't beat me in it.
TINA: Yes I can.
MICHAEL: *(in a playful voice)* Soon as Tina try to punch me ( ), I go in the back of her.
          (As he talks, Michael moves in back of Tina, puts his arms around her without touching her, and pretends to pick her up and smash her down.)
TINA: *(undaunted)* I drop you on your butt.
          (Kristin sees the activity and tells the children to get back to their work. Tina and Michael have a few last exchanges— including more boasts from Michael and a "My-brother-can-beat-you" from Tina—and then return to their work. But Sammy, who has also overheard their conversation, now joins in, affiliating himself with the boys.)
SAMMY: Guess what. I was a Streetfighter. Me, Kevin, and Michael, we could [play]. And when I fight people, I do a flip, and I slam 'em on the ground. That's what I do to bad guys.

Being actually physically tough would be even more difficult for Tina than for Sammy, given her tiny stature (and her big not-always-worn glasses). But being tough was primarily a performance, a kind of boastful storytelling.[11] Tina readily joined in such a performance with the two boys, adopting a playfully competitive stance. She also knew her own limits and invoked her big brother at an apt time. Sammy was much more cautious, affiliating with the boys, declaring his competence as one of them. He did not get a response from either boy, in part perhaps because he did not so much join in as provide a distanced echo.

Sammy's initial appropriation of superhero stories, then, was not a simple reflection of his status as one of the guys, so to speak—he wasn't yet one of the guys. Tina's early stories, which were about love and peace, were not a simple reflection of her identity as a girl—she did not confine her behavior to that of the stereotypical girl.[12] Writing was not so much an expressive medium for individual souls as a tool for social beings whose major concerns were not learning to write. In the sections that follow, I briefly move these social actors centerstage one by one, allowing each a moment in the spotlight before they join their peers and their teacher in the classroom drama to come.

SAMMY: Seeking Inclusion

"If I could say anything about Sammy," said Kristin, "that's it—he really wants to belong. He wants to be part of whatever group will accept him." This was, Kristin reported, an evaluation shared by Sammy's mother, who worried that her son placed too much value on other children liking him. Sammy's concerns, though, did not seem irrational. At least in part, they were grounded in the complex social realities of his life.

Sammy, his parents, and his two little sisters (one a year younger and one just a toddler) had lived in the Deep South. His parents divorced, however, and Sammy's mother had taken her children back to the East Bay, where she had once lived. Living in a neighborhood sometimes troubled with crime, she was protective of her children. Sammy was not allowed to play outside; he ventured into the neighborhood mainly on Sundays, when the family went to church. Religion was an important part of family life, and Sammy himself said he wanted to "save people," in the religious sense, when he grew up.

Sammy's limited opportunities to play in his neighborhood, combined with the never-easy task of entering a school late in the year, may help explain his place on the edges of the unofficial world. It was, I underscore, a world of notable gender, racial, and economic differences—and this was not lost on Sammy. Although Sammy seemed close to his first-grade sister (whom he greeted with a quick hug and a warm "see you later" on the playground), he desperately wanted onto the boys' territory. Perhaps his difficulty breaking into the superhero play—and his perception of Seth's central role in that play—contributed to his sometimes voiced feelings that, if "I was White," kids would play with him. Kristin reported that, when racial tensions surfaced explicitly in the classroom (as they did in other school classrooms that spring),[13] Sammy was one of the most vocal; in their angry discussion, the White and Black children accused each other of only liking members of their own race.

Sammy struggled in the official world as well. His difficulty with school literacy contrasted the seeming ease with which his first-grade sister took to the tasks (a comparison commented on by the school reading teacher, who had worked with both children). Sammy sometimes simply refused to read and write. In his first month in the classroom, he wrote only two brief texts about "having fun":

Once upon a time
I went to Disneyland
and I had fun
and it was great
and I had ride in the
Dumbo and it was fun.
The end.

Once upon a time
I went to Chuck E Chees
and I had fun.
I had [fun] playing with the video games.
and I had lis [lots] of fun.
and we was playing
in the balls and I ride in
the cars and we had pizza the end.

Sammy's way of participating in the composing time period changed abruptly, however, when he first experienced the social possibilities of Author's Theater. As Kristin explained to her study group, when Sammy first presented his own superhero text, all of the other children wanted to be in his story. He was the object of much attention. Moreover, this child—seemingly socially inexperienced—began to display quite remarkable abilities to verbally negotiate a story, as he closely observed the reactions of his actors to the ongoing story line.

KRISTIN: So Sammy suddenly became a writer when he realized the power he had with his peers.... When he shares ... he starts to read ... and then he gets this grin on his face, and he starts adding more things, and he becomes a director.... And his stories orally become more and more developed.

Given the popularity of media figures, and his own desire to belong, to affiliate with the boys, it is not surprising that Sammy chose superhero stories for his productions. But his stories of physically powerful men rendered marginal aspects of his own identity and that of others. Among the most vocal of these others was Tina.

TINA: "Talking Back"

If Sammy was resistant to the official world, Tina was tolerant but often absent. She missed about a third of her second grade year, which worried Kristin. Tina's

the power of pun

absences were, Kristin thought, the primary cause of her difficulties with
math and with reading. Like Sammy, Tina was most comfortable with repetitive, patterned books (like those by Dr. Seuss). Moreover, her absences made
her vulnerable to being "flunked," as the children say, or "retained," as the
teachers put it.[14]

Tina's very first written text in the second grade was about staying home.

I Love win I am alon
I Love Pese [peace]
in [and] my stsrite [sister] is at school
my bothr goes to school
my daddy gos to saf-sekole [San Francisco]
in [and] my momm is at home with the BaBy

And so was Tina. The oldest girl in this family of two teenage boys and three
girls (Tina, her 5-year-old sister, and the infant), Tina loved to play with "my
baby"—and even to change her diapers.

Tina once made her own connection between school attendance, family
life, and reading—a connection different from the one Kristin and other school
faculty were making. She had commented that "I don't pretty much like to
read." And when I repeated that comment (with unmasked concern in my
voice), Tina elaborated, perhaps to reassure me.

> TINA: I just come here to get my home work and to do math. and
> to do everything else except for reading.... I read enough at
> home.
> DYSON: What do you read at home?
> TINA: Dr. Seuss books to my little sister.

Tina knew that school was supposed to help you "be somebody," as the
stay-in-school commercials say. (She wrote such an ad in her journal once: "Be
Somebody. Don't Drop Out.")[15] Tina had every intention of being somebody: Like Sammy, she wanted to save people in the religious sense and,
moreover, to be a minister. Tina's seeming dismissal of the concerns about
her absences—a dismissal that could also have been a defense of her family—seems consistent with Tina's nonruffled way of "talking back," of "speaking as an equal" in a situation where, for one reason or another, she wasn't
expected to (hooks, 1990, p. 337). In fact, it was Tina's talking back that led
to her passionate engagement with writing. But this talk was directed, not to
the school authorities, but to her peers.

Like Sammy, Tina was intensely involved in the peer world. Unlike Sammy,
though, she had been in the school since kindergarten and had a circle of

regular companions. She and her girlfriends declared their relationships in exchanges of phone numbers and "I love you" notes. They even had fake "love letters." Makeda (who enjoyed drawing) "made men" for Tina, Holly, and Rhonda—cards with drawings of possible boyfriends saying "I love [girl's name]." The friends also, of course, had fights—usually silent ones. She and Makeda seemed to have a particularly intense relationship—marked both by warm stretches of shared giggles and whispered secrets and by chilly interludes punctuated with boasts about beating each other up.

Tina's early written texts, like the one above about "pese," were brief texts about her love for family and friends and for doing fun things. In fact, she named her journal "The Peace Book." Like Sammy, she was also very attracted to Author's Theater. She campaigned hard for parts in everybody's stories—including the superhero tales. It was her exclusion from role and relational possibilities in those tales that led to her talking back to "the boys" through writing. And this is when the action started in her own stories (i.e., when she constructed a plot). And this is also when new kinds of social and ideological interactions became visible and audible in the community forum.

In the chapters ahead, Sammy and Tina play complementary roles: Sammy exploits his authorial powers to gain admittance to a valued imaginative world; Tina exploits her authorial powers to rewrite that world. Although Tina seems the more obvious superhero, they both were fueled by the need to be included in a desirable world, and they both faced social challenges and ideological struggles along the way. Moreover, both opened their stories to public witnessing and public participation. Thus their learning to write was mediated by the class as a whole.

With Kristin's help, the children's texts—texts that might seem "not very witty, clever, nor ... poetic"—engendered community discussions about the representation of gender roles, of physical conflict and of power, and of the motivational basis for acts of good and evil. There are grand themes at the heart of this classroom drama that now begins, a drama featuring two children who wanted to save the world from evil: Sammy, a young boy in search of companions, and Tina, a young girl not afraid to talk back.

▼ 3 ▼
▼

The Ninjas, The Ladies, and The X-Men: Text as Ticket to Play

Thirty-one cakes, dampened with whiskey, bask on window sills and shelves. Who are they for? Friends. . . . Like President Roosevelt. Like the Reverend and Mrs. J.C. Lucey, Baptist missionaries to Borneo who lectured here last winter. Or the little knife grinder who comes through town twice a year. . . . [T]he scrapbooks we keep of thank-you's on White House stationery, time-to-time communications from California, . . . the knife grinder's penny post cards, make us feel connected to eventful worlds beyond the kitchen with its view of a sky that stops.

T. Capote, *A Christmas Memory*, 1956, p. 27

When he was Sammy's and Tina's age, the author Truman Capote lived in rural Alabama with his elderly cousins; one of these cousins was his best friend, Miss Sook Faulk. Though sixty-something, she was "still a child" and a fun-loving one at that (p. 13). The two friends made fruitcakes each year and used them as attractive offerings to distant but well-liked others—responsive others who, despite their distance, joined in the fruitcake ritual with them.

Superhero stories were Sammy's fruitcakes, so to speak, a means of entry into a social world beyond his sisters, his caring mother, his supportive teacher. In that social world, mediated as it was by a superhero tale, Sammy had "the courage needed to overcome the enemy . . . and do battle against all the terrors" (Sutton-Smith, 1975, p. 95). Moreover, he was able to overcome what may be the worst "terror" of all, isolation.

In many contemporary superhero stories, the individual hero enjoys the camaraderie of fellow heroes, colleagues in the fight against evil (Lewis, 1991). As Splinter, Master of the ninja turtles, tells his charges:

> Together, there is nothing your four minds cannot accomplish. Help each other, draw upon one another, and always remember the true force that bonds you, the same as that which brought me here tonight. I love you all, my sons. . . . (cited in Lewis, 1991, p. 34)

The "all my sons" is significant here. Superheroes traditionally are powerful men. Even when the media itself offers potential variations on this theme, children may recreate a more traditional gendered world.[1] And so it was with Sammy. Like other children, he was selective in the semiotic ingredients he included in his superhero story. Moreover, since he was using those stories to gain entry into the existent social world, he was also selective in negotiating who was whom inside a tale.

Sammy found a social place—an identity—by "projecting" himself onto and in an appealing story world (McRobbie, 1992, p. 729). In so doing, he seemed to experience the pleasures of inclusion and the powers of the storyteller—along with the objections of those not included in the fun. Thus, the composing period, when Sammy was to receive lessons in the nature of textual worlds, became an occasion for lessons about the nature of social worlds as well.

In the following sections, Sammy, as new kid in the second grade, offers some fruitcakes, so to speak, to his own local versions of "President Roosevelt" and the "Rev. and Mrs. J.C. Lucey." In the process, he gains some access—some points of connection—and, at the same time, receives some early lessons on the functional possibilities and social consequences of both stories and written words.

TEXT AS TICKET: SAMMY GETS TO PLAY

In the early spring of 1993, ninjas were dominant cultural symbols in the second grade. Their popular forms included both the humans and the mutant turtle variety. The humans are three brothers, all trained by their grandfather in the ninja skills he mastered in his native Japan. The oldest brother, Rocky, has a crush on his blonde neighbor, Emily. Throughout the movie, the two younger boys—Colt and TumTum—tease him with the chant "Rocky loves,

Em-i-ly!" The man-sized turtles, who live deep in New York City's sewer system, are all pizza-loving adolescents and street-smart, compared to the suburban innocence of the prepubescent human brothers. The turtles too, though, owe their skills to Japanese ninja training, offered by their benefactor and master, the giant rat named Splinter. These turtle-ninjas also have their female fixation—April, a young Caucasian reporter and, in their words, a "babe," a real "fox."

These ninja stories offered the children clearly differentiated roles for males and females. Both boys and girls explicitly said, and implied by their play, that boys wrote ninja stories because then they got to play karate (play that usually was "fun"—unless some ninja broke the classroom rule about "no physical touching"). Girls, however, wanted to play April, because she "is cute," to quote Holly.[2]

For Sammy, the declared intention to write a superhero story for Author's Theater was an offered fruitcake, a means for soliciting male camaraderie (and, inadvertently, for aggravating girls denied the possibility of playing "cute"). Once he solicited his peers' desire to participate in his Author's Theater, Sammy used his quickly written texts as tickets to that theater—as school-valued artifacts to offer Kristin so that she would allow him entry to the stage. And once on that stage, the public play (and public consternation) began, as illustrated in the following.

Tough Ninjas and Cute Girls

During the composing period, Sammy spent little time physically writing his superhero stories. Most of the time, he was deeply involved in *oral* negotiations. Sammy used planned "good guy" roles to solicit the involvement of others, especially the high status boys. There was an underlying rule (made explicit in disputes) that desirable roles should go to those who first requested them, but this rule was not always followed. Sammy—like his male classmates of diverse heritages—typically allowed Seth and his "sidekick" Jonathan whatever "good guy" role they requested. Usually favored too was Radha, a socially aggressive child, an aspiring actor (as he often said), and a frequent agent for Seth and Jonathan (i.e., he secured roles for them as well as for himself). Sammy gave "bad guy" roles to boys whose involvement was not solicited and who often found out about a planned Author's Theater too late to gain a desired role.

Sammy also found the "cute girl" role useful for negotiating with—and exercising some teasing control over—the boys. In one of his early ninja turtle stories, Sammy offered Seth, Jonathan, and Radha starring roles and then sweetened the pot, as it were.

> SAMMY: And you know who April is? Melissa.
> *(Radha smiles at this, eyes widening, being playfully dra-*
> *matic. He turns and grins at Seth and Jonathan.)*

In the ninja stories, Sammy, Seth, Jonathan, and Radha were all on the same male team, friends united in their toughness and in their admiration of a female.

The admired female was typically either Melissa or Sarah, two White, middle-class, and friendly girls (neither of whom was familiar with ninja stories, because they were not allowed to watch shows with violence in them). These girls did not seek these roles. They were sought. Although looking like a superhero was not necessary for the boys, looking like the featured "foxy babe" was necessary; after all, it is physical features, not physical power, that mark the female role.

In his first ninja story, based on "The Three Ninjas" film (Chang & Turtletaub, 1992), Sammy recruited a good guy team of Seth as Colt, Radha as TumTum, and Nyem as Rocky. (Rocky was the least desirable role, because whoever played Rocky had to contend with the inevitable chant of "Rocky loves, Em-i-ly, Rocky loves, Em-i-ly.") For the Emily role, Sammy selected Sarah, a girl he privately considered his girlfriend (or so he told me).

Despite the pressures of securing his actors, Sammy managed to produce a brief text. This first text was a variant of his early texts about "having fun."

> Rocky and tomtom and
> Colt went for a
> summer vacation when
> there grandpa came.
> And they went to swim and they had fun.

Like many young writers, Sammy had composed his new story by reworking controlled text material (e.g., familiar sentence patterns and known words). The film, as he knew, involves much more raucous adventures than three young boys on an outing with their grandfather. There are the ninja lessons, which occupied both boys and Grandpa during that summer vacation, the varied confrontations with the evil Snyder and his henchmen, and a playground basketball game to win Emily's stolen bike back from neighborhood bullies.

The appeal of these pleasurable events, however, was not lost on Sammy. They were taken-for-granted ingredients, so to speak, part of what he knew would enable him to solicit others' attention and entice them to join in his story. Once on the stage, Sammy would abandon his text and orally draw from these events as he experienced the power of being in charge of the story—and the responsibility of keeping his "charges" engaged.

On the day he first presented a superhero story, Sammy stood with barely concealed excitement and called his actors to the front of the room. First he called his ninjas and then Emily. Sammy grinned widely when the Rocky and Emily chant began, a chant quickly silenced by Kristin (which predictable sanction may have added to the pleasure of it all). Kevin was to be Grandpa, and Melissa was to be Grandma—a designation that immediately provoked an objection.

ALOYSE: There's no grandma!
SAMMY: No grandma?
ALOYSE: No!
MELISSA: There isn't a grandma. *(with amusement)*
    (Sammy smiles sheepishly, seemingly not sure what to do. But Kristin and Penny reinforce his own power to make decisions.)
KRISTIN: Sammy, is there a grandma in your writing?
SAMMY: Yeah.
ALOYSE: But there's no grandma!
PENNY: Aloyse, it's his story.
    (And Aloyse acknowledges this, by asking for [and securing from Sammy] a less-than-prime role for himself.)
ALOYSE: Can I be the bad guy?
    (Sammy nods. And then he calls two other girls—quite persistent girls—for whom he had invented roles: Holly and Liliana are to be "aunties.")

With all his actors at the front of the room, Sammy was ready to begin to read or, more accurately, to compose his story. After reading his opening, he orally played with the semiotic material provided by the ninjas movie, exaggerating its offered human relations for comic effect.

SAMMY: *(reading)* "Rocky [Nyem], and TumTum [Radha], and Colt [Seth] went for a summer vacation. When their Grandpa came" back *(end of literal reading, abandonment of text)* Rocky had jump on Grandpa [Kevin] car. And um—JUMP ON GRANDPA CAR *(directing Nyem, who complies).* And Grandpa got mad. GRANDPA GOT MAD! *(directing Kevin)* And Grandpa wanted to whop Rocky. *(much audience laughter)* Then Emily [Sarah] coming and um and Rocky says "Hi Girl Friend!" *(more whoops from audience)* Rocky said "Hi Girl Friend" to Emily. SAY IT. SAY IT. *(Nyem refuses, while Sarah rolls her eyes.)* ... And then the auntie, the auntie— Liliana is the auntie—
HOLLY: I'm Auntie.

SAMMY: And Liliana is—both of you all is. Two aunties. And um and
              um the aunties didn't know that Rocky was married to
              Emily. *(more giggles and groans)* And um and um Rocky—,
              Rocky—, Rocky—, Rocky, and TumTum and Colt, they went
              to fight all the bad guys.
              *(There is, however, only one bad guy—a problem, given all
              the good guys.)*
SAMMY: I need some more—FREEZE! FREEZE! I need some more
              people to be bad guys.
              *(Girls as well as boys are eager, which surprises Sammy. "You
              want to be a bad guy?" he says to them with evident puzzle-
              ment. He does not allow such gender-shifting, however, and
              picks James, Patrick, Thomas, and Lawrence.)*
SAMMY: Rocky, TumTum, and Colt, they said, "Oh my God. We can't
              fight all these bad guys." And they all start running. They
              was running, and the bad guys was running (after) them and
              the bad guys couldn't catch them. And when they got home,
              Grandpa came down, and Grandpa did karate on all of 'em.
              *(Liliana and Holly begin chanting, "Go Grandpa. Go
              Grandpa. Go Grandpa," as Kevin kicks the air. The good
              guys win the day, and everybody sits down. It's time for
              questions and comments.)*

From his recollections of an early film scene, in which the ninjas-in-
training engage in a mock attack on Grandpa's car, Sammy fashioned his
own opening scene, one in which Rocky (for no apparent reason) jumps on
the car and, shortly therefore, explicitly greets his "girlfriend" (which Rocky
never does in the movie). Thus, the film's loving relation between proud grand-
parent and skilled children became one of blatant misbehaving and desired
disciplining, and the innocent, shy crush became a relation of bold male declaration and female silence. Moreover, in the film, the clever but short good
guys (the three brothers) do run from adult-sized bad guys, but they use their
guile and their physical strength to trip them up as they do so. In Sammy's
story, they are victims who just run, and Grandpa (the true superhero of his
tale) rescues them by tackling the bad guys on his own.

Exaggerating human relations, especially those involving adults, can be a
childhood form of mockery, a means of "express[ing] both power and powerlessness" in the adult world (McMahon & Sutton-Smith, 1995, p. 301). For
Sammy, though, exploiting the relations of the boy heroes seemed more a means
of expressing both power and powerlessness in the peer world. His assertive
stance, his urgent voice, combined with his ever-present grin suggested joy in having children whoop, whop, and be whopped—all at the sound of his own voice.

Still he was anxious to please, and, when the commentary began, he listened intently with no visible signs of distress (except for the moments when he was engaged in intense behind-the-scenes interactions with Nyem, who claimed that Sammy owed him a dollar). As was typical, most of the commentators were child actors, who remarked on how much fun they did (or did not) have.

Kevin had had fun being Grandpa, because "I got to fight all the bad guys," and moreover, "I could like run, like in the movie." Other children, though, were not so pleased. The girls in particular were upset because they had had no role—with the exception of Sarah, who had had a small, in her words, "embarrassing" part as Rocky's loudly claimed girlfriend. Even Seth and Radha, who had had major roles, were not happy, as the following interaction reveals.

MELISSA: For me it was boring, because Sammy put a grandma in the story, and I wasn't doing nothing. . . . I just stood there.

SETH: It was sort of weird um when we were when me and the other kids were doing the stuff because we didn't really have any parts. It wasn't enough action. Kevin [Grandpa] was the one who had the most action in the whole story.
(Seth, who was supposed to be a boy who could transform into a ninja, had just been a boy, misbehaving and running scared—not the sort of "action" he apparently had in mind.)

HOLLY: All me and Liliana and Melissa had to do was to sit there and say, "Go Grandpa, Go Grandpa, Go Grandpa, Go Grandpa."
(Kristin asks whether that action was in Sammy's story.)

HOLLY: No, but we felt like it. We didn't get to talk or nothing. All we had to do was be quiet and let those other people talk.

KRISTIN: But I'm wondering where you got the idea to start saying "Go Grandpa."

. . .

HOLLY: It's kind of something like when you're happy and when somebody on your team is like fighting back.
(Holly notes that the girls in particular had nothing to do. The boys got to talk, which seems a desirable action to her. But Radha, another frustrated ninja, is not impressed with his brief lines and his running.)

RADHA: All he did was call my name. That's it. And there were too much people and they didn't know what to do. So he should make more action and littler people because littler people make a better play.

(When Kristin asked Sammy how he felt the performance
went, he turned his attention to the behavior of the actors.
He commented that Rocky, TumTum, Colt, and Grandpa
had done a good job, although some of the bad guys hadn't
listened to him. And then he acknowledged Melissa's
feelings.)

SAMMY: Melissa was the grandma, and she was mad because she did-
         n't have to do anything. I did have a grandma, but I forgot to
         put the grandma in. She <u>did</u> have a story but I forgot.

Despite the voices of discontent, Sammy's offered story had proven a pretty
good fruitcake, so to speak: It had secured responses from children who had
been elusive on the playground. Moreover, the complaining children wanted
even bigger roles and more action in his next story—and Sammy was eager
to provide that next story.

Sammy was gaining some points of connection to a wider social world
through his story, but, at the same time, both the social world and the story
itself were sources of constraint, for him as well as for others. The social world
Sammy had accessed privileged some children over others, in ways that reflected
the racial and class biases of the larger society. Moreover, the story itself,
with its exaggerated human relations, constricted in particular the roles of girls.
Most limited were the "ladies"—the aunties, cousins, sisters, and other roles
invented by Sammy to appease insistent girls.

The Ladies and Other Extras

Sammy, like most second-grade boys, never included any girl's name in his
superhero texts. The typical superhero story began with a listing of the good
guys and the bad ones; just such a listing comprised the whole of Sammy's
first ninja turtle story.

Ouse upon a time	Once upon a time
ther war Ninja turtle	there were ninja turtles.
ther name war	Their names were
Michoagelo Leonardo	Michaelangelo, Leonardo,
raphal Donotelo	Raphael, Donatello,
and the war nice	and they were nice
and they war friend	and they were friends
and the mean was	and the mean [ones] was
Shredder bebor roke	Shredder, Be Bop, Rat King
and fawt suljs	and Foot Soldiers [the Foot Clan]

Although all of the named characters were male, the possibility of a girl in a ninja story was common knowledge and a potential point of negotiation in the peer talk before an Author's Theater. And, as suggested earlier, Sammy himself was quite capable of improvising a role for April or Emily during a performance—and quite pleased to do so as well. In fact, even before he wrote the preceding text, he promised Melissa that she could be April in his story: This story would be "different" than the last one, he assured her, because she was "gonna have something to do."

There was, of course, only one plum female role. Moreover, the physical qualities required by that role—slender, well-dressed, and White—seemed fixed. Thus, a girl like Tamara, a blue-eyed blonde whose poverty was as marked by her grooming as was Seth's privilege, could never be an April and, initially, neither could a girl of color. Indeed, during composing time one day, Lawrence, who was biracial, commented to his peers that April *had* to be White—a statement that led to immediate and firm objections from Holly, Lettrice, and Aloyse, who told Kristin, who objected as well. (At the very moment that he stated this rule, Lawrence was drawing Professor X—the bald, White leader of the X-Men superheroes—as a Black man with a flat top. [See Figure 3.1.])[3]

The minimal number of female roles was a source of irritation for many girls, especially for Holly and Tina. These two girls saw their exclusion, not as a matter of individual affront ("you never let me play"), but as a matter of collective exclusion ("you never let girls play"). Joined by other girls wanting roles, they began to push hard whenever they noticed any boy offering roles in a superhero story. And they especially pushed Sammy, who "wrote" (i.e., told) long action-packed superhero stories and who also very much wanted to be liked by everyone. Sammy was very vulnerable.

Figure 3.1. *Lawrence's picture of Professor X.*

Perhaps because of this vulnerability or, more particularly, because he shared cultural and racial common ground (not to mention a neighborhood) with most of the girls soliciting roles, Sammy *was* responsive. He gave a rationale for his denial or, more likely, invented a role for the most persistent—usually as some relation or friend of the lead female. In contrast, other prolific superhero writers and Author's Theater participants deflected all protesters with reference to the authority of the text (e.g., "See? [showing text] There's nothing in here for a girl.").

On the day Sammy chose Melissa for his ninja turtle story (and, as readers may recall, secured the approval of Radha), Holly and her classmate Johnetta asked over and over for a part to play. Sammy explained that there were no girl parts, other than April's. But the children continued to demand a role, and Johnetta even said she would be a boy. (Indeed seven of the girls on varied occasions voiced their willingness to take boy parts, if need be.)[4]

"OK, you can be a bad guy," said Sammy, but he immediately changed his mind. "You're Verna," he said. "She a lady. You're not no bad guy. You a lady—Verna, April friend. She [Holly] a lady too."

When Sammy took to the stage for the performance of his story, so too did the good guys (Radha, Seth, Jonathan, and Patrick), the bad guys (Aloyse, Kevin, James, and Michael), April (Melissa), and, of course, "Verna" and "the lady." When other girls (among them Tina) asked for roles, Aloyse suggested that they be rats—the sewer was full of rats. Sammy agreed, and so the rats came to the front of the room as well. Then Sammy began his story.

In that story, though, Sammy did not spontaneously improvise a female role—not even for April (despite the assurance he had offered Melissa). He concentrated on organizing for the display of physical power; he read his piece, introducing the teams of good guys and bad guys, and then had the bad guys invade the good guys' territory.[5] Holly, Johnetta, and Melissa began complaining (and complaining loudly) that they had nothing to do. United in their discontent, they disrupted the play. In response, Sammy improvised.

SAMMY: *(pretending to read)* Verna and April was friends. They used to play with each other.
          (Johnetta and Melissa join hands and play ring-a-round-the-rosy, a common class metaphor for girl play.)
          They used to play with each other. And the lady [Holly]—I don't know who she is. She a lady—she a nice lady too. She April and Verna friend, and they play.
          (Holly joins the ring-a-round-the-rosy game.)
          Until the Rat King is coming.
          (Sammy is now preparing to return to the boys and the fight scene, but Holly whispers frantically.)

HOLLY: Say I got bit by a rat and the turtles have to help me.
(Sammy begins to comply—and Tina delightedly scurries for-
ward to do the deed. But then Sammy decides that Holly
dies. Holly refuses. And as the two whisper heatedly back
and forth, Melissa has what would seem to be a solution.)
MELISSA: READ THE BOOK.
(That is, Melissa tells Sammy to just read his paper and,
thereby, let the written word become the authority. But this,
of course, is not possible. Sammy allows Holly to be rescued,
and then the fight begins.)

Sammy's enacted ninja turtle story was quite long, and discussion quite lim-ited, since it was time for lunch. But there was general agreement that, in Radha's words, Sammy might need to "put littler people 'cause it was too crowded."

"Next time," said Sammy, "I'm gonna put no rats" (the last of the extras).

In Sammy's ninja stories, as in those of other superhero authors, even the female lead had very little (if any) action. There was some possibility of a girl negotiating a role; but, to be successful, that girl had to fit the specifi-cations of a superhero script. And those specifications did not position males and females as equal members of the same team. In Sammy's human ninja story, as readers may recall, Holly had improvised a role as a cheerleader—an improvisation that Aloyse said had made him feel "tough" and like "get-ting" Grandpa. In the story just presented, Holly—a working-class girl of color—had worked hard to gain the right to be publicly rescued.

As for Tina, she seemed to have a pretty good time being a rat, judging by her excited grin when her small part arrived (thanks to Holly). But both Holly's and Tina's ambitions would change notably when Sammy (and other boys) began writing about the X-Men. Indeed, Sammy's own ambitions would change: He would plan such engaging stories that he himself would want a role in them! And it was this changing motivation that made salient the func-tional possibility of text, not simply as a ticket to the superhero game, but as the interactional stuff of, the representational material for, the game itself.

TEXT AS REPRESENTATION: SAMMY'S SHORT STORY

During the spring months, the X-Men craze grew in the classroom, just as it did in the entire Bay Area, from kindergarten through secondary school. A major Bay Area paper listed the X-Men as dominant "in" figures among youth—both boys *and* girls. Contributing to the appeal of the popular comic characters, who were first published in 1963, was the new X-Men cartoon show on Saturday mornings.

Compared to the ninja teams, the X-Men team is huge; indeed, there have been about 200 characters so designated since the series first began (Martin, 1994). Kristin's children, and Sammy in particular, knew best the nine "good guys" regularly featured on the cartoon show, four of whom were women. As Rhonda explained to me, "Most of the girls, they don't like [ninja turtles].... It's meant for boys." When I asked why, Rhonda elaborated, "Everybody want to be April, but—'cause—there's supposed to be *one* April." So, "kids really play cartoons like X-Men ... [that have] Storm, Jean, and all that," that is, all those X-Men characters who, like Storm and Jean, are women.

Her peer Michael concurred, "You [Rhonda] just hate ninja turtles because it's not that much girls on it. But you like X-Men because it's got X-Men girls on it." And first grader Briana, whom I talked with regularly on the playground, explained further. The ninjas only have "one girl that needs some help.... They have *girls* in that [X-Men] show. And they have some ... Black girls and some White girls.... The X-Men are friends and they help each other."

Indeed, all children familiar with the superhero stories agreed that both girls and boys are on the X-Men team. They knew too that, in Sammy's words, the X-Men women are "as strong as men." Moreover, the X-Men stories emphasize mental as well as physical strength; in fact, Professor X, the leader of the X-Men, is in a wheelchair. Thus, the girls had new grounds for demanding inclusion, as Holly made clear to Lawrence.

> *(Lawrence is making a list of characters he plans to include in his X-Men story. He includes only one girl [the X-Men character Storm], which Holly finds quite irritating.)*
>
> HOLLY: That's all! *(with exasperation)* You know some other girls in it *(with definitiveness)*.

Sammy's first appropriation of the X-Men team was directly related to the large number of good guy roles the team made available—but the role of girls in his stories remained limited. For the most part, the usual storyline of tough guys and their girlfriends continued ... except that the enacted storyline now included Sammy (no mean achievement).

The Good Guys and the Rogue

Within a week of the Rocky and TumTum event, Sammy decided to write a Superman story, a decision he announced to his tablemate, Patrick, and to Radha, who was on his way to sit by Seth and Jonathan. Radha immediately requested, and was granted, the Superman role, and then Sammy began to write.

Once upon a time there was superman and bad guys and they wanted to destroy superman.

More so than his earlier ninja texts, Sammy was structuring this text in the basic manner of most children's superhero stories: after the optional "Once upon a time," the good guy was named, the bad guy characters arrived on the scene, and then the "fun" (the fighting) began. However, Sammy's text soon proved problematic, as illustrated in the following.

<blockquote>

(Radha returns to Sammy's table, this time on a mission from Seth and Jonathan.)

RADHA: Make Seth and Jonathan be in it, OK?

SAMMY: OK.

RADHA: Good guys!

PATRICK: They can't be a good guy. There's not enough room. There's only Superman. *(to Sammy)* Is there any more room for good guys?

(Patrick refers to common knowledge of the superhero story as providing "room" for players; the text itself is a sort of ticket to play the story out.)

SAMMY: YOU COULD BE A GOOD GUY! *(yelling at Seth, who is kitty corner on another table)*

PATRICK: WHO? I thought there was only Superman in it.

SAMMY: I'm doing X-Men. *(quietly to Patrick)*

(Radha is still standing by Sammy's table.)

RADHA: Could you [let] Jonathan be Superboy? Pl:ea::se.

PATRICK: NO! He's doing X-Men.

RADHA: Then I'm not playing—oh, X-Men? *(pleased)*

PATRICK: X-Men.

SAMMY: Now good guys can be X-Men.

RADHA: I'm Gambit [an X-Men character].

SAMMY: No you're Wolverine [another character].

(Sammy, as he later confides in me, wants to be Gambit and is hoping to get Sarah to be the female X-Men Rogue.)

RADHA: I want Gambit.

(And, indeed, he maintains Gambit—temporarily; but, as I will explain later, Sammy does succeed in getting Radha to abandon the role of Gambit.)

</blockquote>

Sammy revised his text, making only one change, but an important one; instead of *Superman*, a word which had limited good guy possibilities, he wrote *X-Men*, one that could yield a large team of good guys. Still, for Sammy, the focus on the text itself was momentary; the text remained primarily a ticket. And, in anticipation of the use of that text, he began to solicit an actor for his key female role, that of Rogue.

Sammy's use of Rogue is a dramatic illustration of the power of (and the display of power in) child culture and its enacted societal storylines. Rogue's fate was rooted in an X-Men theme that seemed to me rather minor in the cartoon—that of romantic relationships. Certain X-Men males flirt with and, in some cases, have named relationships with X-Men females. Thus, a boy including a "lady" was potentially making a public statement about romantic love. And, in schoolchildren's social worlds, a boy and girl who *willingly* choose each other's company in public places and without adult coercion are often victims of heterosexual teasing, particularly by boys (Thorne, 1993).

The characters most often affected were not the most obvious ones (i.e., the engaged X-Men pair, Jean Grey and Cyclops). Rather, they were the two characters least likely to act on their flirtations—Rogue and Gambit, both very popular superheroes. The girls who watched X-Men preferred Rogue, a long-haired Southern woman, who is friendly, witty, able to fly great distances and to absorb the power of others, and, moreover, is just plain "tough," as both girls and boys acknowledged. There was some sentiment for Storm, a Black woman who can control the forces of the weather. But, as Tina explained, Storm "be getting knocked out too much." When Storm gets exhausted from controlling the weather—"knocked out"—Rogue regularly saves her.[6]

For similar reasons, Sammy and many other boys liked Gambit, a Cajun who, like Rogue, is friendly, witty, and powerful—able to convert matter's potential energy into explosive power.

Nonetheless, both Rogue and Gambit, power*ful* characters, could become power*less* in the X-Men play. In X-Men cartoons and comics, Rogue and Gambit do flirt with each other, but they have no physical relationship. In fact, Rogue likely would kill anyone she kissed (as she did her first boyfriend). And yet, if a boy moved to put Rogue in his X-Men story, the romantic potential between Rogue and Gambit closed out the collaborative meaning of a tough X-Men team—and the teasing that followed could destroy the team.

To avoid any such teasing, most boys simply left girls out. Indeed, boys sometimes assured potential players, as Nyem did Patrick, that "it ain't no girl gonna be in it." And, conversely, a boy being recruited might ask "Who don't got a girl friend in there?" as Thomas did when Sammy asked him to be in his story. Sammy himself, however, exploited and, indeed, seemed to delight in the tensions he could cause. In his X-Men story, he used the potential role of Rogue just as he had the ninja's April and Emily—as material for gender play.

After the male good guy roles were distributed, with Radha firmly in the role of Gambit, Sammy asked Margaret if she wanted to be Rogue. She did not. (Margaret seldom took any acting role.) Sammy then asked Liliana. She did not want to be Rogue either; she wanted to be Storm (which Sammy allowed). Finally, Sammy asked Holly, but, before she could answer, Tina, who was sitting beside her, begged for the role.

TINA: I want to be Rogue. I wanta be Rogue.
SAMMY: You marry Radha, 'cause he Gambit—

which is how Sammy succeeded in getting Tina and Holly to abandon their desire for Rogue and, moreover, in getting Radha to abandon the role of Gambit. (Radha decided that he would rather be a bad guy.) Sammy thus was free to quietly become Gambit and to solicit Sarah for the role of Rogue.

Thus, in his efforts to gain the attention and involvement of the good guys, Sammy used his text to mark an authorial decision and an appropriation of new cultural material: He revised *Superman* to *X-Men*. That new material raised the possibility of new images of human relations and, potentially, of power itself. But, in child worlds, like adult worlds, meanings do not come in any direct way from stories themselves; meanings are constructed and reconstructed in the social world that takes up the story. And so Sammy, a child deeply attracted to the power of male superheroes, continued to plan teams of "good guys" and to use girls (and the threat of desired romance) to experience his own agency as a male player in the classroom scene.

A Gambit Cut Short

When Sammy's turn for a text performance arrived, he went to the front of the room and attempted to manage the large number of children who had been promised roles in his story—17 in all.[7] There were a few disagreements among the actors, since Sammy had promised several children the same role. Liliana and Holly, for example, had each separately secured the role of Storm (which Sammy bestowed on Liliana, to Holly's great distress). And then there was Kevin's role of Cyclops. Sammy told Kevin that he would be "marrying Liliana." And despite Liliana's protests ("[Cyclops] likes *Jean Grey*. I'm Storm!"), Kevin abandoned the role, and Kristin became Cyclops (and, thereby, the first female to play a good guy role).

When Sammy had all the good guys and bad guys organized on separate ends of the stage, he held his paper up as if to read—but then stopped. He had used his promised X-Men story to solicit a grand collection of classroom members—including Sarah as Rogue. He had no intention of being left out of what promised to be a very good time. He turned to Margaret.

"Can you read this for me?" he asked.

Margaret nodded and took the paper.

"Thanks," he said and took his own place with the good guys.

Thus—quite inadvertently—Sammy's written text assumed a new functional role. No longer a mere ticket, his text was to serve as a representation of the story itself. So Margaret read that story, exactly as it was written (something Sammy never did). The play began—and shortly thereafter, it ended.

MARGARET: "Once upon a time there was X-Men, the bad guys and they tried to destroy X-Men."

(The children [both boys and girls] begin to play out a mock battle, but, after a few minutes, they stop and stare at each other and at Margaret, waiting for her to do what Margaret cannot do: Read more. Sammy's stories are always very long— but not this time, for some reason. The children sit down, grumbling about the short story. Sammy blames Kristin.)

SAMMY: Ms. S. [Kristin] said we have 5 minutes and I couldn't finish it. I'll finish it tomorrow.

(But he immediately follows this with another plan.)

SAMMY: Maybe we could play outside. . . . Maybe at recess if I finish we could play X-Men.

With these comments, Sammy himself explicitly linked "team" games on the playground and superhero stories in the classroom: "Maybe we could play outside." Indeed, Kristin reported (and I observed) that Sammy was now joining in on the recess superhero play. The official composing seemed to have supported his access to this unofficial play: It allowed him an opportunity to display his own knowledge and skill and, moreover, to interact with many members of the class.

However, the official classroom world was different from the unofficial one, in part because of its more inclusive social membership and, also, because of its literacy focus. The story as fruitcake for peers ("Want to play X-Men?") and the text as ticket for Kristin ("I'm done with my story!") were not enough in this public and academic place. Sammy needed a text that could also serve as an appealing representation—especially if he wanted it to function without his own oral improvisation. Moreover, it was not at all clear what an appealing, mutually satisfying text might entail. Group chase games and mock fights comprised a good time on the playground, but they were not pleasing everyone during Author's Theater.

Thus, having linked written and recess play, Sammy (and the classroom community as a whole) would now need to differentiate between them and, moreover, between the role of affiliated player and responsible author. As Sammy, Kristin, and the children talked, Sammy's text was framed and reframed as ticket and as representation, his social goal as affiliation (through the use of common knowledge), control (through the use of authorial direction), and audience negotiation (through responding to others' expectations and desires).

SUSAN: There wasn't so much action.

SAMMY: I know, 'cause it was too short. 'Cause I didn't finish it. Ms. S. said we have 5 minutes and I couldn't finish it when the time was up.

(Sammy is now referring to his text as a representation, as an object to be constructed, a focus Kristin reinforces.)

KRISTIN: Sammy, was your <u>writing</u> any different this time than it was the last time, or was it the same?

SAMMY: It was the same, it was just the same thing.

      . . .

JONATHAN: Well, there was definitely enough action. *(to Susan)* . . . It was just the beginning of the story because first it tells the group [i.e., the team] and then it's probably gonna tell what it does.

KRISTIN: So you're looking at it [a text representation] sort of as in progress?

(Sammy now returns to the use of his text as an opportunity to play. He tells Jonathan that the X-Men play will continue outside [but, perhaps, be more fun]).

SAMMY: When we go outside, we're gonna play a <u>different</u> X-Men. We're gonna still have the same people, but Radha say he don't wanna be Gambit, so I'll be Gambit.

(Johnetta, a girl persistent enough to secure a bad guy role, now questions the nature of the representational stuff of the story just enacted.)

JOHNETTA: The only thing we was doing was just fighting. We wasn't doing nothing good like talking or nothing, but we just fighted through the whole thing.

(This is quite true, since the enacted action was limited to Sammy's brief written words.)

KRISTIN: 'Kay—

SAMMY: Yeah, yeah—they'll be talking when we get outside 'cause we—

JOHNETTA: I wanta hear what Ms. S. got to say.

KRISTIN: Well, I was just gonna let everyone hear what Johnetta said. She said we were fighting but we weren't doing anything good like talking. And now Sammy's responding. . . .

SAMMY: See we did talk, see we would, see all the good guys, but not the bad guys. Yeah the good guys, they talked. You know when they be saying—and Professor [the X-Men leader] is Kevin, 'cause he tell them when the bad things and good things come and stuff.

(Sammy is assuming that the common knowledge of X-Men should satisfy Johnetta. He does not need to specify talk— because talk, the giving of orders, is implicit in the role of

Professor. Johnetta does seem to find this acceptable, but Kristin refocuses his attention on the written text.)

JOHNETTA: Like Splinter [the leader of the ninja turtles].

SAMMY: Yeah.

KRISTIN: So, will you write that into [your text] for next time?

SAMMY: M:: m. But we gonna have, but we gonna, but we gonna keep playing X-Men 'cause I got a long one [story], 'til the bell rings.

RADHA: And also Professor X can read minds [so he doesn't have to talk].

. . .

KRISTIN: So does anybody else have comments and questions for Sammy?

THOMAS: Whose team I on?

SAMMY: You're on the good guys' team. Wolverine [an X-Men character] is a good guy. . . . Yes Jonathan? *(a very sweet voice)*

JONATHAN: Well if Thomas is gonna be Wolverine, I'm just out of it.

RADHA: He's [Jonathan's] Wolverine.

SAMMY: Oh yeah, I forgot.

(Actually, Sammy had promised both Thomas and Jonathan the same role.)

Throughout this discussion, there were suggestions of the interrelated social and ideological processes that would yield explicit authorial issues in the months to come. Some of these issues were about how the social relationships between authors and others are mediated by talk and text. With Kristin's guidance, and in the context of ongoing play, the children would continue to consider the value of detailing action and conflicting views of "interesting" action (e.g., talking vs. fighting). They would also discuss their differing understandings of characters' motivations (e.g., children with common knowledge of media stories vs. those without such knowledge) and the distinction between "fair" players, who allow everyone a turn, and "main" characters, who get more turns than anyone else.

These issues arose from and influenced the children's composing: Individuals' ways of writing, of participating, changed as did the collective's talk about and expectations for "once-upon-a-time" texts. For example, in his very next composing event, Sammy explicitly worried about writing enough "action." He thus began to shift some of the functional load of specifying appealing acts to his writing, rather than relying so heavily on speech or on his audience's knowledge of predictable characters. Such textual deliberations were influenced by both Kristin's deliberate scaffolding and his peers' voiced complaints and pleasures.

However, there were ideological dynamics at play here, as well as social ones. Through his stories, Sammy was positioning himself within the complex of human relations in his classroom. He was, for example, becoming a "typical" boy writer who emphasized male characters engaged in physical action. Moreover, although neither his texts nor his oral stories fleshed out the qualities of those characters, through his choices of actors, Sammy did make visible his perceptions of who best fit the bill of powerful guys and desirable females. The implicit "we experience" underlying his stories—his apparent sense of "the collective in which [he] orient[ed] himself" (Volosinov, 1973, p. 88)—reflected the state of societal play, with its interrelated gender, racial, and class inequities.

And yet, the texture of Sammy's sense of self was more complex than his enacted stories may, at first, imply. His very efforts to improvise roles for Holly, Tina, and other neighborhood girls suggested that he not only desired responses from those perceived as influential, but he also aimed to be responsive himself. A similarly conflicted sense of responsibility was reflected in his decisions to delegate the same desirable role to different boys (e.g., both Jonathan and Thomas were promised Wolverine; both Seth and Patrick were promised Iceman).

Further, the very X-Men material Sammy was drawing on was itself conflicted. Despite its name, the X-Men team of superheroes includes women as well as men. And, although the stories highlight physical action, the characters all are involved in complex relationships with each other: They display and hide affections, they confess jealousies and betrayals, they act out their rages, and rage at each other for such acting out. Sammy himself showed some awareness of this complexity in his very exploitation of the superheroes' feelings for each other.

These conflicts were pushed toward explicitness by a child who has been barely audible in the drama so far—Tina, a child who was becoming quite irritated at "the boys." When no one offered her a fruitcake, so to speak, Tina and her friend Holly made their own. At Tina's urging, they chose ingredients from the media stories (i.e., selected characters and plot events) that revealed different perspectives on—and different representations of—superheroes' lives. In so responding, they displayed a deliberateness of textual action within a socially organized community, a community in which their fates as "ladies" and as aspiring "X-Men" were linked. In the next chapter, then, Sammy will move to the background, and, into the foreground, will come the seemingly quiet, good-natured Tina and her companion in social activism, Holly.

▼ 4 ▼
▼

The Blobs and the X-People:
New Perspectives on
Old Representations

I came to start reading the Bible through my mother. She gave me a licking one afternoon for repeating something I had overheard a neighbor telling her. She locked me in her room after the whipping, and the Bible was the only thing in there for me to read. I happened to open to the place where David was doing some mighty smiting, and I got interested. David went here and he went there, and no matter where he went, he smote 'em hip and thigh. . . . Never a quiet moment. I liked him a lot. So I read a great deal more in the Bible, hunting for some more active people like David. . . . In a way this early reading gave me great anguish through all my childhood and adolescence. . . . I wanted to be away from drabness and to stretch my limbs in some mighty struggle.

Z. Neale Hurston, Dust Tracks on a Road, 1942/1991, p. 40

Born in 1891, Zora Neale Hurston was a folklorist, a writer—and, argues the literary theorist Barbara Johnson (1986), a player with other people's expectations. The actions of the child Hurston suggest a consciousness of the ideological order and a willful decision to act otherwise. Sent to her room, perhaps to reflect on her sin, the child finds in the Bible a character able to gain God's favor in amazingly unmeditative ways. Given a box of books by two young benefactors, White visitors to her all-Black school,

Hurston ignores the ones about pious, frail girls and devours those about mighty Norse gods.

Indeed, Hurston's book *Dust Tracks on a Road* itself defied expectations. She did not construct a childhood defined by the race wars raging in the South; she wrote about a childhood defined by a powerful imagination and a desire to "stretch my limbs" and see what could be felt if not done— an authorial decision that did not please all her readers in either her time or ours (cf., Angelou, 1991; Gates, 1991).

It is this irreverence for others' expectations, and the desire to experience some mighty deed, that links Hurston to Tina and her friend Holly. These girls too made choices in their own social milieu that defied dominant expectations. The two schoolmates and friends had been writing texts about friends and family, about relationships. But they found the boys' stories about superheroes and their adventures quite appealing. And yet they were irritated by the continual reluctance of the boys to "let us play." So Tina and Holly did what excluded but not defeated people have always done—they wrote their own stories, superhero stories.

At first, Tina and Holly used their planned superhero story as an opportunity to play with each other and, then, as a means for gaining the interest of other players. Their anticipated text would be a ticket to the public stage. However, in planning their story, the girls did not make the usual appropriations from the X-Men stories. In fact, their atypical appropriations did not allow easy negotiation with their actors. The very common knowledge that so readily allowed Sammy a shared world with others made problematic Tina and Holly's own entry into the world of the superhero. Their fellow players made understandable but incorrect assumptions about their story's featured characters and its essential plot line.

Holly's and Tina's collaborative team broke up (because of Tina's school absence), and each child negotiated alone with demanding peers. To assert some control, each needed to do more than represent a story on paper; she needed to use her text—and the cultural authority of the written word in the official school world—to disrupt the usual storyline, deeply rooted as it was in unofficial school play. In so doing, the girls' own playful storymaking could become an organizing force in the classroom collective and, also, in their own sense of their powers as active people, social agents, and storytellers and writers.[1]

Thus began a more explicit and polyphonic classroom dialogue of written as well as oral performances, a dialogue in which at least some written texts were clearly linked to previous ones. In Volosinov's words,

> A verbal performance inevitably takes its point of departure from some particular state of affairs.... Thus the printed verbal performance engages, as it were, in ideological colloquy of large scale: It responds to something,

objects to something, affirms something, anticipates possible responses and objections, seeks support, and so on.

> *Any utterance ... is only a moment in the continuous process of verbal communication.* But that continuous verbal communication is, in turn, itself only a moment in the continuous, all-inclusive, generative process of a given social collective. (italics in the original; 1973, p. 95)

As we reenter the classroom collective in the section that follows, the ongoing verbal communication, and its social and ideological state of affairs, as it were, has given rise to a fed-up, defiant Tina. Her own verbal performances, and those of her peer Holly, will in turn contribute to a more inclusive performance from Sammy himself. He ends the chapter—as he ended the first year of the project—with reflections on the possibilities, not of *X-Men*, but *X-people*.

GETTING A TICKET: TINA, HOLLY, AND THE BLOB FAMILY

For weeks, the boys had been writing stories for Author's Theater about ninjas, ninja turtles, and X-Men—and, for weeks, Tina had been begging for a part to play, with limited luck. (She did, as readers may recall, secure a role as a rat.)

Tina had had it. Usually, when she wrote in her journal, she wrote brief texts expressing her love of family and friends. But on this day, Tina enticed her friend Holly to write a superhero story with her. "And no boys," she said firmly, "'cause the boys doesn't let us play."

Sitting side-by-side, Tina and Holly began playfully to plan an X-Men story. As authors, the girls were situated in the social world very differently than the usual male superhero authors, and their story revealed a complex, contradiction-ridden response to the emerging classroom conversation about gender and power.

At first Tina said she would be Rogue. But then she became "the toughest guy in the world. . . . We're all Blobs!" (Blob is a huge, fleshy mutant human, virtually indestructible and a very bad guy in the X-Men's world.) "'Cause if somebody threw a metal ball at me, the energy go right through me, and I would never know. And we're sisters robbing the world. . . . And we'll never get sick. And we'll never die."

The biological sex of Tina's character vacillated, as if she were struggling with the possibility of being a tough "blob" and a female. The cartoon Blob himself is the stereotypical media villain—an unattractive brute, a one-of-a-kind biological deviant, and unambiguously evil (Warner, 1990). In her Blob role, Tina did not stay a "sister" but became an "uncle," one with rather tenuous ties to his niece, played by Holly. In her more familiar female role,

Holly worked to position herself as the needy other in a parent–child relationship, one frequently observed in the girls' play. But Tina had other plans.

TINA: We can live forever.
HOLLY: Unless we want to, Father—
TINA: I'm not your father. I'm your uncle.
HOLLY: But you have—need to go all around the world, but you have
to come with me to look for my mother who died.
(Holly's mother actually had died when she was younger.)
TINA: But she can never die. We're all Blobs.
HOLLY: Yeah. . . . But she's all gone away. I can't drive around the
whole world by myself.
TINA: You don't drive. You fly through the air.
HOLLY: I know. . . . But you'll have to come with me. I'm only 18.
TINA: You're 21. . . . You're old enough to fly all around the world
without having to stop.
*(As the girls became more and more animated, they moved to
the classroom rug, deep in play.)*
TINA: I'm about to go get Rogue! And I'm tying her up and cutting
her hair off.
HOLLY: 'Cause there's fire in there!
*(Uncle Blob [Tina] "drinks" Rogue's hair, absorbing her fire
power—but leaving none for his poor niece Holly Blob.
Holly begs for the right to be like her uncle, to be powerful.)*
HOLLY: Why you drunk it all, Uncle? Why can't I be like you, Uncle?
I want to be like you Uncle.
TINA: You're like your mother, not like me. *(shooting fire)*
HOLLY: Can I be like you?
*(Uncle Blob [Tina] gives her a small bit of fire power in a
[pretend] cup, just a bit, though.)*
TINA: The only thing you can do is just shoot out fire at them [the
X-Men] and then just call me.
*(There are shades here of the ninja turtle stories and of April
who has to call for help.)*

Tina was seemingly in revolt, trying on a role very different from that of a
weak, desirable girl with a heart of gold. She was using her strength, this tiny
child whose journal was entitled "The Peace Book." Although Holly was in the
weaker role, she was also entertaining the possibility of an alternative vision.

Class composing time ended before the children had put pencil to paper,
but they intended to write their X-Men story the next day. Such a story,
however, one where second-grade girls become unapologetic bad guys, would

not survive in the public sphere of the classroom. It would be constrained by the social pressure of girls and boys seeking inclusion as powerful good guys and, then, by the "sexual borderwork" that threatened even a good-guy team of women and men (Thorne, 1993, p. 64).[2]

ASSERTING TEXTUAL AUTHORITY:
HOLLY, TINA, AND THE UNRULY OTHERS

Uncle Blob and his niece did not go quietly into the realm of the more conventional superhero story. Although their performance was held back by the social milieu and its dominant "routes and directions" (Volosinov, 1973, p. 91), the girls' very difficulty in completing their expression helped make salient the functional powers of writing. Thus, for Tina and Holly, as for Sammy, their uses of text were both a result of, as well as a means for, participating in the classroom composing time (Newman & Holzman, 1993; Vygotsky, 1978).

Holly's Tired X-Men

Abandoning the Blobs
The day after the girls had orally planned their Blob story, Tina was absent. Holly tried to write the story herself. But as soon as the word was out that she was writing an X-Men story, Holly came under increasing social pressure to add characters—good guys. At first Holly tried to explain that she was going to have "a different kind of X-Men." But like Sammy, she did not want to disappoint people. As she later explained to Kristin:

> HOLLY: I thought about it, and um I said, I said there should be some other people then this. Then I—when I start asking people, Aloyse, he be all *(excited expression)*, and James kind of following me and saying, "OH! Can I be, Can I be Cyclops?" and all that stuff.

So Holly abandoned the idea of the Blob family. She agreed to allow one character after another into her story; she herself decided to become the once-again powerful Rogue (who, just the day before, had been rendered vulnerable by the Blobs). Unfortunately, Holly's friend Liliana also wanted to be Rogue, and a loud argument began. Radha, Ricky, and Kevin, working nearby, looked over at the feuding friends.

> RADHA: What are you fighting over?
> RICKY: Do you both wanta be Rogue?

> *(Without waiting for an answer, the three boys begin to chant in unison.)*
>
> BOYS: Rogue and Gambit, sitting in a tree. [HOLLY: Shut up!] K-I-S-S-I-N-G.
>
> *(The rhyme goes on, graphically depicting female anatomy—despite the fact that physical contact between Rogue and Gambit is portrayed as impossible in the X-Men stories.)*

Both girls were immediately silenced, and both temporarily abandoned their ambitions to be Rogue. Holly, like most male superhero authors, decided to be "someone who's not married and not engaged." Radha suggested Storm, who controls the weather.

> HOLLY: So? I get knocked down too much.
> RADHA: You know something? You—you [Storm] can destroy this big guy—he was <u>big</u>. He looked like Magneto [an arch-enemy of the X-Men]. Magneto <u>hated</u> him. He was <u>so</u> <u>strong</u>. You [Storm] <u>bust</u> that guy. He made the Sentinels [the immense robots designed to destroy all mutants].
> HOLLY: I don't want to.
> RADHA: You don't get knocked down too much. Rogue saves you. When you fall down, Rogue just comes and saves you. She says, she says um, "You been working too hard, gir'." And then she brings you back to your ship.

Holly, without enthusiasm, adopted the perceived weak role of Storm. (Later Liliana reclaimed Rogue, and Radha confided to Holly that he had wanted to be Gambit, but since he could not get rid of Rogue, he too would be a loveless X-Men good guy: Archangel.)

After settling on a role, Holly began to write her text, with some assistance on spelling and punctuation from Liliana and Radha. Despite the strong social pressures, Holly's text portrayed a distinctly different X-Men team. Not only were her characters predominantly female, they were also people with feelings about each other, just as was typically the case in girls' written worlds. Holly did not begin her text by introducing the good guys and the bad guys but, rather, by introducing "a gro[u]p of people," the X-Men. Moreover, those people were ambivalent about their physical powers, as are the media's X-Men, who sometimes long to be "normal" and bemoan the destructiveness of physical violence. Holly, pressured into the role of Storm, depicted exhausted X-Men, complaining about their responsibilities.

Once upon a time there was
a grop of people it was the X-Men.
Storm said I am tirde [tired] of
changing the weather
but you have to keep working
Arckangel said. I'm tired
of working too, rogue said.
I have to save storm evre time
she fall. I get tired of
fighting bad guys. Ready to fight?
and they all had fun. the end.

The last two sentences had been hastily added when Kristin said composing time was over—and one can wonder how much fun they all were having.

Sparing the Text

Holly had "finished her story," so to speak, but she had not finished the process of taking her writing turn, of eliciting the responsive utterances of others.[3] And this process would not be easy to complete.

Although she had represented her story in a written text, that text had functioned—for Holly and for others—as a ticket to anticipated play. And thus, at the end of the composing period, when the time for Author's Theater arrived, Holly went to the front of the room—and so did the many children whom she had promised roles. In fact, when other children (among them, Sammy) saw the assembled gathering of 12 children, they wanted a part too. Holly obliged by granting them roles as bad guys.

As Holly distributed the last of the roles, a number of male actors began "testing" themselves, in Jonathan's words, seeing "who has more energy and who has better powers." As Gambit (a role finally claimed by Michael) sent his energy-charged cards flying and repeated his favorite line ("It doesn't get much better than this"), Holly thought otherwise and tried to get order. But her low voice was inaudible amid the increasingly excited children. Finally, she yelled the author/director's compelling command, "FREEZE." Only some of the children stopped in their tracks. Johnetta then suggested (wisely, it seemed to me) that perhaps they should not do the story now, because people are "talking too much."

Holly agreed.

Kristin now asserted her own authority and sent the children back to their places on the rug. At Kristin's suggestion, Holly tried again to call her actors to the front of the rug, and, again, Holly struggled with control. Once more, she yelled "Freeze," her teacher intervened, and everyone returned to their seats.

"We need to talk about this," said Kristin.

Part of "this"—Holly's difficulty in organizing the class to enact her story—was related to the minimal functional role of Holly's text in her efforts. Unlike Sammy in his X-Men production, Holly actually did have a text that represented the story she had in mind. But that story featured different characters and actions than the usual superhero drama: Her central action was not good guys encountering bad ones, but good guys encountering each other, offering moral support for sagging spirits. Without using the authority of her text, Holly's storyline—so different from that expected by her public—was overpowered by the narrative grip of the assumed status quo and, more particularly, by the assumed major players (i.e., "the boys").

When all the children had sat back done, Lynn began the discussion with a comment about this problem of organizing, controlling, the players:

LYNN: [The performance] wasn't very organized.
       . . .
HOLLY: I can't think. I have too much things in my mind.
KRISTIN: Can you think of a way to solve that problem?
HOLLY: Yes. Because people ask me can I be in it and stuff.
KRISTIN: Can you think of a way to solve the problem of trying to keep it all in your mind?
MAKEDA: Radha has one!
RADHA: . . . She could write it down, what people for what parts.
       . . .
JONATHAN: She could write [the parts] down. She could add a big long list of Sentinels [robots who are bad guys]. The first person who asks gets to be it [a desirable part], or the first person she asks. And anybody else who [wants a part] is a Sentinel. . . .
HOLLY: Yeah, but see—
KRISTIN: You didn't like Radha's idea of writing the parts down?
HOLLY: I did. But see—
MICHAEL: I know. Gambit.

Michael seems to be saying that "I don't need Holly to write down my part. I know my part"—which is precisely Holly's problem. It is not the writing down but the acting on what has been written down that is hard, especially since the story source is common knowledge, since displaying that common knowledge is a valued means of social affiliation and social fun, and since the story author herself values that affiliation and that fun.

And, of course, it is hard also because her social companion is absent—the very person with whom she negotiated the original story precisely to exclude "the boys." Holly now tries to make the history of her X-Men story clear (although she does not mention—and may not remember—the part about boys).

HOLLY: Tina was not here [today. But when she was. . . .] We was all like pretending there was no good guys in it, just bad guys. . . .

KRISTIN: So what happened to change your mind? Why didn't you keep it like that?

HOLLY: I wanted to change it. . . . I thinked about it, and um I said, I said there should be some other people then this. Then I—when I start asking people, Aloyse, he be all *(excited expression),* and James kind of following me and saying, "OH! Can I be, Can I be Cyclops?" and all that stuff.

KRISTIN: So it was other people asking you?

HOLLY: Yeah, but they didn't really know I was doing the story. . . . [Or, perhaps, "they didn't really know <u>what</u> story I was doing."]

KRISTIN: Have any other of you had that problem where you have a certain number of people . . . and then people start asking you, and you start adding more people? . . . Are you afraid you'll disappoint [people]?
            (Melissa says she has had this happen, but she is not worried about disappointing people.)

MELISSA: Because I'll say, "Maybe next time you can."

JOHNETTA: That's <u>may::be</u>.

Melissa, however, wrote texts about relationships and family experiences. No one followed her around the room, begging for parts. So it was for Susan too, whose Author's Theater performance followed Holly's aborted attempt. Susan smoothly enacted her narrative about a birthday party attended by her mom (played by Melissa), her two baby cousins (played by Jonathan and Seth), and her father (played by Radha).

As for Holly, she explained her failed superhero performance as, in the end, a failure of unruly children. "If [those actors] was all my dad's children," she said, "my dad would give them two chances. That's what I did. If not [if they did not behave], he would send them to their room and make them sit on their beds." Or the rug, as the case may be.

Wielding the Text

The next day, Holly spent the composing period surveying the classroom and compiling two lists: the "people [that] is [acting] *goo::d.* And the people that's [acting] *bad.*"[4] When Kristin came by her table and asked if she was working, Holly declared her story already "done." And, when Kristin asked if she would be performing it that day, Holly said yes, but "I'm only gonna put the people that's supposed to be in it."

In fact, Holly's list making suggested that her mind was on controlling her actors and on using her text to reinforce her authority as author. When her Author's Theater turn came, Holly did just that—she used the text to assert her authority. She was helped in this effort by Kevin (who responded to her request for "somebody to read the story for me") and Liliana (who had to be Storm because Holly, now firmly in control, took back the role of Rogue). Aside from herself and Liliana, Holly called Radha, who had been promised Archangel, and that was that.

> *(Holly has just called her actors.)*
> MICHAEL: I'm Gambit.
>
> ...
>
> ALOYSE: Wait a minute! You said I was Cyclops yesterday!
> HOLLY: No I didn't. I'm doing a different one.
> KEVIN: There isn't a Cyclops in it.
> ALOYSE: How do you know?
> KEVIN: Because I already read it.
>
> ...
>
> KEVIN: Don't you need some bad guys?
> HOLLY: Bad guys, yeah. You're a bad guy, Rhonda. Sammy. And Tina [who has returned to school]. You're not Blob though. You're not Blob. *(Holly is anxious, perhaps, to keep Tina too under control. Nonetheless, Holly has done something quite significant: she has, apparently without conscious reflection, chosen a bad guy team that, like the good guy team, is dominated by girls.)*
> MICHAEL: Can I be Magneto?
> HOLLY: No! ... Now would you stop begging 'cause you don't remember my stories?
> *(Holly now takes her place with her fellow "X-Men," and Kevin begins to read.)*
> KEVIN: "Once upon a time there was a group of people. It was the X-Men. Storm said, 'I'm tired of <u>changing</u> the <u>weather</u>.' ["I'm tired of <u>changing</u> the <u>weather</u>," says Liliana.] 'But you have to keep <u>working</u>,' Archangel said." ["But you have to keep <u>working</u>," says Radha.]

And so the performance went, carefully controlled by Kevin's reading, until almost the end. Holly said her final lines with great feeling ("I'm <u>ti</u>:red of <u>work</u>ing too. . . . ")—much more than that voiced by Kevin. Then the bad guys rushed in, and "they all had fun," to quote Holly's text and, also, Tina's response.

"That was <u>fun</u>::," said the former Blob Tina, as the actors went back to the rug, the performance (finally) successfully completed.

"I <u>know</u>," said Holly.

"When we were fighting," added Tina (which was the part of the story in which she had participated).

Holly had not been able to enact a story featuring Blobs. The original Blob story had reflected Holly's and Tina's views as excluded girls, but it had refracted the ideological status quo. That status quo was "authoritative," that is, deeply embedded in the taken-for-granted world of the social milieu and, as such, impossible to ignore (Bakhtin, 1981, p. 342). Moreover, to gain acknowledgment for her own retelling of a superhero story—her own renegotiated appropriations—Holly needed to exploit the authority conferred in the school context by the written word itself.

In the text finally enacted, Holly was not a nameless nice lady in a superhero story, nor was she a little girl who alternately liked and fought with her girlfriends (the dominant plot of her previous tales). Holly entered into the power politics of classroom superhero stories, armed with a pencil, and became a tired superhero, one who had tangled with the dominant good guy–bad guy plot and rendered it less authoritative. Her written storyline was intertextually linked with her history as a writer of relationships and with her present position as a pressured girl. Holly brought to the public stage—and thereby involved the class as actors and audience members in—an alternative story. In that story, girls and boys could be on the same team; moreover, physical power was not necessarily such fun. Sometimes the good guys just wanted to leave the bad guys alone.

Tina entered a similar social struggle when she attempted to bring the Blob story to the public stage. But more so than Holly, Tina's struggle seemed to be a decisive experience in her own "ideological becoming" as an author (Bakhtin, 1981, p. 341), that is, in her deliberate and selective appropriation of others' words. Unlike Holly, Tina explicitly referred to the ideological tensions about superhero stories, as is detailed in the section below.

Tina's Grieving X-Men

Abandoning the Blobs

When Tina returned to school (on the same day in which Holly successfully enacted *her* text), she was determined to continue to be Blob. She maintained her desire, even when pressure came from her former niece, Holly.

> *(Tina is sitting during composing time with Holly, Liliana, Sarah, and James. She is preparing to make a list of her actors.)*

HOLLY: Can I be Rogue?
TINA: You're all bad guys. I got all the part of you all.
HOLLY: We're not bad guys.
TINA: But so! You can't beat me! Hey-hey-hey-hey! You can try to beat me all you want.
LILIANA: Are you Jean Gray [another X-Men character]?
TINA: No I'm Blo::b. You can't kill me::::.
LILIANA: A BOY::.
TINA: So! I wanta be a boy.

Still, the pressure continued. Holly was determined to be Rogue, and Monique wanted Storm. Sarah said she would be any good-guy girl, and then James asked to be Wolverine. So Tina relented, with evident exasperation, "You don't want to be a bad guy? OK. Fine. You're not a bad guy."

In the midst of these classroom negotiations, in which Blob was abandoned and the X-Men resurfaced, Tina realized that Holly had already written her own X-Men story. And, in that moment of realization, she also acknowledged—and tentatively challenged—the classroom custom of friends including friends (or desirable others) in their stories.

LILIANA: I'm in your X-Men [story], and I'm in Holly's X-Men.
TINA: There's only one X-Men. There's only one X-Men.
LILIANA: Nuh uh.... You're [Tina] doing one, and she's [Holly] doing one.

      ...

TINA: You're [Holly] not in my X-Men.
HOLLY: Yes I am.
TINA: No you're not.
HOLLY: Yes I am. Because I'm your friend.
TINA: No you're not—So! Just because you're my friend, don't mean you have to be in my X-Men.
HOLLY: I'm still your friend though, OK?
TINA: You still can be in the X-Men.

As it happened, Tina gave all the children at her table parts in her X-Men story, parts they found desirable. Moreover, she granted roles to other girlfriends who happened by: Johnetta requested "Black Queen," Rhonda requested "White Queen," and Makeda became "Second Black Queen" (a role Tina invented for her since "Black Queen" was taken). The only boy at her table—James—was promised a role, but when other boys approached her about roles, Tina held firm: "No.... Then other people gonna be asking me, and I'm gonna have to put the whole class in it!"

Faking the Text

Tina had spent the entire composing period negotiating who was going to be whom in her story. She had not yet, however, written a text. Nonetheless, after Holly successfully performed her X-Men story—and, perhaps, because of that successful performance in which she had had such fun—Tina declared herself "ready" for an Author's Theater turn.

Kristin agreed to the performance. So Tina went to the front of the room, holding her ticket, so to speak—her writing book—close to her chest (and understandably so). Tina's actors soon followed. And everyone became very, very quiet. Unusually quiet. The success of the previous Author's Theater performances that day seemed to have settled the children into an attentive rhythm of watch, clap, respond, watch, clap, respond. Everyone was watching now. And Tina, who had never before presented a text, seemed mighty still.

Tina walked over to Kristin, who was sitting off to the side of the rug. She whispered to her teacher that she actually did not have anything written. But yes, she responded to her inquiring teacher, she thought she could make it up.

Tina went back to the front of the room. In a very small, quiet voice, she began reciting a story about good guys and bad guys.

> TINA: Once upon a time there was X-Men. They were *(Tina names her characters, but she uses such a soft voice that it is hard to hear who they are)*. And the bad guys started to fight with the Black Queen.

That plot line made no sense to Rhonda, who said so, loudly. The Black Queen, like the White one, is a bad "guy" (not a regular bad guy on the Saturday morning cartoon but a bad guy nonetheless).

Tina seemed silenced by the correction. As her actors began to complain about her confusing plot and about not knowing what was going on, Tina told Kristin that she would not do her story that day after all. She would wait. She needed "to finish." She needed some written representational material to cue her oral storytelling, and she also needed, it seemed, the authority that having something written could provide.

Tina's peer Sammy could function without a text, making up stories that elaborated on stereotypical relations between good guys and bad ones, males and females. Tina, on the other hand, was drawing on less familiar characters, because of her efforts to provide girl roles for desiring girls. She seemed to have agreed to include characters she did not know (like the "Queen" characters, as will be evident in the following). Moreover, she seemed unsure of herself, in need of support. She found that support in both writing and wielding the text, using that text to reinforce her control.

Wielding the Text

The next day, Tina did indeed "finish" her text and, also, her Bakhtinian utterance—her response to the class. And she did it, like Holly, carrying a text and, buttressed by that text, speaking loudly and clearly.

During composing time, Tina sat next to Holly (who was writing, once again, about friendships). Tina wrote quickly and, for the most part, steadily, producing a text twice as long as any of her previous ones. She knew who was going to be in her story—she had written down her characters the day before. And, for the most part, she resisted others' requests for inclusion in her story (although she did agree to let Lettrice sing a radio soul song at the end of her performance).

Tina interrupted her work only twice: the first time to discuss Aloyse and Thomas's recent suspension (a discussion in which Tina disputed Holly's reference to the "weakness" of girls [see Chapter 1]); the second time to let Michael and Kevin know in no uncertain terms that she too could play the Streetfighter video game (and "drop Michael on his butt" [see Chapter 3]). Like Holly's preperforming activity of making lists of good kids and bad ones, Tina's seemingly unofficial composing time talk did seem related to the social and ideological work Tina would need to engage in if her text was to be heard: She would need to take control and to respond firmly if and when objections to her written storyline occurred.[5]

Like Holly's, Tina's completed text had no evident remnants of the Blob family. But also like Holly's, it was not the usual fare. In Tina's story, all the named characters were female and, moreover, those characters were capable not only of fighting others but also of feeling for others.

ods tare wry 4 x-man	Once there were 4 X-Men.
in the x-man fote othr	And the X-Men fought others.
own x-man died	One X-Men died.
and the rast uavy they wrey	And the rest of them were
sad they criyd	sad. They cried.
Storm flow away	Storm flew away.
rogue stry to criy	Rogue started to cry.
Jeen Gray cam	Jean Gray came.
Black Momy cam to	Black Mommy [a bad guy] came too.
They all fote	They all fought.
and the x-man won	And the X-Men won.
rogue found storm	Rogue found Storm.
She was making weather	She was making weather.
and they all lived	And they all lived
happy eave after the end.	happy ever after. The end.

When Author's Theater time came, Tina declared herself finished and ready for a performance. She went to the front of the room, text in hand, and immediately called her actors. (She had to make some late role substitutions because some children already designated as actors were temporarily out of the room.) Holly was to be Rogue, Monique was Storm, Liliana substituted for Sarah as Jean Gray, Lettrice substituted for Johnetta as "Black Mommy White Queen" (which Tina referred to as one role), and James was Wolverine.

> *(Tina is now reading her story, as her actors listen and act accordingly.)*
>
> TINA: "One of the X-Men <u>died</u>."
> *(No one dies. So Tina repeats the sentence louder.)*
> "ONE OF THE X-MEN DIED." Die! Die!
> *(Tina stares at "Black Mommy," who seems to be a variant of "Black Queen"—not an X-man but a villain. After hesitating, Black Mommy dies anyway. There are no protests.)*
> "And the rest were very sad. They cried." *(Holly cries)*.
> Everybody cry now, even the <u>boys</u>.
> *(Neither James nor Monique are pretending to cry. Moreover, in the real second-grade world, boys are as likely to cry as girls. [And, on the playground, they are more likely to, since their play is more fraught with physical peril.] But crying boys are not common in superhero stories. So Tina marked James' failure to participate, as the failure of the cultural category of <u>boys</u>.*
>
>   *At the end of the story, Tina called "the singing" girls, and Lettrice, joined by Monique and Holly, sang about another kind of power. "Your love so sweet, knocks me right off my feet," they sang. "I tried hard to fight it, now how can I deny it. . . . ")*

After the play was over, the actors returned to their seats, and a very satisfied-looking Tina waited for comments. James spoke first, complaining that he had nothing to do in Tina's play.

> JAMES: You didn't give me no part.
>   TINA: Your part was to cry and to fight.
> JAMES: Uh uh.
> *(As Wolverine, James was the only unnamed X-Men. It is highly unusual in this class for the male role to be unnamed. Tina rejects his complaint. Although she does not explicitly refer to James' sex, her response echoes her own earlier direc-*

*tive. "Everybody cry now, including the <u>boys</u>," she had said.
And now she says:)*

TINA: I said <u>everybody</u>, including <u>you</u>, should cry. <u>Everybody</u>,
         including <u>you</u>, should fight.
         *(Holly now asks about another unusual aspect of Tina's
         story.)*

HOLLY: Why do we have to have all the singing? Because one died?
         That's why?

TINA: Because I was kinda sad.

HOLLY: And she was like singing up there. *(pointing to the sky)*

TINA: It was like you guys were singing in heaven.

Like Holly, Tina had not been able to enact a Blob story. Nonetheless, she was not silenced by others' resistance. She negotiated, given her own affiliations, and, when temporarily overwhelmed, she raised both pencil and voice and tried again. In Tina's vision, like Holly's, superhero teams were dominated by women of color who, nonetheless, served with women and men of different races. Moreover, power itself was tempered with human fragility: People fought, became tired, grieved, and died.

These two activist girls—experienced writers of relationships—were changing the possibilities for superhero stories in the local culture of the classroom. Although conventional male-exclusive superhero stories continued, they were "dialogized," to use Bakhtin's word (1981, p. 426); that is, they were rendered a possibility among other possibilities. And these new possibilities—and the ideological refractions that accompanied their social evolution—elicited a composing time response from Sammy.

TRANSFORMING WORDS AND WORLDS:
SAMMY AND THE X-PEOPLE

It was fitting that Sammy put together the first well-integrated X-Men team. During the second-grade year, he became a kind of social negotiator, anxious as he was both to be included in others' plans and to include others himself. As noted in the previous chapter, he did gain acceptance as a story player both in and out of the classroom.

In the current chapter, Sammy has been barely visible in the preceding pages. But he was in the classroom during both Holly's and Tina's performances. Further, he had had a part in Holly's Author's Theater—along with Tina and Rhonda, he had been a member of the bad guy's team. In that story, Sammy found himself positioned in a very different text world, one organized by a child with whom he had been in much social conflict over the proper role for a "lady." And that conflict—and the experience of literally being in her alternative world—-seemed to make salient for him new kinds of authorial choices, new possibilities for portraying human relations. (In fact, the next year, in the third grade, Sammy "made up" Holly's text about the dutiful X-Men doing their work despite exhaustion—he included the same characters and the same exchange between Archangel and Storm, evidence that appearing in her story was a significant experience for Sammy.)

In Sammy's first completed text after Holly's and Tina's performances—and his first after his own previous X-Men story—Sammy once again appropriated this superhero team. He wrote the following text.

> Once upon a time there was X-Men.
> And they was friends.
> And the bad guys was mean.
> And the X-Men went to Pizza Hut.
> And the bad guys come in
> and they started to fight
> and the X-Men won.

While writing this story, Sammy explicitly planned to write some fun "action" for the X-Men (getting pizza)—he had, as readers may recall, been criticized for having so little "action" in his previous X-Men story (see Chapter 3). Moreover, he deliberately planned to include all the major female X-Men. He did not specify their names in writing (something he would do in the third grade), but he did orally *solicit* (i.e., he asked in an open-ended way who wanted to fill) both the male and the female roles; the girls did not have to beg.

Thus, Sammy gave roles to the boys sitting at his work table, including Nyem (as Wolverine), Aloyse (as Cyclops), Kevin (as Beast), Thomas (as a bad guy), and James (as Gambit's brother)—Sammy himself was Gambit. And Sammy gave the female roles to girls who *asked* for them, including Tina (as Rogue), Johnetta (as Storm), Monique (as Jubilee), Liliana (as Jean Gray), and Lynn (as a bad guy). When Sammy asked for a volunteer reader, he took the first person who raised a hand: Melissa.

As a result of this social process, this affiliating with a diversity of others in the context of a superhero story, Sammy took to the stage an unusual X-Men drama. The X-Men themselves were gender-balanced: there were four girls and five boys; the performers were racially balanced as well. Moreover, of the two bad guys, one was a girl and one a boy. (And, although the children on the stage were predominantly African American, the girls and boys were racially integrated too.) Further, the romantically linked characters—Liliana and Aloyse, and Sammy and Tina—ignored the teasing that began when their roles were known. Thus, the children took the roles they wanted and stayed with them. The teasing stopped, the story was read, the drama enacted.

After the play was over, Kristin asked if there were any comments. A number of children noted that acting out the story had been fun, and others noted that it had been fun to watch. For example:

MAKEDA: I like when [the X-Men] went to the pizza place. And I like when they fighted. And it was good that you picked X-Men. And I know people watch X-Men. So do I, and I like it.

MELISSA: I liked your story, and I like that you picked me to read it, and reading is about my favorite thing.

LYNN: My favorite part of the story—because I was in it, my favorite part of the story was when we got to fight.

(Then Sammy himself, with no prompting from anyone, says:)

SAMMY: And there were really more X-Men. The X-people were boys and girls, and the um bad guys were boys and girls

—a spontaneous semantic transformation to mark a cultural one. Thus Sammy seemed conscious that something had changed—that he had found new social and textual possibilities for human relations. At their roots, the conflicts generated by superhero stories were about these relations; they were about inclusion, exclusion, and the right to play in a story, "to stretch [one's] limbs in some mighty struggle" (Hurston, 1942/1991, p. 40).

CODA: THE END OF YEAR ONE

There is a literary parallel of sorts in Jules Feifer's (1993) book *The Man in the Ceiling* to the interactions between second graders Tina, Holly, and Sammy. The lead character in that book is Jimmy, who feels he is a rather "[un]successful boy" (p. 39), given his lack of athletic prowess, but a nicely budding cartoonist. Jimmy uses his cartooning skills to impress Charley Beemer, who he views as a *very* successful boy and a playground leader. Charley finds Jimmy's "Mini-Man" superhero adventures boring, and so he suggests "Bullet Head," a bullet with human features that can propel itself through people and property with remarkable speed.

Jimmy's sister Lisi is not impressed with this new adventure series, as the following exchange reveals.

"What's with you and all this blood and stuff? And bodies and things blowing apart? This guy's head being shoved into a ship's propeller!" [This is Lisi talking.]

Until that moment, Jimmy thought this was his most successful drawing.

"He's a bad guy," Jimmy said.

"It's disgusting! What's the matter with you?!" Lisi shouted. She was back to shouting but had not yet returned to screaming.

"I'm just—I'm just drawing it for somebody. It's not as if it's my own idea.... "

"You're drawing it <u>for somebody</u>?! ... <u>Who</u>?"

"Charley Beemer," he said.

"CHARLEY BEEMER?!"

Lisi screamed. She was back to screaming. "CHARLEY BEEMER HAS NO TALENT! YOU SHOULD DO MY IDEAS BEFORE YOU DO CHARLEY BEEMER'S! ... "

Not for an instant did Jimmy dream that Lisi would not be impressed—impressed? bowled over!—by the news that he was collaborating with Charley Beemer. She was like no other kid he knew. She was <u>so</u> weird. (pp. 126–127)

In the dialogic vision that underlies this book, everyone writes *for somebody* or somebodies. Writers, like speakers, orient themselves in social space. Their words "presuppose others"—the others from whom they have learned the words and those whom, in the moment, they are addressing (Bakhtin, 1986, p. 72). Still, if they are to avoid mindless domination by others' discourse, they must become mindful of their appropriations and orientations—indeed, they must become playful, willing to apply those words to "new conditions," to new "relationships with new contexts" (Bakhtin, 1981, pp. 345–346).

People like Lisi, who view the social world differently, provide ideological wake-up calls to those immersed in the taken-for-granted. As "weird" as Lisi seemed to Jimmy, she made him take notice—and he made her take notice, articulate her own views of Charley, cartooning, and her brother.

In a similar way, Sammy, Tina, and Holly's ways of speaking and writing during composing time were interwoven. Sammy contributed to the "particular state of affairs" that Tina and Holly took as their "point of departure," to return to the Volosinov quote in this chapter's introduction (1973, p. 95). These girls were certainly not impressed that Seth and Jonathan were in Sammy's stories. *They* wanted to be in his stories. The girls did not object to the violence of the superhero tales (although such objections would be forthcoming in the third grade), but they did have their own ideas about how such stories might go.

The girls' "written verbal performance[s] engaged, as it were, in ideological colloquy of large scale"; in their authorial choices of male and female characters and of those characters' own words and actions, Tina and Holly "respond[ed] to something" and, in Tina's case in particular, "object[ed] to something." In their struggles to bring their stories to the wider public, they learned to "anticipat[e] possible responses and objections" and "to see[k] support" (Volosinov, 1973, p. 95).

In seeking support, all three children—students in a writing class—turned to the text itself. Sammy became more conscious of the representational function of writing, which allowed him some independence from his own oral storytelling. Thus he was better able to join in the anticipated social play of Author's Theater. Tina and Holly also used the text to mark—to represent—their authorial decisions and, also, to cue their oral storytelling and, moreover, to reinforce their authority in the unruly crowd. Just as the children's enacted texts were shaped by the demands of the classroom social life, so too that life was shaped—and reshaped—for display by the relational possibilities offered by the children's texts.

In these ways, the children were beginning to exploit the dialogic nature of texts—their potential as a means for deliberately regulating authors' relationships with others in the social and ideological world. Their ideological awakening—their awareness of a gap between their own thoughts and those assumed by others—was audible in comments like Tina's "Everybody cry now, even the *boys*," and Sammy's "The "X-people were boys and girls and the bad guys were boys and girls."

The children, however, were *just* beginning to exploit the dialogic potential of texts. All three children, like the children in their classroom more generally, were primarily appropriating the cultural material around them, selectively reproducing available roles and relations but not inverting or transforming the given. In the next chapter, based on the children's experiences in the third grade, Tina stretches her authorial muscle and begins to turn the given on its head.

▼ *5* ▼
▼

The "Trials and Tribulations" of Emily and Other Media Misses: Text as Dialogic Medium

"Good day, Granny. I've brought you a hot loaf of bread and a bottle of milk."
. . . "Undress yourself, my child," the werewolf said, "and come lie down beside me."
When she laid herself down in the bed, the little girl said:
"Oh, Granny, how hairy you are!"
"The better to keep myself warm, my child."
. . . "Oh, Granny, what a big mouth you have!"
"The better to eat you with, my child!"
"Oh, Granny, I've got to go badly. Let me go outside."
. . . "All right, but make it quick."
The werewolf attached a wooden rope to her foot and let her go outside.
When the little girl was outside, she tied the end of the rope to a plum tree in the courtyard. . . . [The werewolf] jumped out of bed and saw that the little girl had escaped."

An oral tale recorded in France, about 1885; published by Paul Delarue and cited in J. Zipes, *The Trials and Tribulations of Little Red Riding Hood*, 1993, pp. 5–6.

L ittle Red Riding Hood, that disobedient child who dallied in the woods, was not always a helpless little thing, badly in need of a hunter, a woodcutter, or a bit-brighter granny. At one time, argues Jack Zipes, she was quite capable of saving herself.

Little Red Riding Hood, Cinderella, and other folk characters have origins traceable to the teaching tongues of old women, who warned their young charges of the dangers around them (Warner, 1994). Young girls especially needed to be wary, and not only of actual beasts in the woods. Forced unions, on the one hand, and a dependency on male resources, on the other, made their relationships with fathers and husbands complex and contradictory. No less complex were their relationships with other women, their work companions and their competitors for the security men could provide. The commonness of mothers' deaths in childbirth meant that young girls often negotiated these complexities on their own, helped along, perhaps, by ghostmothers returned as fairies.

Over time, these old, cautionary tales, which had originated in the countryside and been passed on mainly by women, were written down for the edification and pleasure of the children of the bourgeois. Of the new composers, it was the now-famous men, like Perrault and the Grimm brothers, whose vantage points most shaped the stories' continuing evolution. In their hands, curious, self-reliant, and formerly triumphant girls became helpless before the wolves they themselves lured; in the end, they received their just deserts (Zipes, 1993). Good and lovely girls lost their tongues and suffered in silence, awaiting their princes; their suffering was caused less often by men and, much more, by wicked and ugly women (Bottigheimer, 1987; Tatar, 1992; Warner, 1994).

In contemporary times, the men and (less often) the women of media—the Walt Disneys and Steven Spielbergs—have become the major retellers of old stories. In their hands, folk figures, like Little Red Riding Hood and Cinderella, have become the commercial cousins of more recent and ephemeral characters, like April and Storm, added to children's "image store" (Warner, 1994, p. 418). These commercial producers aim not only to edify the young but mainly to sell to them (Kinder, 1991). Thus, the diversity and malleability of stories may wane even further, fixed by the forces of commercialism and the seductive, and marketable, images of the dominant cultural storylines (Warner, 1994).

And yet, the available female characters are marked by the contradictions of our own times. There is still the disobedient Red Riding Hood, the long-suffering Cinderella, and her sinful sisters, but there is also a wisecracking superhero like Rogue, with girlfriends tried and true.[1] Contemporary girls (and women) are "presented with an array of media archetypes, and given morality tales in which we identify first with one type, then another," suggests media studies scholar Susan Douglas. We "have grown accustomed to compartmentalizing ourselves into a whole host of personas," who may have contradictory desires (Douglas, 1994, p. 13; Fisherkeller, 1995; Luke & Roe, 1993; Turnbull, 1993).

Moreover, this self disarray is not necessarily ideologically stultifying. In fact, it is potentially liberating, *if* the images that mediate it become ingredients for one's own stories, one's own response to confusing times. In fact, from a Bakhtinian perspective, play with appealing but contradictory voices evidences a coming to consciousness, a resistance to the authoritarian and the set. By "turning persuasive discourse into speaking persons," composers explore and "expose the limitations of both image and discourse" (Bakhtin, 1981, p. 348). At its most expansive, this is what modern novels and other media forms can do; the composer displays not so much a truth as an "orchestration of discourses," of characters talking to, past, and over each other (Stam, 1991, p. 253).

Herein, the concern is not with how the privileged men have appropriated Little Red Riding Hood and her folk relations, nor with how adult literary or cinematic artists appropriate complex discourses. Rather, the concern is with how children themselves appropriate available cultural resources (whatever their origin) to answer others in their own social spaces (Mukerji & Schudson, 1991).[2] Among the most pervasive of those cultural resources are the images provided by video and television (e.g., Grider, 1981; Sutton-Smith, 1975; Tucker, 1980, 1992).

One central female character in Kristin's classroom was Emily—the well-mannered and unaffected girlfriend of "The Three Ninjas'" Rocky. Emily was not a main character in the film, but, as illustrated in Chapter 3, she was a main character for girls seeking a role in ninja stories. Moreover, like her less ephemeral folk relations, Emily was "interpreted and reinterpreted," subjected to "trials and tribulations" (Zipes, 1993)—not by different selves over the centuries, but by the children in this classroom collectively and, in particular, by Tina.

Unlike the famed artists studied by Bakhtin and Bakhtinian scholars, Tina was a small child and a beginning writer. She did not write a grand tale with complex characters for the official world, nor did she retell a story that would itself be retold in the unofficial one. But through a series of stories, she did appropriate, exaggerate, invert, and, eventually, bring together the relational lives of a "whole host of personas." In fact, given her second-grade social activism, Tina seems to qualify as the sort of "case" in which, according to Bakhtin, play with provided images is "especially important": "those cases where a struggle against such images has already begun, where someone is striving to liberate himself [sic] from [their] influence" (Bakhtin, 1981, p. 348).

Tina's manipulation of Emily and other media characters—her marking and elaborating on their actions, qualities, and feelings—were her means for (and the result of) her participation in grand cultural dialogues about power, goodness, and love, as particularized in her local classroom community. In that community, the children's concerns over access to the fun of enacted texts (i.e., who has, or can use, a ticket to play) were increasingly complicated by conflicts over the nature of fun and, in this chapter in particular, about gender roles (i.e., how child authors represent the possibilities and qualities of males and females). Thus, before I return to the exploits of Tina, I describe the changes evident in her classroom community in the third-grade phase of this project.

A NEW MIX: CONTINUITY AND CONTINGENCY IN THE EVOLVING COLLECTIVE

On my first day back in Kristin's room in the third grade, I noticed Tina, Liliana, and Sammy sprawled on a corner of the rug, writing in their journals. As they worked, they were playing "dogs," a game started in the second grade by Makeda; in this game, girl owners bossed around and chased after often-difficult boy dogs. With two girl owners and no dog companions, Sammy was very cooperative.

> *(With her eyes on her paper and her hand forming the letters of a word, Tina says quietly to Sammy)*
> TINA: Hey dog! You hungry?
> *(Sammy nods his head.)*
> *(to Liliana)* Go get him some pork chops, and some ground beef, and some fish.
> *(Liliana walks over to the shelf where the children's writing folders are kept, retrieves not a folder but some pretend food, brings it back to the rug, and places it in front of Sammy.)*
> LILIANA: Here go your food.
> TINA: *(after a few minutes of quiet writing)* You still hungry?
> *(Sammy shakes his head.)*
> Bark, Sammy, bark!
> SAMMY: Arf!
> TINA: *(in a very quiet voice)* Bark sometimes, OK?
> *(Sammy nods.)*

As the preceding scene-within-a-scene suggests, the unofficial world of play and peers seemed alive and well in Kristin's room, as did the official world of composing. However, there were changes in the classroom community, including in its membership and its "image store" from the popular media.

Changes in the Cast of Characters

Sammy was no longer at the edges of the unofficial social world. He played regularly with the boys on the playground, who were into sports (especially football), as well as superhero games, this year. He even had a best friend, Aloyse. Moreover, Seth, who had been such a significant figure in the second-grade class, had left the public schools; he was now in a private school. Of the five new boys, there were two who themselves were notable classroom figures (both Mexican American and from low-income homes): Victor, a physically large child (once retained) and a dominant (and sometimes dominating) voice on the playground and in the classroom; and Edward, a physically much smaller and interactively less dominating child. Like Sammy and Tina (and unlike Victor), Edward loved to act and, often, was quite the ham. (Demographic information on all third-grade children can be found in Table A4.)

As for Tina, she was most often found with Makeda this year. Her fellow activist, Holly, had moved, and Johnetta, who had also spoken up for the girls, had been retained and was in a different classroom. There was, however, a new girl who, by the end of the year, would emerge as a classroom force on gender issues—Lena, an immigrant student from Eritrea.

The new year had brought new media figures as well. From television came the superhero team "Power Rangers" (Saban, 1994), who were popular with some boys, among them, Sammy and Aloyse. From the new videos available came the characters of *Aladdin* (Musker & Clements, 1992), whom Tina in particular liked very much. Popular videos included films made for adults, most notably *Jungle Fever* (Lee, 1991); the racial and romantic tensions featured in this film figured into the imaginations of some girls (as highlighted in Chapter 7). Video games also provided new images for composing. These images were appropriated by a number of boys, among them Edward, Victor, and Victor's good friend Bryant; their plotless scenes of one physical encounter after another generated classroom discord (as discussed in Chapter 6). (For more detailed descriptions of all movies, TV shows, and video games, see Appendix B.)

Developments in Texts as Products

The children's texts themselves were generally longer than they had been in the second grade. The average story length of a second-grade text (for all children) was 49 words; of a third-grade text, 77 words. More particularly, Sammy and Tina, who had written brief texts of about 35 words in the second grade, now wrote longer stories—Sammy's averaged about 50 words and Tina's about 115. Tina was especially proud of these new page-long stories. As Radha told her one day, she had become "a heck of a writer." On my first day back in her room, Tina interrupted her story writing (and her dog play) to show me her writing book.

"I used to write *short* things," she said.

"I remember," I responded.

As will be evident, collectively, the children's written story orientations had more elaborate introductions of characters, and their plots more extended series of actions. There is nothing particularly remarkable about these text changes. In classrooms where young children regularly write, one would expect longer, more elaborate tales (see, e.g., Chapman, 1994; Dyson, 1989b; King & Rentel, 1981). What is remarkable is the social and ideological dynamics that undergirded children's authorial decisions and made those decisions significant markers of, and contributors to, individual and community growth.

From Accessing the Action to Questioning the Details

The year before, in the second grade, Kristin had provided the word "action," the children had provided the word "fun," and, in the interaction among teacher and children, the textual representation of action became associated with having a fun story. Ideological tensions were generated when children perceived themselves as being denied access to that fun because of their group membership (i.e., their sex and, less markedly, their race). In the third grade, Kristin provided a new word—"details." Since qualities of characters and actions were becoming more detailed in texts themselves—and less dependent on spontaneous invention by playful actors, ideological issues associated with access (e.g., the availablity of parts for girls) were also becoming issues of representation (e.g., the nature of a "girl part").

The particular issues generated were contingent on the particular chemistry of the real and imagined characters in this classroom community. For example, one day James decided to write a story based on the video-game-turned-cartoon *Sonic the Hedgehog* (Bohot Entertainment, 1993). When Aloyse volunteered for the role of Sonic's sidekick, Tails, Sammy reacted quickly.

"Oh, you that little girl who be with Hedgehog," he said—a comment that inspired a rigorous denial from Aloyse and, then, an intense discussion that spread through the class. Tails' sex, it seemed, was debatable. As Sammy shouted that he had "more witnesses" for the truth, Kristin noted the commotion and called everyone to the rug. She asked the children to brainstorm what clues the cartoon offered as to sex identity. Each item—each representational element—the children generated (e.g., way of walking, talking, size of ears and nose, the length of hair) was met with resistance (e.g., "Boys don't always. . . . "), until finally it seemed to all that Edward had the best suggestion: Listen and see if Sonic says "he" or "she" in reference to his friend.

The discussed issues were also contingent on the children's continuing experiences as urban children in a socioeconomically, racially, and culturally complex school. Most notably, in the third grade, the children more often referred to racial issues in both official and unofficial talk, and so did Kristin, who built such issues into the school curriculum. For example, during a class discussion of a child's proposed "Bruce Lee" story (DeLaurentis & Cohen, 1993), Lettrice reacted to the story's Chinatown setting. She had never read a story set in "Africa Town." She had, in fact, never heard of a place called Africa Town, and she planned to "invent" one when she grew up. In the ensuing discussion about Chinatown, many misconceptions surfaced, including about the founding of Chinatown and the "Americanness" of its residents. These misconceptions were the basis for future classroom experiences, including a field trip to Oakland Chinatown.[3]

Differences in the children's use of media source material also influenced their discussions. For example, in an official discussion of the criteria for a "good" story, Lynn suggested originality was important, "not like, you know 'X-Men.'" From my perspective, Lynn's singling out of X-Men was notable, since a number of children had written similarly "unoriginal" stories based on books. In fact, Lynn herself had written stories based on *The Sideways Stories* (Sachar, 1985), a chapter book about the not-quite-sensible—the "sideways"—children and teachers at Sideways Elementary School. Other book-based stories included Sarah's featuring Nancy Drew, Jonathan's on *The Chronicles of Narnia* (Lewis, 1950), and Adam's on *The Jolly Postman* (Ahlberg & Ahlberg, 1986).[4]

A number of children reacted to Lynn's comment on X-Men. Lettrice pointed out that sometimes people change the stories and, even if they don't, "it's not like . . . you could be sued," since the stories were only for school, not for the wider public. Edward agreed, and then Tina offered her own opinion. "You *can* [write a good story about X-Men]," she said, "but only if you have enough courage in yourself."

As was illustrated in the preceding chapter, in the second grade, Tina's writing and, moreover, her public presentation of an X-Men story *had* taken a great deal of courage—the courage to write the story differently, to talk back. In the third grade, Tina would display such courage again. However, when I first returned to the school for the third-grade phase of the project, I did not find the tiny social activist who had so riveted my attention the year before. Instead I found a Tina who seemed to have decided to write "girl" stories.

THE APPROPRIATION OF EMILY AND OTHER MEDIA LADIES

On my first day in the third grade, I noticed that Tina had written X-Men on the back of her journal, and, above those letters, the words "no no." No more X-Men. "Too boyish," she had told her teacher. Underneath this negation, she had drawn pictures of Aladdin and Princess Jasmine. (See Figure 5.1.)

Tina was the *only* girl in her class who, by this mid-December date, had written a superhero story (a short variation on her second-grade story featuring Storm and Rogue). But now she seemed to be playing with more traditional gender roles and relations. During composing, she often sat next to Makeda, who primarily wrote rescue stories featuring such traditional roles (including one in which poor Emily was trapped in a closet by the bad guys, a fate she was spared in the film). Tina, however, seemed less than serious about her own portrayal of traditional roles.

Figure 5.1. *Tina's picture of Aladdin and Princess Jasmine—and her commentary on X-Men stories.*

For example, Tina wrote a superhero story from the perspective of "us girls," that is, the female victims. In so doing, she used a new textual feature—the spoken words of the main characters, who were quite desperate for help. The very desperateness of the girls, suspended between rescue and death, suggested a parody, a revoicing of a victim's plea, infused with a sharp directive to the "boy."

> "Batman is going to save us girls.
> Hurry Bat man hurry.
> We are about to die."
> Penguins came too . . .
> "Batman, wrap them up, kill them.
> Hurry, boy, hurry."
> *(Spelling and punctuation corrected for ease of reading.)*

Moreover, during Author's Theater, when Tina played the role of victim in fairy tales (e.g., Snow White) or superhero stories, she consistently exaggerated the role for dramatic effect—and she also consistently made the children laugh. In Sammy's ninja story, for example, she played the role of Emily. Sammy actually had written a sparse text that appropriated the movie scene in which Rocky and Colt play basketball to win back Emily's bike from two school bullies.

During Author's Theater, Sammy fleshed out his story (adding dialogue and plot details), but he moved quickly from the scene in which Emily's bike is stolen (a scene that features Emily) to an elaborate retelling of the basketball scene and an even more elaborate presentation of a fight scene. Tina, however, played her brief part to the hilt, so to speak (pun intended), as is illustrated in the following.

> *(Sammy is presenting his "Three Ninjas" story, which features Aloyse in the lead role as Rocky. Patrick is TumTum, Bryant is Colt, Radha is Grandpa, Jonathan is the boys' father, and Michael is playing the roles of both bullies. Sammy has come to the bike scene.)*

SAMMY: *(improvising)* Rocky, Colt, TumTum, and Emily was riding their bikes, and then Emily went to school [i.e., Emily took the straight and narrow path to school, unlike Rocky and his brothers who ignored a KEEP OUT sign and took a less paved route through an abandoned lot]. . . . The fat boy and the skinny boy [the bullies] had take Emily's bike.

MICHAEL: *(playing both roles)* Give me that bike.

SAMMY: And then—and then Emily screamed and called Rocky.

> *(Tina screams shrilly and calls out in a high-pitched, pathetic voice for Rocky.)*
> SAMMY: Rocky said, "What's wrong, Emily?"
> ALOYSE: What's wrong, Emily?
> TINA: *(Boohoo's with enthusiasm and then says in a choked-up voice)* They took my bike!
> *(Rocky gives Emily a ride to school where the two older brothers play a basketball game with the bullies "to get the girlfriend's bike back." Emily is not mentioned again.)*

In the actual movie, Emily does not weep (nor does she completely disappear from the action). Rather, she is perturbed with Rocky for leaving her alone while he "showed off." Through exaggeration of stereotypical human relations, Tina avoided boredom; as she told Sammy after the performance was over, "even if a person has a little part, make it so they're not just sitting there doing nothing, 'cause that's boring." Just as importantly, though, Tina was playing to her audience. In Warner's words, storytellers "may well entrench bigotry" (i.e., storytellers may play to an audience's prejudices) "if that is what is expected: how thrilling is the wicked queen . . . let her dance in her red-hot shoes" (1995, p. 409). Or, in Emily's scene, let her weep pathetically.

Tina also appropriated and exaggerated romantic encounters for performative purposes, just as Sammy often did. Unlike Sammy, Tina had not exploited romantic relations in the second grade, and, moreover, she always avoided romantic acting roles (i.e., those involving loving, kissing, marrying). In the third grade, however, she was initially concerned, quite explicitly, with not being "too boyish"; thus, the exaggeration of rescue and romance may have been a particularly appealing form of mockery, of expressing her own "power and powerlessness" as a girl in the peer world (McMahon & Sutton-Smith, 1995, p. 301). Although it "may well entrench bigotry," to return to Warner's words, exaggeration is also a way of not taking too seriously the very stereotypes one is exploiting.

Affiliating with the Crowd Through Jasmine

As already noted, Tina was very taken with the movie *Aladdin*. In that film, based on the old fairy tale, a street boy (Aladdin) falls in love with a wandering princess (Jasmine), outwits an evil sorcerer and his parrot companion, and, with the help of a genie in a lamp, wins the princess' love. Unlike the ninja movies or X-Men, Aladdin was not a widely retold story in this classroom community, but Tina seemed preoccupied with the character of Aladdin.

In her two completed Aladdin texts, Tina highlighted a brief opening scene in the movie, when a nurturing Aladdin befriends small urchin children by sharing broken bread with them (which scene seems almost Biblical to me). In her first story, Aladdin, an admitted "street rat," steals bread (as he does in the movie); in her second story, Aladdin, no longer nonchalant about being called "a street rat," buys his bread—suggesting that this moral digression was problematic to her. After all, Tina had ambitions of being a person of God, a minister to the people, like her aunt. (Indeed, to my knowledge, the only time Tina herself wept pathetically at school was when she thought Thomas, her cousin, was literally full of the devil.)[5]

Tina gave less attention to the romance between Aladdin and Jasmine. In both her texts, Aladdin and Jasmine meet and marry and, in one story, Jasmine rejects "the bad guy" as a husband before she and Aladdin marry and have five kids (which, in the film, they do not). Tina gave no written attention at all to Aladdin's encounter with the forces of evil. Following are her two completed texts, written within a week of each other.

Once upon a time there
was a boy named Aladdin.
People called him a street rat.
So. He did not care.
Well, he was a street rat.
Abu was a monkey. One day
Aladdin and Abu had went to
the store. Abu stole a
watermelon.
The store man caught him.
Abu put it back.
Then Aladdin steal one.
He steal some
bread and broke it in half for
Abu. Then he saw two little
kids. Aladdin gave his bread
to the girl. Abu gave his to
the boy.
Princess Jasmine came
and her tiger and her
was in the back yard.
And the tiger was playing with her.
And they [Aladdin and Jasmine]
met and get married.

Once upon a time there
was a boy named Aladdin.
People called him a street rat.
He did not like that.[6]

Abu was bad.
Abu got a whooping by
the tiger.
Abu cried.

Then Aladdin bought some
bread.

He gave it to the little
kids. They play and jump
and ran and ran and ran.

Princess Jasmine was
in the backyard with her
tiger.

The bad guy wanted to marry
the princess. She didn't want to
also. The prince [Aladdin?]
wanted to also. They met
and went to the palace and

got married and had 5 kids.
Angie, Asia, Tina, Damon, Derick.

The end.   The end.

(Spelling and punctuation corrected—and bracketed phrases added—for ease of reading.)

Despite her written attention to Aladdin, when Tina brought her second Aladdin story to Author's Theater, she did not mention the "street rat's" distribution of bread but, rather, played up Abu's misbehavior. Moreover, she emphasized Jasmine's relationships as victim-to-be-rescued and as lover and soon-to-be wife and mother (the latter a role she does not play in the film). Thus, as her story of Aladdin entered into the social milieu of the community as a whole, Tina played with, rather than against, the dominant storylines in her class.

The following excerpt from her performance illustrates Tina's skill at anticipating audience response. She is a very different performer from the child overcome with shyness on her first attempt in the second grade.

(Tina is assembling her actors. She chooses Radha for Aladdin and black-haired Susan for Jasmine because of "how they look." [Tina has never before made choices of actors explicitly based on physical resemblance to characters—but neither has she presented a story that highlights romance, with its concomitant emphasis on physical appearance.] Tina tells Radha as he comes to the front of the room, "You're gonna have to be married to Susan." Susan rolls her eyes [and I am surprised, since Tina has so actively avoided romance as author and actor]. Other players include Patrick as the father, Makeda as the tiger, Jonathan as the monkey, James as the genie, Sammy as the magic carpet, and Victor and Kevin as the bad guys.

Tina starts to read her second Aladdin story, "Once upon a time there was a boy named Aladdin," but she soon abandons her text.)

TINA: "One day they went to the store," a hundred (dollars) in their pockets. "Abu stole some bread. . . . So . . . he got a whooping by Jasmine's tiger." *(much laughter)* That Abu, *(sigh)* he stealed. He cried and cried and cried. And tiger had left. So one day Princess Jasmine escaped from her castle. Climbed down the ol' walls she did. The tiger followed her.

MAKEDA: Mmmm. I wonder where she's going.

TINA: So one day Princess Jasmine got lost.
        (Susan walks around.)
        Bad guys came behind her.

(Pauses as Victor and Kevin creep come up behind Susan; then adopts a dramatic voice.)
So her tiger barely killed them and scared them away.
(Pause; lots of laughter as Makeda growls and scowls and runs after the two boys.)
FREEZE! So the princess ran before the bad guys caught her. . . . Princess Jasmine and Aladdin . . . lived in a castle. The father came in, caught 'em kissing.
(Susan moves to one side of the rug, Radha to the other. They both stand cross-armed; Radha is smiling but Susan just looks deadpan. They will not act out this scene. Tina does not press them to act but continues her story.)

TINA: They got in trouble. The father left. Then Jasmine went with Aladdin and so they got married.
(Audience members begin singing "Here comes the bride.")
Three days later *(pause)* Aladdin found a lamp, and he rubbed it.
(Radha now performs his part.)
And his brother the genie came out . . . And they flew on the magic carpet.
(More laughter as Radha straddles Sammy, who is lying on the floor.)
They got off. The genie granted them five wishes. ( ) Eight days later, they had five children.
(Most children are laughing very hard now. Kristin intervenes, telling Tina that it is time to end her story. Tina, however, uses her text to reassert her authority as author and to finish her performance.)

TINA: Wait. *(to Kristin)* I'll tell you what the kids' names was. *(looking at her text)* . . .

LETTRICE: Tell us their real names.
(Lettrice seems to be suggesting that Tina will simply make up, rather than read, the children's names.)

TINA: I'm telling you.

RADHA: Tell us the names!
(Radha is almost mocking in tone, as if he does not believe Tina has the names written.)

TINA: You read them.
(Tina hands Radha the paper.)

RADHA: OK. *(visibly startled; Tina has written these names)* "They had 5 kids: Angie, Asia, Tina, Damon, Derick. The end."

Tina had used evaluative techniques (Labov, 1972), like repetition ("That Abu; he stealed"), repeated adjectives, and unusual syntax ("Climbed down the ol' walls she did"), to underline the misbehavior and the vulnerability of both Abu and Jasmine. As a group, Tina's audience responded with audible glee. There was evident pleasure in the communal witnessing of the forbidden and the dreaded. And, unlike her Author's Theater presentation featured in Chapter 4—about the strong but vulnerable X-women—there was nothing in this story that directly challenged the ideological status quo.

However, in her Aladdin presentation, Tina had had the tiger, not Aladdin or some other male human, rescue the vulnerable Jasmine. Moreover, she had never stopped campaigning for roles as an X-person, as a strong woman who takes on the evil other, in the boys' stories. In fact, Tina's return to the public role of social resister and her reappropriation of tough girls as an author dated from a tense encounter with her new peer, Victor.

Talking Back with Storm

The encounter with Victor took place one day in early March, when Kristin asked the children to look over their writing folders and choose a "good story," one worthy of revision, editing, publication, and display in the classroom library. In response to Kristin's query about the qualities of such a story, Lynn had made the aforementioned comment on originality, and Tina had followed with her own comment on courage. In the discussion excerpt that follows, Kristin has just asked Tina to explain what she means by a "good" X-Men story.

> TINA: It should be more about the girls winning instead of the boys.
> KRISTIN: So should every story have the girls winning instead of the boys?
> TINA: No, not <u>all</u>, just some, just some of 'em, not all of 'em. Because in every story the boys always have to win. And that's really not fair to the girls.
> VICTOR: Not <u>fair</u> to the <u>girls</u>? Not <u>fair</u> to the <u>boys</u>.
> *(Victor has a disgusted look on his face and grumbles inaudibly after he finishes. Kristin intervenes to keep the peace and, also, to bring the children back to the task at hand and to Lynn's "original" comment.)*
> KRISTIN: It seems to me what you're talking about . . . [is] that the story should in <u>some</u> way be original. It should be a little bit different. You should put some of your own ideas into it. And one idea might be to have the girls win instead of the boys. . . .

(Tina seems to be talking about the public good—about fairness, but Kristin here emphasizes textual goodness—being original.)

TINA: Yeah, 'cause in <u>most</u> stories, like X-Men and all that—
(Victor interrupts.)

VICTOR: There's girls in there too!

TINA: I know but the boys are always doing things for the girls, and it seems like the girls are weak.

VICTOR: Look at Storm! Look at Rogue!
(Victor has his face right up in Tina's face, but she is not blinking.

Animated and incomprehensible conversations erupt, quite heated, among all the children. Kristin now emphasizes textual and authorial choice: She says that the issue is "not necessarily [about] what happens on X-Men [television cartoon], but [about] what you choose to write about."

Lynn seems moved to explain why her novel-in-process is about boys.)

LYNN: In the story—the baseball story [about the Oakland A's], there aren't any girls because they don't have teams for girls, just for boys.

KRISTIN: I'm not saying that you would want to do this, [but] could you imagine a story where a girl became a member of a baseball team?

LETTRICE: It's not—

MICHAEL: Now they got girls in wrestling. They got girls in wrestling.

VICTOR: Oh yeah. They got 'em in basketball too!

BRYANT: They got girls driving race cars!

MICHAEL: Of course girls could be in tennis. *(laughs)*

In the discussion, which had been dominated by boys, the general response to Tina's point about "fair" X-Men texts was to refer to the source material for those texts, the media stories themselves. In that material, female characters *were* physically powerful. And when Lynn justified her baseball stories with reference to her source material, many boys noted sports that included girls (although not necessarily on the same playing field as boys).

For her part, Kristin worked to underline the power of the author's imagination and textual decisions, another sort of power implicit in Tina's comment. Moreover, Kristin tried to clarify the tension between Victor and Tina—the tension between what is offered by, and what is taken from, commercial culture. In essence, Kristin was saying, "There are about as many powerful female X-Men as male X-Men in the cartoons and videos, yes. But those females have nonexistent or minor roles in the boys' stories." Indeed, in the third grade, child-composed X-Men stories included 104 references to male characters, but only 24 references to females; moreover, female roles in narrative action were quite limited. (See, e.g., Edward's picture [Figure 5.2] of the X-Men Wolverine, Cyclops, and Storm "too," so to speak; appearing strikingly shapeless, she stands quietly behind her two teammates.)

The class discussion ended, composing time began, but neither Tina nor Victor was done with the conversation. Victor's mind was on the media stories; he muttered over and over that "they" just didn't know about the X-Men; it was well known among the children that Kristin didn't even have a TV! But Tina's mind was on her classmates. During composing time, she asked the boys at her writing table, "Is a girl gonna win? 'Cause you guys—Why don't you guys let a girl win? . . . I make you a deal: If you write a story with a girl winning, I'll make a story with a boy winning."

In fact, like Victor, that very day Tina chose for publication—for her "good" story—an X-Men piece she had written. Tina's featured the female character Storm, and she approached it with great seriousness and no evident parody. In the story, Storm rescues the X-Men's male leader, Professor X, who is, unfortunately, possessed by a demon, or so Tina explained to me. At the same time,

Figure 5.2. *Edward's picture of the rebel Wolverine ("They make me mad!!!"), the responsible Cyclops ("Chill out."), and the usually shapely but very dignified Storm.*

Storm saves the life of another male character, Gambit, whom the deranged Professor X is attacking. At the edges of Tina's text is symbolic material that echoes from earlier stories, stories about everyday life and "loving" its pleasures.

> Once the X-Men were
> taking a walk in the park.
> They love to walk in the park.
> So when they got done
> they went home to eat pizza from Pizza hut.
> They love pizza from Pizza hut.
> So they went to Professor X. Gambit was going to him,
> and Professor X shot at him. Storm came and pulled him [the pos-
> sessed Professor X] out of his chair, and turned him upside down, and
> shook him and shook him. Then the bad guy [the demon] came out
> and he died. The end of this one.

THE INVERSION OF HEROES

In her stories about victims and heroines, including Storm, Tina was composing within the relations provided by the media stories; she was selecting appealing roles, and exaggerating more "boring" ones, for performative fun. However, a few weeks after the initial tense encounter with Victor, Tina began to write exclusively stories that featured strong female characters. In these stories, Tina not only appropriated but inverted expected relations (Babcock, 1993). This consistent transformation of female roles began after a class revival of the "fairness" discussion.

Resisting a Weak Rogue

The discussion resurfaced the day Victor brought *his* "good" X-Men story to Author's Theater. It was a long story (approximately 163 words), requiring nine characters; among them was one girl, Rogue, played by Tina. Unfortunately, Rogue had but one action, or, more accurately, one line: At the end of a long battle, in which the male characters engaged in an intricately detailed fight scene, Rogue said to the escaping bad guy Magneto, "You are not going to get away, Magneto." But he did.

> One day Juggernaut and Colossus [X-Men characters, a bad guy and
> a good guy, respectively] was fighting and Colossus punched
> Juggernaut. And he fell down. And then Juggernaut ran into
> Colossus. And then Colossus got up and punched Juggernaut again
> and he ran. The next day Colossus had his friends. And their name

was Wolverine and Gambit and Bishop [all good guys]. And Juggernaut had his friends. And their names are Sabertooth and Morf and Magneto and Nightcrawler (bad guys).... [A detailed battle follows, in which Wolverine fights Nightcrawler, Juggernaut fights Colossus, and is assisted by Bishop, Gambit fights Sabertooth, and then Bishop shoots Morf. Finally:] **Rogue said You're not going to get away Magneto.** Bishop shot his bullet but it did not hit him. Magneto threw powers at him [and] flew away. *(Spelling corrected for ease of reading.)*

Victor's performance went smoothly. His actors, including Tina, acted out their carefully detailed parts. But, after the performance, Tina did not have praise to offer Victor. Rather, she wanted to know why her part was *so* short. "I didn't have time," said Victor; otherwise, he implied, her part would have been much longer. Victor's explanation was met by an unusual reaction: A number of girls, across lines of race and class, objected to his excuse, which, like his Rogue, seemed quite weak.

As is evident in the discussion excerpt that follows, the children were concerned with access to an imagined world, an issue related to the text's function as a ticket to play. However, with support from Kristin, the children also focused on the nature of the text as representation, particularly its depiction of female and male roles in the plot's action.

KRISTIN: How do you feel about Tina being the only female X-Men— X-person [a name change related to that first made the preceding year by Sammy], and yet she didn't fight? ... Why did you put it so she didn't have a part?
          (Kristin here echoes Tina's earlier raised issue about fair texts in which girls are tough and sometimes "win.")

VICTOR: Why?
          . . .

ADAM: He already explained that.

TINA: Explain it again.

VICTOR: I didn't have enough time....

KRISTIN: What do the rest of you think about that? ...

MELISSA: I think you [Victor] kinda meant to do that because um she was before a lot of people [i.e., other characters came into the action after Rogue] and um ... all she got to do was say a couple of words....

LYNN: I would've been Wolverine if Thomas wasn't.
          (With this comment, Lynn shifts attention temporarily away from the text itself.)
          . . .

RADHA: Well, it's OK to have a <u>girl</u> play a boy's part because—
VICTOR: I wasn't thinking of nothing like that.
RADHA: Well, if you [Lynn] want to play Wolverine, then, it's per-
         fectly, oh, natural for a girl to be a boy....
VICTOR: *(misunderstanding Radha)* It's not natural. I know what you
         mean. Yeah. It wouldn't sound right. Say, watching X-Men,
         and Storm played Wolverine.... *(much laughter from children)*
LILIANA: Because Storm's kinda skinny and Wolverine! *(See James'
         depiction of the muscle-bound Wolverine, Figure 5.3.)*
LYNN: Well, I think that ... when Tina just said "You're not going
         to get away," what—
         (Lynn is now refocusing on the text itself.)
VICTOR: I told you that's all the time I had. I had to rewrite it [copy it
         over and prepare illustrations for the published version].
LYNN: Well, next time, you should write more because the males
         were like fighting, the other boys get to, so the girls
         should.... You had a little time to write some more. You
         could have left out one of the male actors.

Figure 5.3. *James' depiction of the muscle-bound Wolverine.*

VICTOR: Alright, alright.

BRYANT: I know what you mean. The girls feel left out.

THOMAS: Well at least she had a part.... Some people don't even have a part.

KRISTIN: My concern isn't that Tina didn't have a part. My concern is
that all the X-people—all the ones who were boys, they were
all fighting. But when it came to a female part, to Rogue's
part, she didn't fight. She just had words to say.

ADAM: But she's [Rogue's] so powerful.

*(Adam has moved the discussion away from Victor's text,
referring to the nature of the source material [i.e., the media
character]. Bryant then concurs with Adam, adding that talking can be "fighting without no movements." In so doing,
Bryant echoes class discussions about the power of speech.
But Kristin poses a question that refocuses the children on
the specifics of Victor's text.)*

KRISTIN: So, in Victor's play, did she have any effect on the bad guys?

BRYANT: *(to Tina, in a kind voice)* Well next time she's gonna get
revenge, alright?

(Tina stares straight at Victor, a deadpan look on her face.)

. . .

KRISTIN: Could a male X-person do that, be powerful without fighting
and win?

VICTOR: Yeah, like Jean Gray.

*(Giggles break out, since Jean Gray is a girl, and soon there
are many references to funny movies in which men dress like
girls. Eddie Murphy, Martin Lawrence, Robin Williams,
among other actors, have played roles that exaggerate stereotypical female qualities for laughs—just as, in fact, Tina herself has done. Indeed, Tina is laughing now. She then makes
a comment that inspires Victor's own objection to the limit-
ing of gender role possibilites.)*

TINA: I think it wouldn't look as funny if a girl played a boy's part,
but it would look funny if a boy played a girl part, like [the
TV show] Martin.

VICTOR: Why is that?

. . .

Tina, I gotta question for you. Just a while back you said
"Girls don't look funny in boys' clothes but boys look funny
in girls' clothes." Well, I mean, what's the difference? Just
look at me. Just look at Aloyse dressing like you. Would that
be funny?

*(There is much laughter, but Victor is very serious. And, after
all, all three children are wearing t-shirts and jeans.)*

The specifics of representation (i.e., which character does what) was not the sole focus of the children's discussion. Lynn's comment on girls playing male roles and Victor's reference to Jean Gray both shifted attention away from the text. The issue of fair participation—of opportunity to play—was then separated from the issue of text representation. Females playing males (as Lynn suggested) might make participation in social play more gender "fair," and males playing females might be "funny," but neither would problematize the text world itself. Indeed, Lynn considered herself a girl who was "not girly," as she told me—she wanted to play *boy* roles. For this reason, Lynn did not challenge the ideological order to the degree that Tina did.

Tina was wrestling with the notion of what *was* "girly," so to speak. In her first public encounter with Victor, Tina had objected to the fact that girls seemed weak in X-Men stories—not to the fact that girls did not get to play in those stories (her objection in the second grade). Superhero stories feature physical power—a traditional male possession. Other definitions of power are not so important in that narrative context. In Victor's story in particular, Rogue's part—her spoken words—were not those of a winner, as Tina had wanted, but of an onlooker to the action.

Kristin, in echoing and amplifying Tina's concern, continually reinforced and, at times, refocused the children's attention on textual images of power and gender. In fact, the discussion did seem to lead Victor to reconsider his own actions as an X-person author. Victor may not have deliberately turned tough Rogue into an ineffectual superhero, but he deliberately revised her role in his plot. Without Kristin's knowledge, and despite his own dislike of copying texts over, he revised his story so that Rogue engaged in physical action and no one yelled a warning at Magneto. Instead the warning became a defiant parting shot from the gloating bad guy: "You will not get me, X-Men!"

To Be—and Not To Be—Emily

Tina herself now began consistently to write stories that included strong females and, moreover, transformed expected gender relations in some way. Tina's first ninja story illustrates such a transformation, since Emily herself becomes "tough." Emily does, in fact, have a moment of physical glory in the *Three Ninjas* movie, when she follows up TumTum's swats to a couple of moronic bad guys with a kick and a punch of her own. But this is only a moment in a movie in which she is mainly a love-smitten (if not entirely impressed) girl, an easy target for bullies, and a victim to be rescued. In Tina's story, Emily *is* the rescuer. Tina inverted the expected gender relations of rescuer and victim but stayed within the basic relational structure of the story: physically abusive perpetrators, victim, physically powerful rescuer.

Indeed, as evident in the following text, Tina provided evaluative commentary that emphasizes Emily's physical power: in the story orientation ("she was tough"); and in the narrative plot itself ("she can whip some butt"). In this, she balances Emily with the "bad boys," whose tendency toward violence also is emphasized (in a style reminiscent of her oral storytelling).

> Once there was a girl named Emily. She was tough. Her and her boy friend was eating pizza. They love to eat pizza. So one day they were going to school. They love school. Emily's mother walks them to school. She was nice. She love little kids. Kids love her. Then they went into the room. Bad boys, they love to beat up kids. . . . School is over now. Rocky, Emily, TumTum, and Colt. Colt was going away. Emily found him. The bad boys had him. Emily can whip some butt. So she did. So they all ran away. She is tough I said. So they walk home again. The end. *(Spelling and punctuation corrected for ease of reading.)*

Despite the featured physical encounter, in Tina's Emily story, as in her X-Men stories, there are potential signs of "differance" (Derrida, 1978), signifiers of other relational roles and other kinds of power, seemingly ignored but, nonetheless, there in background details. Emily and her boyfriend share a pizza. (In the children's stories, as in films marketed for children, sharing pizza is a sign of friendship.[7]) Moreover, the major adult figure is not a wise grandfather who taught karate but a "nice" mother—*Emily's* mother, a nurturing one who loved and protected kids, male and female. This mother, who is not in the film, does not allow children to go off unaccompanied to school; she walks them.

Tina did not present her story about tough Emily in Author's Theater.[8] However, she did present the very next one she wrote—a story that was intertextually linked to a diverse set of characters from the community "image store," all of whom assumed positions outside their usual relations. Moreover, these characters' relations were not fixed in Tina's stories but subject to reinterpretation and reconstruction in the community of the whole. As I will illustrate, Emily's textual predicament became the site, first, for ideological simplification and, second, for complication in a grand community dialogue. Her fate was not sealed within appropriated or inverted relations; rather, she (and therefore her appropriators, her authors) had some agency, some possiblity of choosing actions from an expanded range of possibilities.

THE DIALOGIC RECONSTRUCTION OF LADIES AND HEROES

Tina's story involving Emily and Batman was on the very same page in her writing book as the story featuring the tough-acting Emily. But this new Emily was passive and grown-up, marked as pretty and married, with no specific occupation. Emily's husband, though, did have an occupation; he studied bats. His name was Batman ("like in the cartoon," as Tina explained to me). In the story, Batman does not save "us girls" but is, in fact, victimized by them and avenged by a man-obsessed baby-girl bat named Bebe.

"Bebe" is the name of a girl in a chapter book the class had read, *The Sideways Stories* (Sachar, 1985). Bebe had tiny toes and a fast "draw" (literally—she drew real fast) and, perhaps most important, she had a name that rhymed with Tina's given name. To Tina's delight, Sarah even wrote a version of the *Sideways Stories* chapter, replacing Bebe with Tina's own name. In a sense, then, Tina herself may have been the powerful, protective baby bat.

Following is Tina's Batman story.

> Batman. Once there was a man that studied bats. He loved to study bats. He was married. His wife name was Emily. She was pretty. So her husband went to the lab to study a baby bats. It was a girl. Her name was Bebe. She was very very big. She love men. She would eat the women if they would be bad to the man. Emily man came home. She was mad then happy again. The end. *(Spelling and punctuation corrected for ease of reading.)*

As will be evident in the excerpt from her Author's Theater presentation, Tina considered this story both funny and scary—a horror story about a scientist and a crazed bat. As will also be evident, her actors and audience also seemed to find the story very funny. Tina incorporated her actor's improvisations into her own oral storytelling, exaggerating Batman's fear and Bebe's ferocious love—and silencing ever more the passive Emily, who waits at home for her man.

> *(Tina takes her place in the front of the rug and calls her actors. Edward is to be the scientist, Makeda the wife, and Rhonda the baby bat Bebe. Tina begins to read with great expressiveness.)*
>
> TINA: "Once there was a man that studied bats. He <u>loved</u> to study bats. He was married."... ["O::h," says the audience.] "Her name was Emily."
>
> EDWARD: Just like "Three Ninjas!"
> *(Tina grins very widely.)*
>
> TINA: "She was <u>pretty</u>. So her husband went to the lab" and was studying a bat named Bebe.
> *(Tina stops reading and begins improvising but stays very close to her text. Her written text has confused syntax at this point and perhaps that influences her decision to abandon the text.)*

RHONDA: I'm Bebe. I'm a bat.
          (Class laughs enthusiastically. Everyone seems to be enjoying this story very much. Edward, apparently responding to the class's playful mood, gasps, runs off to the far corner of the rug, and stands shaking. Tina then responds to his actions, improvising her next line.)

TINA: He was afraid of her. She <u>lo::ved</u> him.

PEER: The bat loved him? *(incredulous audience member)*

TINA: Whoever messed with him she would kill them. One day the man went back home. He told his wife about the bad day he had.

EDWARD: I had a bad day! That bat is messed up. She tried to kill me, man!
          (The audience laughs. Edward may have misunderstood Tina's text, since his improvisation suggests that the bat was trying to kill him, which was not the case. However, Tina once again picks up on Edward's improvisation.)

TINA: He went back to the lab. And the bat killed him. And he died. The End
          (The audience laughs, except for me, who wonders about the disappearance of Emily.)

I, however, was not the only one who wondered about Emily. Tina presented her story in May of the school year—a month and a half after it had been written. By that time, the classroom community had had much experience discussing the worlds represented in texts. As will be documented in the next chapter, superhero stories in particular had raised complex questions about the motivations of human beings and the worthiness of their actions. For example, Kevin's story based on *Biker Mice from Mars* (Unger, 1994) led Tina to wonder why the character Grease Pit was *so* evil and, thus, to a class discussion about character motivation and, also, about the possibility of redemption and change. A commercial "X-Men" book, in which Professor X declares his purpose in life—to combat evil—led to a discussion that Kristin initiated about the children's views of their own life purposes.

These questions about the inner lives of characters and the ways in which characters respond to their own life circumstances could complicate the simple characters and the morally unambiguous worlds of superhero stories, and they complicated Tina's story of Batman, Bebe, and Emily as well. In the discussion following the performance, a number of children audibly wondered about Emily. Indeed, the first questioner was Emily herself (Makeda), who asked about the motivation of her husband's killer.

MAKEDA: Why did Rhonda—no, the bat have to kill um my husband?

. . .

TINA: 'Cause he poked her, and she didn't like it. And so she just
            killed him.

. . .

LETTRICE: How come you didn't tell that thing you told, that he poked
            Rhonda?
            (Tina does not respond to this inquiry about the representa-
            tion of her story but calls on Jonathan, who has his hand up.)

JONATHAN: I think you should tell how they met.

TINA: The next chapter is where they met.

JONATHAN: But if there's a next chapter—the guy died, so he couldn't tell
            that part.

TINA: I know. I'm telling it without him.

KRISTIN: Could you tell a flashback? Have you ever seen a flashback?
            (Many assents in the audience—and references to movies;
            Tina herself recalls one.)

TINA: Like Jason [reference to a horror movie], yeah Jason. The girl
            had a flashback to when she was a little girl and she didn't
            know her father.

. . .

MAKEDA: I have flashbacks a lot of times. 'Cause my grandmother, she
            had died while I was over there, at night. And the next morn-
            ing I didn't know where she was. She had died. So I had
            flashbacks that she was alive that time. That was the only
            grandma I had. I used to go over to her house every day.

KRISTIN: And do you think that could apply to Tina's story. Somebody
            died in her story? How could Tina use that in her story?

LENA: She could've like, she could've like, Makeda [Emily] could've
            like um write her story about her husband and then start
            crying.

MAKEDA: But I didn't really know.

TINA: But you just could've start crying 'cause he died.

. . .

KRISTIN: In the beginning of the story, you said that Bebe the bat was
            protecting the man from other people. . . . And then, all of a
            sudden, she killed him. And I wondered, how did she change
            from loving him . . . ?

TINA: And so—he didn't like her. And so he—when he was study-
            ing her, and she had rabies in her, and when he was studying
            her, he poked her, and she didn't like that. . . .

MELISSA: I liked your story. Um um—When Edward was scared of

Rhonda, he looked funny, and Rhonda was like *(raising her arms into a bat-like arch)* like that.

. . .

KRISTIN: So that's something she could write?

MELISSA: Yeah, I think Tina could write "and then the bat Bebe gave whatever-his-name-is ["Mike," says Tina] a scary look like—" *(makes the bat-like arch and widens her eyes)*.

KRISTIN: "with her eyes open really wide." *(Melissa agrees.)* You could describe what Rhonda was doing in your writing.

TINA: OK. I'll have a chapter 2, so be ready! It's gonna be <u>scarier</u> though.
(Lynn then asks for more information about the lab, which she thought was interesting, and Rhonda suggests "more detail about the characters," and then Kristin asks the class if they think Tina's characters "had a purpose in life.")

JONATHAN: Well, Mike's might've been to study bats . . . to figure out which bats to avoid. . . .

LYNN: Well, one for the bat might've been—two purposes, to either be studied and to be sort of an example for other bats on how to be studied and, also, to um—fall in love with Mike and to kill him.

KRISTIN: So maybe to kill him had some larger purpose?

LYNN: And Mike's—Mike's wife um, Emily, Emily's purpose might have been—maybe she didn't follow her purpose. And it might've been that she should've gotten there and saved him some way.

. . .

THOMAS: Um, mine is not no purpose. But I think she killed him because she was jealous [of Emily].

. . .

TINA: I forgot to put in um ( ) the part where um she wanted to marry him, but she forgot that she couldn't marry him because she was a bat. And you [Rhonda] realized that you couldn't marry him because you was a bat. And the other thing is that you were jealous of Emily and you wanted to kill her too.

KRISTIN: What you guys are talking about now, and what Tina is offering us now, is motivation . . . motivation of characters to do something.

In the preceding interaction, both Tina and her audience carried on a dialogue with and through her characters, trying to understand their sense and sensibility. This was not a discussion of general issues raised by stories (e.g., Do human beings have a purpose in life? Can people who do evil change?); this was a discussion of the specific dilemmas faced by the characters themselves. Perhaps the complexity of the discussion was owing, in part, to Tina's liberation of her characters from their usual plots, where actions were known and motivations assumed (to get one's bike back, to defeat the bad guys, to marry the desired).

At this point in the community's evolving history, the text itself could function as a clear mediator of community dialogue. Tina, as author, referred to "the next chapter," when characters and their relations would be clarified. Some of her audience members requested more explicit textual representations; others suggested possibilities that changed or at least challenged implicitly Emily's silence and her passive relationship to her husband and to Bebe.

No one explicitly objected to Emily's role in Tina's story in the way that Tina had explicitly objected to Rogue's role in Victor's story. Perhaps little was expected of Emily. But, in this classroom community, it was now possible—it was not ideologically out of the question (or out of the text)—for an Emily to whip some butt, so to speak. And with new possibilities come new responsibilities. Perhaps, thought Lynn, Emily missed her chance.

There was, alas, no "next chapter" about Emily.[9] But Tina did go on to write other stories featuring powerful women. In these stories, Tina herself reconstructed relations, making new selections from available possibilities—negating, extending, foregrounding, and recombining them in new ways.[10] One such story, about Venus Tina, will appear in my own next chapter. Venus Tina's emergence was linked intertextually to the increasingly precarious position of the media superheroes in this classroom community. The actresses who had dominated the role of Emily in the second grade were, in the third, quite critical of superhero stories. Moreover, the portrayal of physical conflict was itself a matter of much social conflict, as is illustrated in Chapter 6, in which Sammy and the superheroes once again take center stage.

▼ 6 ▼
▼

The Coming of Venus Tina: Texts as Markers and Mediators of Tough-Talking Kids

All of a sudden, it hits me—I conceive a character like Samson, Hercules, and all the strong men I ever heard of rolled into one. Only more so.

J. Siegel, co-creator of Superman, in M. Benton,
The Comic Book in America, 1993, p. 22

For Jerry Siegal and Joe Shuster, Jewish high school students, Superman was a graphic response to the Nazi concept of the superior man who could lead the masses to glory. The two friends conceived of their own superior man, one with a social conscience who would use his strength to battle evil others (like Nazis) and to help those in need (Boichel, 1991). For Sammy and his male peers, superhero stories were mediators of their social affiliation and markers of their ideological common ground, their desires to be superior men able to save the world from those who would destroy it. Like the Power Rangers (Figure 6.1), they stood ready to transform themselves into warriors whenever duty (or, rather, an appealing opportunity for play) called.

Stories, however, offer more than symbolic substance (e.g., characters and plots). They are also potential markers of social "taste" (Bourdieu, 1984) and, thus, potential resources for the construction of societal divisions (Jenkins, 1992; Levine, 1988). Like words, stories "taste of the context and contexts in which [they] have lived [their] socially charged life" (Bakhtin, 1981, p. 293).

Figure 6.1. *Michael's portrait of the Green Power Ranger.*

Some of that "taste" comes from the medium itself—a television screen, a cartoon strip, a library book—and from the voices of peers, teachers, parents, and other adults that may surround both medium and message (Buckingham, 1993; Hodge & Tripp, 1986).

In the words of the media scholar Ellen Seiter, in contemporary societies, all citizens depend on commodity consumption, "not just for survival but for participation, inclusion, in social networks" (1993, p. 3). Highly educated, affluent parents who have access to alternative forms of such consumption (e.g., cable station "educational" programs or "educational" toy stores versus Saturday morning cartoons and Toys " Я " Us chains) may feel guilty about their children's desired media productions and media-inspired toys—desires that are linked to peer group affiliation. As children grow older, they may "catch on to the way remarks about television are evaluated by adults and learn to emulate [those] higher-status, negative opinions" (p. 108).

In the official world of the third grade, children's use of media-based stories was linked to their identities, not only as boys and girls, but also as members of different sociocultural referent groups. Media-based stories were written primarily by boys. However, as discussed in Chapter 2, in the third grade, non–middle-class girls, all of whom were children of color—unlike their middle-class female peers—all of whom were White—also drew relatively often on the popular media for their "free" writing, and working class boys of color did so almost exclusively. (See Appendix C.)

Moreover, during Author's Theater discussions, some children distanced themselves from peers' superhero stories in ways that suggested a dominant criticism of middle-class adults about children's television (Seiter, 1993). They did not initiate objections based on gender or racial stereotypes but, rather, on the amount of fighting in such stories. As Sarah said, citing her mother, they are "too violent." Since the objecting children usually were White and middle-class, the Author's Theater became a potential stage for the display of stereotypical class divisions in taste, divisions that, in Kristin's room, were interrelated with race as well as gender.

These stereotypes were deceptive. In the unofficial world, *all* of the children engaged in at least some play involving violence inspired by the popular media. For example, Sarah, Melissa, and Jonathan, all middle-class children, enjoyed playground chase games in which they ran (or pretend-swam very fast) from the unmitigated evil of powerful sharks and violent dinosaurs on the loose.[1] Jonathan, who sometimes sat on a chair reading a book during superhero performances, carried *Star Wars* (Lucas, 1977) and *Star Trek* (Roddenberry, 1966) action figures in his back pack to play with before and after school.[2]

As illustrated in Chapter 5, ideological gaps among children could be mediated by social negotiation, that is, by efforts at mutual accommodation and connection. In the third grade, this social negotiation could be realized through textual negotiation, through decision making about the possibilities of a story's characters and plot. It was just such negotiation that mediated the gender tensions articulated by girls like Tina, excluded from superhero worlds. Tina resisted the gendered nature of physical power, even as she affirmed its potential fun.

But children distancing themselves from superhero stories—and from their own play with physical power—did not *want* access to those stories in the official world. To negotiate these ideological gaps about the appeal and the nature of physical power, children of diverse socioeconomic and cultural backgrounds, girls as well as boys, would need to find themselves desiring inclusion in a common story world, a world in which physical power played a role. Such a situation occurred in April of the school year, when Kristin introduced stories featuring heroes akin to those of the superhero tales (as Jerry Siegal suggested in the opening quote)—the Greek myths. These stories, however, are cultural classics, associated with the educated elite, not with the masses, and taught through the written word (despite their oral origins), not through the television or movie screen.

In the chapter sections to follow, children will be seen using stories to mark their affiliations with others, to disassociate themselves from others, and to negotiate with others across societal divisions. The presented classroom drama will feature Sammy and other children involved with superhero stories, and, then, those involved with Greek myths. Tina, who did not find the Greek myths so appealing, will appear in small scenes—until the last section, when she will emerge as Venus Tina, a superhero constructed from the expanding possibilities in the classroom "image store" (Warner, 1994, p. 418). To begin, however, I briefly focus on the place of physical power itself in the school social lives of the key characters in this book—Tina and Sammy.

BEING TOUGH IN AND OUT OF STORIES

Sammy was a fan of Rosa Parks and, in particular, of Eloise Greenfield's (1973/1995) biography of Mrs. Parks, which Kristin had introduced to him. (His elaborate story maps of this book appear in Figure 6.2.) Rosa Parks, a hero associated with nonviolent resistance in the civil rights movement, is also a human superhero as defined in this book: She was someone who resisted the ideological status quo and who did so in response to, and in collaboration with, others. Nonetheless, Greenfield's biography begins with a scene of the child Rosa defiantly standing up to another child—a White boy accompanied by his mother.

> Rosa was not afraid, although the white boy was near his mother. When he pushed her, Rosa pushed him back.
> "Why did you put your hands on my child?" the mother asked.
> "Because he pushed me," Rosa said.
> "Don't you know that I could have you put in jail?" the mother asked.
> "I don't want to be pushed by your son or anyone else."
> And she walked on.
>
> (Greenfield, 1973/1995, p. 1; see also reference to the scene in Sammy's story maps in Figure 6.2.)

In Greenfield's book, the child Rosa voices a sentiment expressed often by Kristin's children: the desire not to be pushed around. An aspect of all children's growing up is figuring out the kinds of power that are possible in a society, and which kinds of power—be they physical or verbal—allow which people to "impose their will, even against oppression" (Foucault, 1978; Jordan, Cowan, & Roberts, 1995; Weber, 1978, p. 22).

As noted in Chapter 2, in unofficial social worlds, acting tough—acting like someone who could stand up to and, indeed, take on others—was primarily a performative act, a means of verbal display and play. Sammy appreciatively listened to such verbal banter but did not engage in it himself. Tina, on the other hand, was very skillful in such verbal play, as were many chil-

Figure 6.2. *Sammy's story maps for* Rosa Parks *(Greenfield, 1995).*

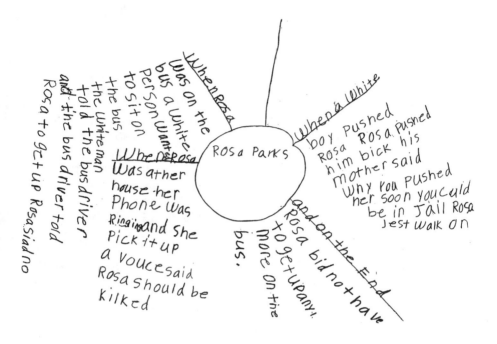

dren from her neighborhood; variations on such play are well documented among children from working class neighborhoods of diverse heritages, whose parents want them to be able to stand up for themselves (Heath, 1983; Miller, 1982; Rizzo & Corsaro, 1991; Walkerdine, 1986).

In the following exchange, Tina talks tough to Edward (whom others have accused her of liking), but she switches her tone immediately when Bryant bumps his head.

TINA: *(to Edward, who has been talking with Bryant)* Do your work!

BRYANT: I know. Do your <u>work</u>, or <u>I'm</u> gonna <u>tell</u> the <u>teach</u> er.

TINA: I'm not gonna tell the teacher.

EDWARD: She might belt you.

TINA: Who?

          (Like Tina, I'm unsure who Edward thinks might belt whom.)

EDWARD: She might whip you.

TINA: Who?

EDWARD: She got a belt.

TINA: No, but I don't need a belt. I don't need a belt.
(Bryant leans too far back in his chair; it tips over, and he hits his head on a table.)

EDWARD: You alright, Bryant? *(laughing)*

TINA: You OK, Bryant? *(very sweetly)*
(Tina calls for Kristin, but Bryant says he is alright.)

EDWARD: Ah, you belt him! *(teasing to Tina)*

TINA: No I didn't. . . . I don't need no belt. All I need is my shoe. Take off my shoe. Bang, bang, bang! It hurt so much.

Once Tina even responded to an insult from Thomas with a threat to beat him up—Thomas was the largest child in the class and one with an earned reputation among teachers and children for physical aggression.

The performative quality of being tough does not mean that actual physical fighting did not happen on occasion. Since physical aggression was strictly prohibited in school, threats to beat up others *before* or *after* school were sometimes voiced, and they were matched with counterthreats, and those threats could be carried out (although this happened very rarely). As Makeda told Sammy one day (when he said he would get "my daddy" if anyone beat him up), "If you can't fight for yourself, well, then you're just gonna get beat up." Projecting an air of confidence—and pushing back *if* you're pushed—is important to keeping away those who prey on the weak.[3]

Nonetheless, children, like Thomas, who were perceived as routinely handling problems by hitting others were not admired but criticized as "bullies" (just as in James' [1993] British study). Moreover, children who moved from the verbal display of toughness to physical fighting also received no peer praise. Sammy, a small boy, sometimes made such a move with (or, rather, to) Edward, a boy who was even smaller than he was. But, when he did, the other boys expressed concern and gave sympathetic pats, not to Sammy, but to Edward ("You OK, Edward?").

Sammy punched Edward—but he may have had Thomas on his mind. The punches to Edward came in the spring of the year, when Sammy was under some pressure from his stepfather to stand up to Thomas if the latter child threatened him. Kristin pointed out to Sammy that Thomas was "twice his size"—and so physically fighting him was not a good idea. Sammy himself seemed to negotiate his relationship with Thomas just as he did most other boys—not by fighting him with fists or with words but by trying to affiliate with him, to get on the same team, so to speak. During composing time, Sammy jointly recollected with Thomas and others the "good" scenes from popular superhero stories, provided appealing roles in superhero dramas, and, in the third grade, sat alongside them and wrote about the same superhero team.

(Sammy's longest story in the third grade [143 words] was written alongside—and with the support of—Thomas.)

In superhero stories, good guys only pushed when they, or those weaker than they, were pushed. They stood up for others, as they themselves stood side-by-side. Thus, these stories "with too much fighting" were major mediators of collaborative and peaceful play and, also, of the evolving community dialogue happening through and about texts. In the third grade, that dialogue included explicit discussions of the textual and moral sense of physical conflict and, moreover, of physical power itself.

Like dialogue about the representation of gender, dialogue about the representation of power was generated, in part, because of the third-grade emphasis on textual details. When variations of "the good guys fought the bad guys" became blow-by-blow descriptions of the action (quite literally), texts generated discussions of text sense and human sensibilities. Initially, the most active participants in those discussions were those most affiliated with the fighting good guys, as illustrated in the next section by the class response to Sammy's X-Men story.

QUESTIONING AUTHORIAL DECISIONS:
TEXTUAL SENSE AND SENSELESS VIOLENCE

When the project began in the third grade, Sammy was still heavily engaged during writing time in the oral negotiation of who could be whom in his upcoming Author's Theater performances. In the third grade, unlike the second grade, Sammy did not save roles for particular children; for example, he gave female roles in superhero stories to the girls who sought those roles. But he did continue to try to please as many people as possible—which meant that, in his enacted stories, the good guys tended to outnumber the bad.

Sammy's free writing texts usually were short, relative to those of his peers (about 50 words, relative to Tina's 115 words, and the class average of 77). In a typical story, he introduced the good guys and the bad guys, had the good guys go out for pizza and the bad guys plan the destruction of the world; then he announced the fight and the (predictable) winners: the good guys. However, Sammy's oral performances could be much more elaborate than that. As a third grader, he demonstrated his ability to control both a complex storyline and his actors: In his stories, people were wounded, died, or went home for a nap or a sandwich before returning to the action. Sammy wanted to give everyone something to do (thereby fulfilling the text's function as a ticket to play), but he also wanted to keep his players under control, or Kristin would stop the production. As he told Patrick one day, if players became unruly, the author could "just make 'em go home."

Sammy's first observed third-grade performance was based on an X-Men episode well known by fans in Kristin's room—one in which the bad guys (robots named Sentinels) wound the X-man Beast and kill his teammate Morph (who later returns, transformed into a bad guy). The performance involved a large cast: Aloyse, Bryant, Edward, James, Kristin, Liliana, Makeda, Michael, and Radha. (Tina was absent this day, or perhaps she would have had a role.) In an apparent attempt to keep this large cast under control, however, Sammy had many X-Men die in a series of fight scenes, despite the fact that there were only *two* designated "bad guys" (both of whom, Radha and Edward, also played good guy roles).

> *(At this point in Sammy's story, the pizza-eating X-Men have already chased "the bad guys" off. Two team members, Beast and Morph, go for a walk, and then the bad guys kill them.)*
>
> MICHAEL: They <u>killed</u> them? *(distressed)*
> SAMMY: Yeah. The bad guys had Beast on the ground and Morph on the ground. And Beast got wounded, and Morph got wounded. And they die.
> *(Consistent with the textual values of the official community, Sammy responds with more details.)*

Eventually, Rogue and Gambit are taken captive by the bad guys and transformed through a machine into bad guys themselves; at the direction of a resurrected Morph, they "destroy the X-Men."

Kristin then tells Sammy it is almost lunch. He protests briefly ("How come I can't read a little [more]?") and then ends with a "the bad guys won" and "to be continued."

After the performance, as the actors returned to the rug for a quick discussion before lunch, Edward commented to Michael, "That was fun. That was cool."

But a very serious Michael disagreed, "But the X-Men <u>died</u>."[4]

As illustrated in the following, during the discussion, Michael and other actors commented on—and complained about—the text as an object, a representation whose details were of questionable sense and sensitivity.

> MICHAEL: You just said "and the bad guys won." You didn't say which bad guys.
> JAMES: The bad guys. You know, the bad guys.
> MICHAEL: Yeah, but bad guys—what kinda bad guys? Are they mutants or not?
> ALOYSE: Mutants.
> MICHAEL: You don't know that.

ALOYSE: Were they mutants?

SAMMY: Yeah.

MICHAEL: You didn't say it in your story.
(Like Michael, Sammy is not smiling. He looks straight ahead, his mouth grim. He is also, I infer, quite perturbed. Makeda now offers her comments.)

MAKEDA: Your story was alright. Your story was alright. Your story was alright. The part that was alright to me was—the first part started off and they were at the pizza place eating. But ... I gotta say ... you guys didn't even have that much people. You know, all the X-Men couldn't get beat up by 3 or 4 people [i.e., the two bad guys plus the transformed X-Men] . . . .

LILIANA: It was sort of boring when we were just laying there [dead].

KRISTIN: I'd like to say that I was impressed with your story, that you were able to carry a story through and keep something else happening. To me, the story itself was not boring, whether or not Liliana herself got bored lying there.
(Michael has been muttering about how Sammy did not name all the X-Men who were fighting and all the X-Men who died. Kristin now directly addresses the issue that seems to be bothering Michael.)

KRISTIN: Have you ever seen a story where somebody dies? *(general nodding)* It might be that a person who's acting in [the story] doesn't like it that they had to die, but is it OK for an author to make people die? *(general nodding)*

MAKEDA: It's his story! You don't have to say names or nothing.
. . .

RADHA: Well I liked the story because, you know, you don't have to tell all the names, because, you know, you don't have to say like this person died, this person died, this person died—it will take, you know, too much time. . . . Everyone should be happy because at least they had a part. You had a part 'cause he said "Everyone," and all the good guys, you were one of the good guys and then you had a part! He didn't want to say the names because it was most, it was all of us. If it was, you know, part of us, then he would say the names, but if it was all of us, he wouldn't say all of them.

Radha's comments implied the relevance of a number of potential text functions in the Author's Theater. "You" should not complain because you had a part—the text offered you a ticket to play. "You" might feel that more textual details—a more carefully represented world—would have allowed you a better part but, actually, that would have been boring. And, anyway, as Kristin also emphasized, Sammy wanted or didn't want to do certain things; the text was a symbol of his authority.

And yet, Sammy's goal had not been to isolate himself with his "own" text. He had taken appealing superheroes from the common image store and constructed a story as a social "bridge"—a dialogic symbol—to link himself and others. "If one end of the bridge depend[ed] on [Sammy], then the other depend[ed] on his addressee" (Volosinov, 1973, p. 86). He did not own his words' meaning, in part because he could not own other people's responses to those words.

For example, Michael—regarded by children as an expert in superhero matters—continued to voice his discontent with Sammy's story as he got in line for lunch. He recited a litany of all of the X-Men who would have to die for there to be no more X-Men. (And Michael knew many, many X-Men characters in great detail.) This was too much, it seemed, this massive death of his idolized superheroes. In the ideology of the superhero story, the good guys do not permanently disappear from the face of the earth.

Before getting in line himself, Sammy plopped on the rug beside me, looking quite dejected. "Michael acting like he didn't like it," he said. Sammy had had criticism of his stories before, criticism from people wanting more of his story, criticism that could be addressed by adding more parts or more action (see Chapter 3). But Michael had not liked "it" —the story itself (especially the plot). As will be evidenced later in this chapter, concerns about text sense and actors' sensitivities—and Michael's sensitivities in particular—surfaced in a future composing event. (On my next visit, Sammy reported that he had promised Michael the role of the Green Power Ranger in his next story, and so they were friends again.)

The discussion of Sammy's Author's Theater had engaged only Sammy, his actors, and other superhero fans. Most presentations generated comments mainly from children somehow implicated in those stories, as actors or people knowledgeable about the story's content. Audience members who did not claim such knowledge usually did not speak. When they did, their social distance from the media-based authors was clear, as illustrated by the response elicited by Edward's and Bryant's presentations of very detailed stories inspired by the video game *Streetfighters* (Capcom Games, 1991).

In the boys' video game-based texts, characters engaged in street fights that had no particular good guys or bad guys. The basic text pattern (both written and presented) was: [One character] was fighting [another character]. [One of the characters] did a [kind of move] and then [the other character] lost. Listen, for example, to Edward reading his text. (For an accompanying drawing, see Figure 6.3.)

Figure 6.3. *Edward's picture of Ken and Ryu fighting and throwing fireballs.*

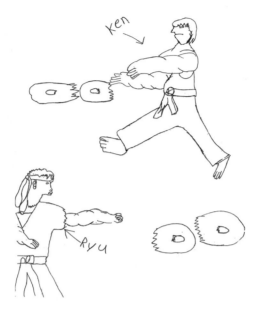

EDWARD: Ryu and Ken was fighting. Ryu did a Ha Do Ken [a move
          involving pelting an opponent with a fireball]. Ken did a
          [indecipherable kind of move] and Ryu lost and Ken won.
          Chun-Li was fighting Vega and Chun-li did a king-sized kick
          and then Vega lost. . . .
          (At the end of his presentation, Edward asks:)
          Did everyone get a turn?

The stories based on video games did allow everyone a turn, so to speak.
However, the turns, like the text itself, seemed monotonous to me, to Kristin,
and to some class members not caught up in the fun of turning a video game
into text and play. When Kristin asked if anyone had noticed anything about
Edward's plot, Lynn noted it was repetitive ("People kept fighting and winning, not that they went for pizza or something"). After Bryant's very similar presentation, Sarah noted the lack of character motivation ("I couldn't
really tell *why* everybody started fighting"), and Melissa and Lynn echoed
her comments.

"It's *Streetfighters!*" responded Aloyse, with exasperation in his voice.
"That's how it is!"

A particularly stark contrast in response between those involved with media stories and those more removed was evident in the class commentary on an X-Men story presented by James. The presentation garnered alert attention from all, because the bad guy—a Sentinel—was played by the very tall and very popular Jason, a college student volunteer. The following comments, in chronological order, are illustrative.

TINA: That was very funny. . . .

BRYANT: I like how you wrote the story so that everybody got a part. . . .

JONATHAN: I didn't like the fact that it was just fight fight fight. . . [5]

MAKEDA: The part that was funny to me was when Wolverine got squashed. . . .

SUSAN: . . . I also agree that you should not have just fighting. . . .

SARAH: I agree with what Jonathan was saying.

To gloss the children's comments, Makeda, Bryant, and Tina characterized the play as fun; Jonathan, Susan, and Sarah characterized it as violent. Soon, however, out on the playground, an unusual social configuration of children found themselves negotiating their mutual inclusion in another kind of story featuring fighting men: the Greek myths.

IMPLICATING NEW PLAYERS

In April, Kristin decided to read a Greek myth to her children. As she explained to them, the Greek myths "were told centuries and centuries ago," but they were similar in some ways to superhero stories. Greek myths also featured powerful beings trying "to solve some problem."

Nonetheless, the Greek tales presented a society whose moral sense was quite different from that of contemporary superhero stories. The gods themselves were not defenders of human beings; their "relation with mankind rested on power, not on righteousness or justice" (Guthrie, 1950, p. 123). They committed acts of great violence against mortals to salve their own pride. Mortal men and women considered beautiful were for the gods' taking—and for the gods' and goddesses' jealous rages. Moreover, although the mortal heroes were fighting men, they also were "playthings" of the gods—of forces beyond their comprehension (Zimmerman, 1991, p. 102).

The Greeks may have viewed their Olympian gods as something akin to the rich clans on television soap operas. In the words of the literary artist and scholar Robert Graves (1960):

[The Greeks] thought of Heaven as ruled by a divine family rather like any rich human family on earth, but immortal and all-powerful.... In remote European villages even today, where a rich man owns most of the land and houses, much the same [attitude prevails].... Every villager is polite to the landlord and pays rent regularly. But behind his back he will often say: "What a proud, violent, hasty-tempered fellow! How he ill-treats his wife, and how she nags at him! As for their children: they are a bad bunch! That pretty daughter is crazy about men ... ; that son in the Army is a bully...." (p. 8)

From an adult point of view, the gods' moral precariousness is evident in the first myth that Kristin read to her class, the story of Athena and Arachne. In that story, the goddess Athena struck the country girl Arachne, who had boasted that her own weaving was better than the goddess' (which it was). With that blow, Athena turned poor Arachne into a spider. Her action seemed to inspire genuine awe in Kristin's class; the children leaned forward after Kristin read of the goddess' deed, eager to see the book's accompanying picture.

However, this violent act garnered quite different evaluations. For example, Tina, who did not object to the physical force of superhero play, found Athena's transforming force unfair, to say the least. But Jonathan, who (as a third grader) did object at times to the superhero stories, found Athena's action justifiable, given what he deemed the unfair action of Arachne:

> *(Kristin has just read that Athena turned Arachne into a spider. Many children gasp, and some, like Sammy, look quite shocked.)*

SAMMY: They turned her into a spi:der? *(incredulous)*

MICHAEL: Let me see.

LETTRICE: I don't see why the goddess turned her into a spider even if she was better than her. How come she wanted to turn her into a spider? *(quite disgusted)*

   · · ·

MELISSA: Because she was ... so upset and jealous that she just couldn't stand it anymore.

TINA: ... I know that she was mad and upset that she could weave better than her.... So I mean she should have—the woman, the goddess, could have said something like, something <u>nice</u>, instead of turning her into a spider, because that wouldn't be appropriate if the <u>girl</u> would turn the <u>goddess</u> into a spider. *(Tina seems to be arguing for fair play here. Since the girl should not turn the goddess into a spider [and also could not], the goddess should not do so either.)*

   · · ·

JONATHAN: Well, I think maybe like um when somebody takes somebody else's <u>pride</u>, (if) that person is much better, (you) would feel a little jealous.

      . . .

TINA: Instead of her turning her into a spider, they could have fought with their powers . . . like with their hands.

KRISTIN: Isn't that kinda like what they did, they fought with their powers—with their weaving? And who won?

TINA: The <u>girl</u>.

KRISTIN: The girl won—

TINA: <u>Yep</u>! *(with definitiveness)*

KRISTIN: But Athena still had more power so she could change her . . . because she's the goddess.

JONATHAN: Well, I don't think it's <u>fair</u> if somebody gets you better, especially if you're trying to be the first best. You'd lose respect.

In the story of Athena and Arachne, Tina seemed to sympathize with Arachne—the weaving girl, who was treated so dastardly by the goddess. But Melissa and, especially, Jonathan seemed relatively sympathetic to the goddess, who was confronted by such an upstart. Perhaps their reactions were influenced by Athena's role as the main character, the triumphant being, in a school-introduced book. This was no video game character, no cartoon superhero, but a being who had actually been in stories for "centuries and centuries." After all, an adult-authored children's story featuring the triumph of an evil act is highly unusual (as is a child-authored one).

The class had responded with evident interest to the Greek myths, so Kristin continued to read them. Almost immediately after she began doing so, Greek figures began to appear in the writing books of Jonathan, Melissa, Sarah, Susan, and Liliana—all middle-class students. Moreover, a different—and unusual—combination of children began to play a child-invented game of gods and goddesses out on the playground. (An annotated list of figures the children appropriated from the Greek myths is contained in Appendix C.)

"Gods and Goddesses": The Game

One day, as I arrived at the school, I witnessed Sammy dragging Susan across the playground; she was screaming but happy. A large group of children—a group I had never before seen together at recess—was playing "the gods and goddesses game." Among the gathered children were Susan's best friends Sarah and Melissa, along with Jonathan, Liliana, and Lena (the only girl of color who had joined the play).[6] However, the players also included boys of diverse backgrounds who enjoyed superhero play, including not only Sammy but his best friend Aloyse.

The Greek myths offered children reoccurring characters, interrelated in complex family relations and engaged in familiar storylines of physical opposition and rescue. Good guys and bad guys, great quarrels and grand rescues, marriages, births, and deaths—all were abundant in the myths. The core of the playground game was appropriated from two stories. The plot was influenced by the story of Persephone, the daughter of Demeter, who was kidnapped by Pluto, dragged to the underworld, and, partially at least, rescued by Jupiter. The cast of characters, though, included those central to the story of Psyche, an earthly maiden whose marriage to Cupid (son of Venus) was saved by Jupiter.

In the game, each child consistently took the role of a particular character. Radha, for example, was Jupiter, Demario was Jupiter's cousin, Jonathan was Cupid, Sammy was Pluto, and Aloyse was his cousin. Among the girls were Sarah as Psyche, Lena as Persephone, and Susan and Melissa as Psyche and Cupid's children. Since the game was set in motion by Sarah and her usual playmates, Sammy and his usual playmates were left with minor good guy roles—or major bad guy ones (like being Pluto). Following is a brief narrative of their play (constructed from field notes).

The "game of gods and goddesses" (so named by Sarah) is taking place on a large expanse of the playground. Mount Olympus is on the grass in the far southeast end of the playground, against the fence and under a large tree. The underworld is on the hot sand, beside the climbing structure, on the west end of the playground. As I enter the drama, Pluto (alias Sammy) is coming up from the underworld. "Earthquake! Earthquake!" he yells, as the ground opens up for him. He quickly grabs Callisto (Susan) and, just as quickly, is off to the underworld. Immediately Jupiter (Radha) rushes off to the rescue. "Don't go there, father," screams a distraught Persephone (Lena), "You'll die." But it is too late. He is gone.

In the meantime, another of Psyche's children, her baby (Melissa), is tossing and turning on the bench in the gods' palace. She is quite sick, and her father Cupid (Jonathan) realizes that he left the baby's medicine in the underworld. "You left it in the underworld!" says the incredulous Persephone (who knows of the dangers in that place). "You stupid—" "I'll go get it," replies Cupid, and soon he too is off.

In the midst of the screaming and the running, Edward runs here and there, turning the handle of an old fashioned (and invisible) movie camera. "Good horror film! Good horror film!" he says with enthusiasm.

The gender roles in the preceding play were stereotypical: the boys found power in physical display; the girls in family management. Nonetheless, those roles were interwoven in the same collaboratively constructed story. Moreover, the roles did not always remain stereotypical. There were, after all, often as many as 11 children to be accommodated, boys and girls with different desires for story roles and different attractions to the pleasures of the myths. In part because of the need to negotiate each other's desires if the play was to continue, and in part, perhaps, because of their limited knowledge of Greek myths, roles and storylines were transformed. (Sometimes, of course, things got out of hand, and the play dissolved in quarrels and massive quitting.)

For example, in the preceding narration, characters were invented by boys desiring parts, just as characters were invented in recess superhero play: by the inclusion of twins and cousins. In the superhero play, however, being a twin or cousin became immaterial as soon as one was on a team and engaged in chase games and (pretend) battles. In the gods and goddesses game, being a twin or a cousin positioned one in a complex family drama.

In addition, children with less appealing roles sometimes proposed transformations (and character transformations do occur in X-Men stories and in Greek myths). Thus, on one occasion Pluto (Sammy) was "transformed" [the children's word] into a good guy, which made Jupiter (Radha) mad, and so Jupiter was transformed into a bad guy. Cupid (Jonathan) was going to try to control Jupiter, explained Psyche (Sarah). But if Cupid failed, and an angry Jupiter attacked Olympus, "then we'll have to fight"—*we'll* meaning all grown-ups, and Psyche assumed a karate stance to demonstrate. Clearly, within the gods and goddesses game, where physical violence was a common place, Sarah was willing to engage with physical power—and even to assume a physical stance reminiscent of the ninjas and the Power Rangers.

"Gods and Godesses": The Book

Although the Greek myths mediated new social configurations and story possibilities out on the playground, inside the classroom, these new social and literary complexities unraveled. Children separated into their usual social circles. Family relations, on the one hand, and grand battles and rescues, on the other, also separated into their usual texts.

Child-initiated mythology texts were produced by the members of the family, so to speak. Sarah, Melissa, Susan, Liliana (all regular writers about human relations), and Jonathan made "Family Albums" featuring Venus, Jupiter, Psyche, Cupid, and their children.[7] During their production (which continued on and off for the rest of the school year), the children sat together on the rug, huddled in a small circle. Each child produced a separate album, marking their drawn characters with the name of both the Greek figure and the human child who played that role. (See Figures 6.4 to 6.6.) Jonathan, for example, drew a robed figure named both Radha and Jupiter; Sarah drew a small winged child named both Melissa and Blis.

Figure 6.4. Jonathan's portrait of Cupid, played by himself.

[Jonathan]

Cuped

Figure 6.5. Jonathan's portrait of Jupiter, played by Radha.

[Radha]

Jupiter

Figure 6.6. Sarah's picture of Blis, played by Melissa, and Psyche, played by herself.

[Melissa]

Blis

[Sarah]

Sicky

These myths served the child authors as a means of affiliation, similar in ways to how the superhero stories served Sammy and his fellow fans. All of the children worked with great care on these drawings, consulting the classroom's collection of mythology books for physical details, just as many superhero fans (especially Michael and Edward) drew their characters just so, informed by cartoons, comics, and trading cards. As they worked, the children clarified the complex relationships among the characters, similar to the talk among X-Men fans about characters' interrelationships. In fact, the mythology writers talked and drew much more than they wrote, transforming the complex playground dramas to oddly costumed domestic scenes.[8]

Only Susan wrote extended texts about the Greek figures. Her stories, written from the perspective of her playground character (a child of Psyche and Cupid), literally brought the myths into the realm of the everyday. The child Callisto goes for walks with her mother and her siblings (Blis and her twin Venus [who is "named after my Grandmother"]). Her father takes her to nursery school, just as Susan's own father brought her to school each day.

> My Daddys name is Cupid. He makes people fall in love wen he shoots an arow. He battles with plouto and still manegas [manages] to take me to nusry scool at 9:00. [Psyche and Cupid's wedding day is presented in Figure 6.7.]

Sammy admired the family albums produced during writing time, as did other recess-time players of the god and goddess game. The first day Sarah and her friends began making them, Sammy, Aloyse, Radha, and Edward sat and watched for a while, their composing books in hand—but not in use. They commented on the drawings and joined in on talk about the god and goddess game. In the excerpt from the composing talk that follows, Radha [Jupiter] has just clarified Sammy's powers ("You can go underground and you can't fly.") and is now discussing his relationship to Liliana [Venus].

LILIANA: *(to Radha)* I'm your step mom. I'm your step mom.
RADHA: But I'm a dad.
LILIANA: Who's your child then?
RADHA: Aloyse! He's Mercury! [actually, Aloyse played Pluto's cousin and, therefore, is Jupiter's cousin]
            (Susan has been quietly bemoaning the quality of her drawn picture to Melissa. Sammy has overheard.)
SAMMY: OH! That's cute!
MELISSA: See? Everybody likes it.
SAMMY: That is cute.
            (Kristin comes over to the rug, notices Sammy's closed writing book.)

Figure 6.7. *Susan's picture of Cupid and Psyche's wedding day.*

KRISTIN: Sammy, what are you writing? You need a new book?
              (Sammy nods.)
              OK, I'll get you a book.
ALOYSE: *(to the group as a whole)* This is fun! Look what Jonathan
              drawed!
RADHA: Oh, that's Archangel [of the X-Men]!
JONATHAN: It is <u>not</u>. It's Cupid.
              *(Soon Kristin returns with a new writing book for Sammy.
              He, Radha, Aloyse, and Edward move to other corners of the
              rug or to tables and begin their own stories. They are, to a
              child, writing about the adventures of superheroes.)*

On occasion, the superhero authors included Hercules or Pluto as a bad
guy in their stories. And, as will be discussed, they all produced assigned
essays, detailing the traits and powers of their chosen Greek figure. One evening,
Aloyse even called Kristin at home, telling her that a movie about Hercules
was on the television. He himself was going to watch the Warriors basketball
game; but, since she liked the myths a lot, he thought she might want to know
about the movie. But Aloyse, like the other god and goddess players, went
back to his usual social circles and textual sources during composing time.[9]

Still, Sammy, Aloyse, Sarah, Melissa, and other children *had* at the very least witnessed, if not engaged in, great battles together out on the playground. Their social worlds and cultural coordinates did have new possibilities after the playground game of gods and goddesses ... or so it seemed when unexpected social connections were negotiated in response to a superhero story presented by Sammy and Patrick.

NEGOTIATING "THE COMPANY WE KEEP"

One day, Sammy and Patrick decided to write a superhero story together. This was the children's idea, but one Kristin encouraged—and one that generated extensive planning, monitoring, and, more broadly, concentration on text, as has been documented among other young collaborating authors (see especially Daiute, 1989, 1993). Moreover, this concentration was not an alternative to, but very much furthered by, Sammy's social concerns.[10]

As will be evident, the boys considered social affiliations (having appealing roles and fun actions for their actors) and social control (not having so many characters and so much action that things would get "out of hand"). However, the boys—and the male peers who negotiated a part in their story—did not question the appeal of physical power itself. Such questioning would emerge only when the boys' story was performed for the community as a whole through Author's Theater—and, then, the usual ideological gaps, linked all too neatly to societal divisions (i.e., to gender and class), would be newly complicated. And Sammy's Greek alias (Pluto) would have something to do with this complication.

Local Negotiations: The Gathering of Tough But Good Guys

For two composing periods, Sammy and Patrick worked side-by-side on their Power Rangers story. The boys negotiated the story's content, but each wrote the text in their own writing book. On their first day of working together, the boys introduced the Power Rangers in their story and decided on Hercules as the bad guy. In the following excerpt, from their second day, Sammy is sitting at a table, waiting for Patrick, who's on his way to the table with his writing book. Sammy's excitement about their story—and the planned Author's Theater—is clear in his voice, as he urges Patrick to hurry up.

> SAMMY: OK, Patrick.... Let's do it! OK, come on. Let's finish writing about Hercules.... *(Patrick has settled in his seat.)* We could put, we could put, we could put, um, "and Hercules was the bad guy."

PATRICK: [How about instead] "And Hercules was trying to kill the
           Power Rangers"?
SAMMY: No, "and Hercules was" um—
PATRICK: "Trying to kill the Power Rangers!"
SAMMY: No, "and Hercules was the bad guy." Then we're gonna say
           he was trying to kill the Power Rangers. Yeah, please. . . .
           Please Patrick. (giggles) . . . That's [your way's] gonna be
           short.
PATRICK: Oh. OK.
SAMMY: And we gotta make it long.
PATRICK: OK.
           *(Both boys begin to write Sammy's suggested sentence. They
           move collaboratively forward, orally planning their words,
           helping each other spell, and orally rereading. Then Patrick
           again suggests his sentence.)*
PATRICK: "He was trying to kill the Power Rangers"?
SAMMY: No. "He didn't know the Power Rangers." Then "he saw the
           Power Rangers. They start fighting." Right?
           (Patrick looks displeased.)
           Yeah. OK? Come on.
     . . .
PATRICK: But this is just gonna sound like, describing the story, and we
           wanta do the story.
           *(Patrick is bringing up a long-standing community concern
           about having enough action in a story.)*
SAMMY: *(proposing the next sentence)* "And the Power Rangers didn't
           know him." Then we could write what you wanta write.
PATRICK: O: kay. *(resigned)*
     . . .
SAMMY: *(the proposed line now written)* OK. Now we could do what
           you wanta do. What you wanta do?
PATRICK: And um, "The Power Rangers saw him wrecking the city. . . . "
SAMMY: Destroy, not wrecking. . . .
           (Bryant now comes over to the boys' table, seeking a role.)
SAMMY: Bryant, you could be [Hercules'] friend. . . .
BRYANT: I'm a bad guy? . . . Take me off.
SAMMY: Man! Why you always have to be a bad—see, you always
           wanta be a good guy. . . .
BRYANT: Pretend like he's a bad guy, and I'm a good guy. And when
           he wanta do something bad, I don't. I don't wanta join him.
SAMMY: OK. Yeah.
PATRICK: But you always do.

SAMMY: Yeah.
BRYANT: No, I don't join him. But only if you pull a gun on me, then
           I'll—
SAMMY: Look how I'm doing this, Ms. S. [Kristin]!
           *(Sammy is quite pleased with how hard he is working and
           with his page full of writing. Thomas now comes by the
           table, his attention having been captured by Sammy's call to
           Kristin.)*
THOMAS: O:h! O:h! Can I be Hercules in your story?
SAMMY: Radha is.

           . . .

THOMAS: Can I be in it?
SAMMY: OK. You could be a bad guy, 'cause there's no more good
           guys.
PATRICK: Sammy! Sammy! I don't like so many people in my story. . . .
           It's too hard to control. Everybody gets out of hand.
SAMMY: If they do, let's just make 'em go home.
PATRICK: NO! If they do [get out of hand], Mrs. S. makes us stop. And
           we won't be able to do the rest [of the story]. . . .
SAMMY: But there's only two bad guys! That don't make sense [given
           the number of Power Rangers].
           *(Sammy's comments here recall those Makeda made about
           his X-Men story: A small number of bad guys have no logical
           chance against a team of good guys. Patrick is insistent, and
           Sammy agrees that Hercules will have one friend—Zeus.
           Patrick, however, writes only Zeus's name in his piece, and
           Sammy writes only Hercules. Both boys plan but leave out
           parts of their story, seemingly because the writing takes such
           effort and, in the process of planning, spelling, rereading, and
           planning again, they lose track of their planned text.)*
SAMMY: *(resaying the planned story and suggesting a next line)* "And
           they turned into Power Rangers. And they fought Hercules
           and his friend. And Hercules still won."
PATRICK: No, Hercules didn't win. It was a tie.
SAMMY: No—
PATRICK: 'Cause that would be fair to both [teams].
SAMMY: Yeah but that ain't gonna be the end. [That is, Hercules can
           win now; the Power Rangers will win later.] We gotta have
           more parts. Let's do it longer, until lunch.
           *(As the boys continue to plan their story, they disagree on
           whether or not the [original] Power Rangers should immedi-
           ately call for help from their sometime teammate, Tommy—the*

> *Green Power Ranger [Michael]. Sammy, trying to make the*
> *story last as long as possible, wants to wait. But not Patrick.)*
PATRICK: Michael's gonna be complaining like, "When it's gonna be
>   my turn? When it's gonna be my turn?"
SAMMY: Hey Michael!
>   *(Sammy recites both plans for Michael. Michael suggests that,*
>   *since the Author's Theater turn really is Patrick's [i.e.,*
>   *Patrick's name, not Sammy's, is next up on the Author's*
>   *Theater list], they should go with Patrick's idea. The boys go*
>   *with Patrick's idea.)*

Sammy and Patrick, then, worked to meet their social goals with the cultural material provided by the superhero genre. They tried to be inclusive and fair to their actors; for example, they deliberated on how many characters to include and what sort of plot developments would allow all the characters an opportunity to win. And they also worked to make a "good" story, one with sufficient action and sensible human relations (i.e., between the good guys and the bad ones).

Indeed, the pressure of the immediate social milieu helped transform the text so that it served, not only as a ticket to social play, but also as valued representation and as dialogic medium, that is, a means to negotiate with others' desires. And yet, despite their deliberations, Sammy and Patrick were not questioning their depiction of power. This issue was not salient in the social world their text reflected. But it *would* be during Author's Theater, when their texts were brought to the community of the whole.

Public Negotiations: Questioning the Tough, the Good, and the Guys

After composing time was over, Sammy and Patrick went to the front of their classroom to organize for Author's Theater, as the rest of the children gathered on the rug. The boys called their actors. The seven male actors were superhero regulars, but the two females, Melissa and Sarah, were not. Melissa and Sarah had been chosen for female roles during the second grade year (see Chapter 3). During the third grade, however, the superhero authors were much more responsive to children who *requested* roles in these stories, especially Tina and Makeda.

When the play finally began, the two boys took turns reading sentences. However, Sammy, a much more experienced Author's Theater director, took the lead in anticipating potential social problems in the enactment of their imperfect text. For example, he smoothed over the difficulty with "Hercules" and "Zeus"—and kept in control both Radha (listed as Zeus in Patrick's list, as Hercules in his own) and "friend" Bryant.

SAMMY: *(reading)* "Once upon a time there were Power Rangers."
         (improvises but keeps reading intonation) And their name
         was Billy, Jason, Tommy, and um Sarah—I mean Trini,
         Kimberly, and Zack. And the bad guys' name was Zeus—
         (orally comments) Radha, you the boss!—and Hercules *(nod-
         ding to Bryant, who has now become Hercules).*
BRYANT: Hercules is a <u>nice</u> guy.
         . . .
SAMMY: Now you read.
PATRICK: *(reading)* "But the Power Rangers didn't know Hercules" —
SAMMY: *(improvises)* and Zeus.
PATRICK: Oh yeah, *(back to reading)* "But the Power Rangers didn't
         know Hercules and Zeus"—no wait. "But the Power Rangers
         didn't know Zeus."
SAMMY: Zeus and Hercules.
PATRICK: What do you mean?
         *(Patrick points to his paper, indicating that there is no
         Hercules. The child actors begin to get out of hand, as mock
         battles begin. Sammy immediately begins to read and impro-
         vise. He not only includes both Hercules and Zeus in the
         action, but also clarifies the action and substitutes character
         names for pronouns without referents.)*

The following is an excerpt from Sammy's written version; bracketed
sections were added orally, or substituted for the preceding boldface words.

Once upon a time there were Power Rangers. [And their name was Billy,
Jason, Tommy, Trini, Kimberly, and Zack.] **and Hercules.** [And the bad
guys name was Zeus and Hercules.] But he didn't know the Power
Rangers, and the Power Rangers didn't know Hercules [and Zeus]. The
Power Rangers saw him and his friends [destroying the world]. Jason said,
"It's Morphin' Time." And they turned into Power Rangers. And **they**
[Zeus and his friend] fought the Power Rangers. The Power Rangers were
getting beat up. And they turned back into their selves [like kids]. And **he**
[Jason] called Tommy to their side. And they were Power Rangers. The
Power Rangers won. *(Spelling corrected for ease of reading.)*

Despite Sammy's social attention and rhetorical skill, all the child actors
were not happy when they sat down. Kristin opened the floor for questions
and comments, and Sarah immediately raised an objection, an objection that
emphasized her distance from—her lack of affiliation with—the social group
that watched superhero shows.

SARAH: See, I don't watch the show, so I don't know what to do. It doesn't make sense to me. I couldn't hear you, and it's like all of a sudden people are fighting.

. . .

KRISTIN: Sarah's comment is that she doesn't know how to do [act out] the character because she's never seen it [the television show] before. So, Sarah, what would help you out there?

SARAH: If there were more details.

KRISTIN: What kind of details?

SARAH: Like, what led to what. They didn't say what they did bad. It's more like, this character did this. But <u>why</u>?

. . .

MELISSA: And one thing that I really don't like is, I don't like when the story is just fighting, 'cause that's what that story was mostly about.
(A number of boys immediately make faces, among them Edward and Aloyse [who is Sammy's best friend].)

KRISTIN: When she said that, I saw you guys kinda go "Uh!" Why did you react that way?

. . .

ALOYSE: Because that was his story and that's how he did it. You [Melissa] don't have to tell them what to do.
(In a move toward compromise, Demario suggests perhaps nonphysical fighting—"arguing"—would be acceptable. [It is hard, though, to imagine a superhero calling others to battle with some variant of "Come on, boys. Let's argue!"]. Kristin probes further.)

KRISTIN: How many of you don't like fighting in stories?
(Sarah and Melissa's friend Susan raises her hand. Like her friends, Susan has spoken out against fighting. But now she has a different comment.)

SUSAN: In this book I'm writing, Pluto will go to battle.

KRISTIN: You're saying that this is a story where there is some fighting in it that you like? *(Susan nods.)* Those of you who like fighting . . . do you like the story when all it is is fighting. . . . ?

ALOYSE: Just fighting.
(Aloyse has kept a firm, grim look on his face.)

VICTOR: No way. Like, sometimes if you write a story like that, it's boring when it's just fighting.

. . .

MICHAEL: I don't like stories just fighting. In <u>my</u> X-Men story, I'm gonna make 'em fight for the Professor [their leader], and then they gonna stop fighting and they're gonna become friends.

When Sarah made her original objection, fracture lines appeared in the class, lines that accentuated not only gender but also the interrelated borders of race and class. Those objecting to the story were White, middle-class girls; those reacting to the objections were Sammy's regular playmates, all non–middle-class boys of color. But, even as the community fractured and social distance was revealed, a complex discussion of authorial decisions began.

A consensus seemed to be forming (a polymorphous one, but a consensus) that, to be good, stories must have more than *just* fighting, and that that fighting also must have a place in an evolving story. The "good" in question had, in part, to do with being a coherent story—a story with a narrative structure, a thematic point, and enough variation to keep audience interest. But it also had to do with being a worthy world—one in which any fighting has some motivation and eventually is ended. After all, being good *was* important to the superhero fans (as Bryant illustrated with his fervent efforts to become a "good" friend of the designated "bad" guy; goodness, like strength, is inherent in the concept of the superhero, the people's savior).

This consensus continued to evolve even as Edward fractured the community once again.

EDWARD: But I know why kids want that fighting.... 'Cause, you know how boys are. They get bored. They like fighting.

LENA: Oh God.

KRISTIN: Why're you getting mad, Lena?

LENA: It's sick. There's some girls that like fighting.

. . .

EDWARD: I think boys like all that fighting.
(But Edward's friend Demario disagrees.)

DEMARIO: I don't like a story that has all just fighting in it, 'cause it wouldn't be a story. It would just be fighting, and you wouldn't know when to stop.

KRISTIN: Good point.

SARAH: It seems to me that if it's just fighting from beginning to end, without any story, it wouldn't be like "So one day they go into battle."

KRISTIN: So it wouldn't have the narrative part of the story?

SARAH: Yeah.
("Going into battle" is the language of the Greek myths, not the superhero dramas; and, indeed, Sarah herself [somebody who does "not like fighting" in stories] has gone to battle in a playground game of "gods and goddesses," as have her friends Melissa and Susan.)

So Sammy and Patrick had gotten together to compose a good story—a fun story—for Author's Theater. But when that text was displayed in the public forum, social tensions emerged and, with teacher guidance, so also emerged talk about authors' decisions about the representation of human relations, about stories. The goodness of the superheroes was opened to question, as the children negotiated their ideas about the kinds of displayed power that seemed morally defensible as well as textually interesting. At the same time, pleasures in physical power were displayed as *not,* after all, the province of only one kind of story or one group of children.

Thus, talk about text reconnected class members as decision-making children informed by certain shared values. As the discussion evolved, they did not make "flat judgments for or against" certain works, to use the words of Wayne Booth (1988, p. 18) but, rather, had "a fluid conversation about the qualities of the company [they] keep [in their stories] and the company [they themselves] provide."

The relative inclusiveness of the children's discussion was evident in the very way they linked their turns across social and ideological lines. Susan, for example, characterized herself as someone who was writing a story that included fighting, and, in so doing, she positioned herself somewhere other than in a dichotomous relationship between a "them" who like fighting and an "us" who don't. Demario declared that too much fighting was indeed boring, thereby moving away from Edward and also positioning himself in a complex dialogic space. As a community, the children referenced both Greek myths and superhero stories, suggesting that their play with diverse sorts of stories in the unofficial world—and the openness of the official world to that diversity—contributed to this social positioning and textual reimagining.[11]

As the talk generated by Sammy's and Patrick's superhero story continued, it included a discussion of actual (not perceived as play) fighting and a naming of powerful nonviolent political leaders, including Rosa Parks, Sammy's nonviolent hero. By this time in the year, the class had discussed the power of speech and, moreover, the power of internal determination and the way in which it may defeat the power of physical force, as in the civil rights movement. As Aloyse said at the end of the excerpted discussion, if we want to win in life, we have to "fight with the inside of [our] head[s]." That is, if we want stories in which those who are not physically strong (like the very slight Aloyse) are "powerful," then we need different kinds of stories. Superhero stories, video games, Greek myths, and biographies of varied historical heroes— all feature different kinds of conflicts and different kinds of resolutions as well. Collectively, they offered the children symbolic material with which to explore the complexities—the ambiguities—of goodness and power and, also, of their own relationships with each other.

FASHIONING A NEW SUPERHERO:
"ALL THE STRONG WOMEN I EVER HEARD OF"

Noticeably absent from the preceding discussion were the voices of girls of color, with the exception of Lena. Unlike most male superhero fans, these girls never joined the gods and goddesses game on the playground; they stayed with the jump ropes and the metal bars. Nonetheless, even in their very silence, these girls were responding to the recent inclusion of gods and goddesses in the classroom store of powerful images. Not surprisingly, it was Tina who offered a textual response to this new "state of affairs" (Volosinov, 1973, p. 95) and, in so doing, provided a fitting end to this chapter on physical power.

Like the traditional superhero stories, the classroom Greek myth books (particularly d'Aulaire & d'Aulaire, 1962) featured many good-looking characters of both sexes, but they emphasized male strength and female beauty. In the d'Aulaires' book, most of the myths' beautiful women (like the ninjas' Emily) were pale-skinned, with flowing golden hair. In the children's essays on their chosen Greek figure, they verbally retained the qualities of their character's appearance—even when they invented additional physical features.[12] Following are excerpts from Thomas's enthusiastic description of Bellerophon and Makeda's of Venus.

BELLEROPHON

Bellerophon was a mortal warrior. He really good looking, brave and strong. He has light skin and brown hair black eye and a diamond earring. He wear glasses he take them off when he put on his mask [his helmet]. He does exercises. He has big muscles and He work out when he wakes up....

Bellerophon work for the king the king's wife fell in love with Bellerophon, who was a warrior he turned her down She going mad and told a lie on Bellerophon. The king sent him to another king as punishment and was told to kill the Chimera.... *(Spelling corrected for ease of reading.)*

VENUS

Venus is the goddess of love and beauty.... Venus is tall she has white skin she has thin tight eyes her hair covers her body and she has yellow hair fingers are long and fingernails are long and painted yellow like her hair she has a tattoo on her thigh it looks just like her....

After Venus came out of the foam she was taken to Olympus. Hera was jealous of Venus because she was prettier than her so she told Zeus to tell Venus to pick a husband. The guys lined up. They told her all the wonderful things they could do. When she heard

Hephaestus could make jewelry and works late, she chose him. They got married that night. At the party she told the other men to give her their gifts later. She told the men when Hephaestus might be coming home at night.... *(This latter paragraph was dictated to Kristin.)*

Thomas' Bellerophon is a rather modern warrior, with a diamond earring and a work-out routine. Makeda's Venus is a more modern woman as well, with a more active role in finding her mate than the original myth allows (i.e., Zeus, not Venus, chose her husband; as for Venus herself, she preferred Mars). (In this modernization, the characters recall Susan's stroller-pushing Psyche and her responsible Daddy Cupid). Bellerophon and Venus were also depicted explicitly as light-skinned.

This emphasis on lightness and, for the women, on long blonde hair, may have contributed to the racial division in the girls' involvement with the Greek myths.[13] Lena, Makeda, and Tina made this racial emphasis explicit one day, when they were sitting side-by-side, supposedly working on their gods and goddesses project. As noted earlier, Makeda and Tina had chosen Venus as their project character. Lena had chosen Persephone. The following description of the three girls' actions is based on field notes.

Lena has begun drawing her picture, but Makeda and Tina are pretending to be "killer Venus's," play fighting each other. Kristin comes by to help them focus on their work. She tells the girls to draw "how they imagined" their goddesses looked. "It doesn't really matter what somebody else drew." But, after Kristin leaves, all three girls suggest that it does matter.

Tina and Makeda begin drawing their blonde goddesses, concentrating on their long hair. "[Long] like Tina's," says Makeda to me, "but not twisted. Like yours."

I am very embarrassed; my own reddish mane has implicated me in this hair business. "Venus *could* have braids [like Tina's two long ones]," I say. Moreover, I continue, "it could be *black* hair [like Tina's and, also, like Makeda's shorter, swept-up twist]."

"I don't think so," says Makeda kindly.

Lena has been outlining her Venus with a black color. She explains to Makeda and Tina that she has chosen black because white did not show up well on her paper. She is sure this is not right. "People from Greece are not White—I mean, are not Black."

"Yes they can be!" counters Tina.

"I don't think so," says Makeda, now to Tina. "I think she's [Venus is] white."

"Well maybe she's white to you, but not to me!" responds Tina.

Kristin's comment that the children could "use their imagination" had no apparent effect on the girls' imagined Venus. A potentially patronizing comment from the usually quiet me elicited only a kindly, seemingly patronizing comment back. But Lena's and Makeda's remarks, comments from inside the peer social world, elicited a strong response from Tina. She talked back to them—a typical Tina response to a peer's exclusion from a narrative world.

Tina drew and wrote back as well. Immediately, she began to draw a Black Venus (see Figure 6.8), and, then, so did Makeda. Her friend became frustrated with her drawing, but Tina finished hers, making a goddess with long hair and dangling earrings. Further, at home after school, Tina wrote a long story of perpetrators and victims and of a grand rescue, a story featuring a transformed goddess, a heroine named Venus Tina.[14] Following is the story, which was displayed on the classroom bulletin board.

> Once there was a boy and girl in the park and two men was walking by the park and the men saw the two kids. So the two men started to run after them, and the kids ran. One man chased the girl. The other ran after the boy. The boy name was Aloyse and the [girl] name was Asia [her sister]. So when Venus Tina heard about this she was mad. So she came down. She saw the men running after the kids. She got mad-

Figure 6.8. *Tina's picture of Venus Tina.*

der. She came faster and picked the kids up on her magical flying horse named Makeda. It was a girl horse. And she took the two kids in the sky. There was a big park on a cloud. There was a lot of kids play[ing] on flying horses. It was kids from [Tina's] school. They had ice cream and candy. Then she took them home. They said, "What about those two mean men?" Venus Tina made them nice. And on earth was fun again. She made parks safe for us kids of the world. By Tina. Love Tina. *(Spelling and punctuation corrected for ease of reading.)*

Venus Tina seemed to be, to use Jerry Siegel's words, "all the strong women Tina ever heard of rolled into one. Only more so"—and with a strong social conscience. Like Storm and Rogue, Venus Tina flew through the air, but (like Bellerophon) she used a magical flying horse to do so—a horse specifically marked as a *girl* horse, a horse named Makeda. Like "tough" Emily's mother (see Chapter 5), her own mother, and, in fact, like Tina herself, Venus Tina took care of little kids, sweeping them out of harm's way.

The world of mortals was terrorized by the traditional "mean men," who, nonetheless, terrorized equally a girl and a boy. And Venus Tina saved them both. Moreover she did not "kick butt," like the appropriated Storm or the inverted Emily. (See Chapter 5.) Like the powerful goddesses in the class-shared myths, she transformed them. But this was not a jealous goddess like Athena, who turned a human into a spider. This was a kind goddess, one who made the bad good, recalling, at least for me, Tina's aunt the minister (or Tina's own transformation of Aladdin from street rat to boy saint). "And on earth was fun again."

Tina was a participant in a classroom community in which appropriated heroes—whatever their cultural source, "classic" or "popular" —were subject to critical reflection and, moreover, a community in which child heroes were continuously urged to "use their imaginations," to feel free to venture beyond the given. Kristin's urgings, however, in and of themselves did not push children beyond familiar ground (beyond assumptions about the worthiness—or disrepute—of story heroes and their actions). Her openness to diverse cultural resources and her consistent references to their own authorial power helped them push *each other* beyond their usual storylines.

Venus had entered the classroom image store, along with the Power Rangers, the X-Men, and Rosa Parks. That store held for each child the symbolic means for examining an aspect of themselves. But their use of those symbols was not an act of individual self-expression but of an evolving social response to those around them. The symbolic material of books, cartoons, video games—of all aspects of our consumer culture—is useful only if it is used in everyday practices as a means for affiliating, differentiating, and negotiating a social place in a world of others (Douglas, 1994; Seiter, 1993; Willis, 1990). In Kristin's classroom, those everyday practices included composing and dramatizing stories—practices that, by late in the third grade, engaged all the children (although, of course, not all the time, nor in the same way).

In their unofficial play, their official dramatic enactment and follow-up discussions, and in their own individual contributions as writers, the children could not only appropriate, or invert, available roles and relations; they could reconstruct them, imagining new choices from expanding possibilities. Through marking, elaborating, and transforming the features, actions, and circumstances of powerful characters, children themselves gained some power— some ability to have a say—in the evolving community dialogue.

For Sammy, such reconstruction was most visible when he was negotiating his stories face-to-face with other children, composing along side them or reconsidering his story in the exigencies of the dramatic moment. Then, the good guys did not always win, and both good and bad guys were subject to the human condition: They needed food and sleep; they worried, mourned, loved, and died. For Tina, this reconstruction was most visible when, resisting another's imagined world, she determinedly put forward her own in writing. Then—or, at least, now, near the end of the school year, superheroes were not necessarily "guys," and their power did not necessarily bruise.

In this chapter, the major dialogue has been about physical power—the capacity to inflict one's will on others because of one's might, and the interrelationships between might and right, might and gender, and between might and other kinds of power. Physical power was a relevant ideological issue in the lives of children, whatever their sex and socioeconomic circumstance; and it was present as a symbolic element in school-introduced stories as well as television-introduced ones. There was another important issue, however, one that has been pervasive but sidelined in all the chapters to this point, and one that will be increasingly important as the children move toward adolescence: the issue of who loves (and who should love) whom. In the last chapter of the children's drama, this issue takes center stage.

▼ 7 ▼
▼

Transformed and Silenced Lovers: Texts as Sites of Revelation and Circumvention

I was thinking about the matter of cultural archetypes and positive black images as I came out of the subway not long ago. Just ahead of me I saw a little black child of about seven accompanied by her mother. She was wearing a bright pink hat that said "Barbie" in white knit letters, with a little white knit copyright symbol just after the name. I wondered if this might mean there is a black Barbie doll on the market, hunkered down in her Barbie Dream House waiting bravely for Ken. Or if there might even be a black Ken doll out there, clean-shaven, crewcut, with knees that don't bend. . . . Does [the black Barbie] look more like Diana Ross or Janet Jackson? . . . Is Barbie, that anorectic instrument of white women's oppression, *capable* of being black?

Patricia Williams, The Rooster's Egg:
On the Persistence of Prejudice, 1995, p. 133

Patricia Williams, a lawyer and cultural critic, looks with understandable worry at the young Black child with the Barbie symbol on her hat. Little girls' private desires are expressed through the use of cultural icons like Barbie and her boyfriend Ken. These icons represent romantic archetypes, and, as such, they are undergirded by seldom-articulated but very powerful ideologies of beauty, social class, and race (Christian-Smith,

1993; Gilbert, 1994; Moss, 1989, 1993; Walkerdine, 1985, 1990). Thus, a Black Barbie doll—which does, in fact, exist—cannot symbolize what the White Barbie does; she is not the real thing. Perhaps this is one reason Williams, who is African American, only had White dolls as a child—and why "my favorite toy ended up being a stuffed dog named Cicero" (p. 184).

Although not previously featured, the complexity of public meanings associated with romance have been evident throughout this drama about Kristin's children. The diversity of the classroom community—the children's own differing positions in relationship to shared cultural figures—generated critical response akin to that Patricia Williams herself was aiming for with her comments about Barbie. For example, as illustrated in Chapter 3, a key question in the second grade was, "Does a superhero's 'foxy babe' have to be White?" In dialogue with each other, the children were more explicitly confrontational, and more apt to playfully mock cultural images, than Williams seems to anticipate.

However, the girls who raised the "foxy babe" issue were more concerned about gaining access than critiquing images; that is, they were concerned about their right to appropriate an available role. (In the end, they found foxy babe roles quite boring.) For their part, second-grade boys did not even include April's or Emily's name in their texts—such an inclusion would have led inevitably to much teasing. Thus, romantic relations—and their underlying ideological assumptions—were not a central topic of reflection in the second grade.

In the third grade, though, some children, especially Tina and her friends, began to write and present stories that textually represented and, in fact, highlighted romantic encounters. These stories anticipated the personal and social issues that will become increasingly important in these children's lives, as they edge toward preadolescence in their urban environment. Moreover, the interactions generated by those stories suggested the ways in which writing, as a means of community participation, might help the children explicitly confront—or deliberately avoid—the ideological complexities of romance.

As will be evident in the pages to follow, in the third grade, playful teasing about who liked whom continued, but more seriousness accompanied the pairing of people. For example, Tina was quite upset when peers teased her about liking Edward. She wrote in her journal that "they thike [think] that me and Edward are in love. But we are not in love in [and] I feel sad mad bad." When Makeda and Aloyse teased Sammy about having liked Sarah in the second grade, Sammy told them that his new girlfriend (who remained unnamed) was Black. Just as close peer relationships tended to be among children from similar sociocultural backgrounds, so too did potential romantic pairings. According to Holmes (1995) and Schofield (1989), in our society, even in integrated schools, interracial romance seems to be atypical.[1]

Also evident in the coming pages is the third graders' relative sophistica-
tion as writers and community members. As Sammy and Patrick illustrated
in the last chapter, observation of third graders' composing processes revealed
their monitoring of, not only the sense of their words, but also the ways in
which others might react to their words. The wrong details—too many bad
guys, senseless death, unmotivated fighting—could lead to disruption and/or
discord. In the most ideologically charged romance story to be presented, Lena's
anticipation of audience discord will lead, not to deliberate textual mediation, but to deliberate textual silence on a sensitive issue—the issue of interracial romance.

Learning to circumvent the controversial, like learning to deliberately
respond to it, is a potential developmental outcome of learning to write in a
community of diverse others. Like adult writers, child ones may exploit written performance as a means of furthering, challenging—or avoiding community dialogues (Freire, 1970; Graff, 1987; Volosinov, 1973). After all, children are not "silenced" only by society's schools (Fine, 1987). They are also
silenced by society's words, words like "Black" and "White," embued as
they are, even for small children, with unarticulated but complex meanings
likely to generate friction in our "genderized, sexualized, wholly racialized
world" (Morrison, 1992, p. 4).

Thus, in this last chapter of the children's drama, child composers will
be seen using familiar figures and popular characters as a means for expressing, exploring, and, at times, reconfiguring romantic relations. And both
textual explicitness and textual silence will figure into their efforts. In the
first major section to follow, I consider the ways in which children represented human relationships in their romance stories (i.e., stories about people "wanting" or enacting romantic involvement). Then, against that back-
drop, in the second section I present the drama of Lena's text about, and yet
not about, interracial romance.

REVEALING LOVERS' RELATIONSHIPS

In Author's Theater, love, kissing, and marriage had great "splash value"
(Henderson, 1996, p. 198). Just their very mention was sure to elicit playful
"oohs" and "aahs" from audience members, even if the actors were not so pleased.
Children's references to "bodily parts, bodily functions, sexual differences, and
sexual activities" are often a great shock to adults (Sullivan, 1995, p. 157), but
they are very very funny to children. Such shared humor allows children (just
as it does adults) a way of controlling the uncontrollable, of exercising some
power over the unknown and the feared (Sullivan, 1995; Tucker, 1995)—and,
perhaps, of outwitting adult suppression (McMahon & Sutton-Smith, 1995).

The third graders sometimes chose to actually write romantic actions, among them "liking," "loving," sweet talking (e.g., "You look good"), kissing, and marrying. On occasion, they even featured romance as their main storyline. The number of representations of romantic actions was relatively small— only 27 of the children's products (about 13%) included such representations, and only 13 (10 by girls, 8 of whom were girls of color) featured romance as the main storyline. In contrast, 111 (or 50% of all completed products) featured physical encounters. Still, the very appearance of romance in the children's written stories suggested the functional importance of texts themselves in the third grade. Through those texts, children marked, mocked, and, sometimes, dialogically engaged with ideologies of romance.

Children's representations of romance occurred primarily in familiar textual territory: Most were representations of—or exaggerations of—relationships between well-known media figures. For example, Michael, always a stickler for accuracy, included a romantic detail (i.e., Wolverine "loved Jean Gray") in a descriptive introduction to an X-Men story. In a more dramatic vein, Sammy wrote that *The Three Ninjas*'s Emily kissed Rocky for getting her bike back (something the original Emily most definitely did not do), and Radha rewrote in great detail an episode about Kimberly and the Green Power Ranger Tommy, adding a dismissive line (said under the evil Rita's spell), "Get lost, girly."

None of the preceding may seem funny to an adult reader, but any reference to romance during Author's Theater provoked at least a few giggles from this child audience. Rhonda was the most explicit and the most explicitly playful in her romantic prose, which drew, not on the traditions of popular culture, but on the verbal silliness of child culture. For example, she elicited much delighted laughter with her story of the boo boo man and the pee pee girl.

> ... "You look good," [said Rhonda's boo boo man]. The pee pee girl said, "I know I look good." And then they started dating. And then he said, "Will you marry me?" She said, "Yes." And then they had a baby. Her name was Melissa. Melissa was born on June 17, 1994. And they live happy ever after. *(Spelling and punctuation corrected for ease of reading.)*

There was, however, textual material about romance that was neither straightforwardly descriptive nor solely humorous. In composing such material, child authors articulated, or avoided, longstanding community issues through new kinds of texts, texts that were relatively realistic.[2] As illustrated in the two sections to follow, issues of gender and race could now be explored, not only in the context of superhero play and rescue plots, but also in the context of "gender play" (Thorne, 1993) itself and plots about men seeking, liking, or loving women—and, sometimes, vice versa.

Continuing the Textual Dialogue About Gender

In most children's appropriations of media material, they (like the media stories themselves) foregrounded the male as the active lead in romantic encounters. Jasmine attracts, but Aladdin takes action, Rocky and Emily share a puppy love, but Emily's imagined kiss is a reward for Rocky's more vigorous display of affection—even the boo boo man makes the first move. However, near the end of the year, Tina articulated her ongoing concerns about gender and equality in two texts of romance. She wrote the story of Batman, Emily, and Bebe, in which Bebe was the active (if deadly) pursuer (story presented in Chapter 5). And she wrote another about teenage lovers; in this latter story, Tina reconstructed (rather than simply inverted or reversed) the expected nature of romantic encounters.

The story was written in large part after school, at her kitchen table, or so reported Tina. It did not in any explicit way include intertextual links to the popular media. And yet, it was deliberately linked to ongoing class dialogues initially generated by media-based stories, a deliberateness suggested by Tina's manipulations of details, of relations and actions, and by her interactions with her peers about her text.

The characters of the story, "Asia and Mike," were named for her siblings: Asia was her baby sister, who "kept messing with me when I was writing, so I put her in it"; Mike was her teenage brother. Tina was *serious* about this story, unlike her playful dramatization of Jasmine and Aladdin's romance and of the terrorizing bat, Baby Bebe. When her classmates acted out her Asia and Mike story in Author's Theater, Tina became quite distressed at their improvisations, which she usually very much enjoyed. She wanted all concerned to attend to her text, not to the actors' funny lines, a text in which she had taken great care to make her gender roles "fair."

> *(Tina has called her actors to the rug. Makeda is Asia,*
> *Demario is Mike, Rhonda and Edward are the parents.*
> *Tina's text is visually displayed in the following in a way that*
> *highlights its detailing of gender relations.)*
>
> TINA: Ready? *(begins reading)*
> "Once there was girl and her name was Asia."
> You're not a baby!
> *(to Makeda, who has begun to crawl around the floor)*
> You're a big girl. So stand up.
> *(again reading)*
> "She was bad to her mom
> and her dad.
> Her mom was always good to her.
> So was her daddy."

EDWARD: *(acting)* Say! I buy you a Barbie Doll.
RHONDA: *(acting)* Come on and I'll take you to the hair dresser to get
            your hair done.
            (Much laughter from the audience)
TINA: Ok ok! FREEZE! SEE? Where am I?
            *(Tina is irritated. "Freeze," is the order given by
            authors/directors when they feel the actors are out of line.
            Her "SEE?" implies that their silliness has made her lose her
            exact place in her text—which usually does not matter; she
            usually does not read her texts but improvises on them.)*
            "And her mom name was Mary.
            And her daddy name was Tom.
            And **they** love her."
            *(Edward says nothing, but Rhonda says, "I love my darling
            girl, but she needs to get her hair combed." The audience
            laughs, Tina sighs and keeps going.)*
TINA: **"The mom was going to work**
            and Asia daddy was going to work also.
            The mom work at Taco Bell.
            And Asia dad work at Burger King."
EDWARD: *(acting)* What you want? Well, we outa that, Man. Get you
            something else.
TINA: WILL YOU <u>SHUT UP</u> AND <u>LISTEN</u> TO WHAT I'M
            SAYING?! *(exceedingly irritated; returns to reading)*
            "And Asia mom was 33
            and Asia dad was 33
            and Asia was 15.
            And she work at a Christmas tree lot.
            She love to give people trees.
            Once there was this boy.
            His name was Mike
            and he was nice and quiet.
            He was 15 too.
            He love Asia
            and Asia love him too.
            The next day
            Asia mother was coming home from North Oakland
            and she saw Asia's daddy
            because he worked there
            and Asia's mom saw Mike and Asia kissing."
DEMARIO: *(playing Mike)* I gotta go. I gotta go. I forgot I got football
            [practice].

> *(Tina keeps reading.)*
>
> TINA: "Asia mom kicked Asia in the butt
> And Asia daddy came home and did the same thing.
> Kicked her butt.
> Asia and Mike ran away
> and got married
> and had no kids
> and die May 32, 1996
> at Asia 96
> Mike 96 also.
> The end."

In the children's acting, there was an undercurrent of gender stereotypes; and, indeed, many children, including Tina, relied on these stereotypes for improvisation when acting. But Tina's text explicitly marked equality of male and female action. Although Asia's mom was mentioned first, she and her similarly aged husband both worked, and both loved and disciplined their daughter; Asia and her similarly aged boyfriend loved each other; both ran away and married; they even died on the same date, each still exactly the same age ("at Asia 96, Mike 96 also"). Moreover, Tina's text explicitly negated common narrative expectations; in most children's stories, marriage was inevitably followed by many children. But "Asia and Mike . . . [though married] had *no* kids."

Both actors and audience members were impressed that Tina's piece "had a lot of details," as Makeda said. After head nodding all around, Jonathan elaborated: "It described the names, the jobs, and a lot about their personalities." Personalities, I would add, that are complex, that are sometimes loving and sometimes not. In the context of the history of the class and of Tina's own storylines, those details offered an alternative vision of relational possibilities in the ongoing conversation about gender.

Implicating a Textual Dialogue About Race

Unlike gender—which is difficult to avoid, since individuals are inevitably "he's" or "she's"—race as constructed semantic category is not woven into our grammar. It is, however, coded into our narrative images, which reverberate in particular ways in our society (Morrison, 1992). For example, race as well as gender was present in the way April, Emily, and Venus were, and were not, imagined in the children's community.

Race did not seem salient in the children's superhero stories when the emphasis was on physical encounters. The children's media source material, including both *X-Men* and *Power Rangers,* depicted males and females of varied races and ethnicities as physically powerful, even though their out-of-battle behavior sometimes fit cultural and gender stereotypes. For example, since the children appropriated the fight scenes from these sources, they neither reproduced nor discussed the Pink and Yellow (White and Asian girl) Power Rangers' trips to the mall, nor the Black (African-American boy) Power Ranger's cool hip hop dancing.

Race became salient only when sexuality or romance entered the superhero stories—and, then, only because the children dramatically recreated these stories. Since children tended to give roles in appropriated media romances to those who looked the part, their choices of actors articulated race as an aspect of media grammar, that is, of the pattern of who is included and who is excluded in certain narrative contexts. To reiterate, when race became an explicit issue (after Lawrence said that April *had* to be White), it was articulated as a matter of dramatic access—of who could play a White character—not as a matter of textual transformation of the image itself.

In fact, the interplay between ideologies of race and of romance (if not love) are seldom deeply explored in mainstream commercial art forms for adults (Barrera & Larsen, personal communication, March, 1996).[3] When it is, the particularities of a relationship are often reduced quite literally to a matter of "Black and White" or a matter of "love" (Guerrero, 1993; hooks, 1994). In bell hooks' words,

> Hollywood's traditional message about interracial sex has been that it is tragic, that it will not work.... *Mama, There's a Man in Your Bed* [Serreau, 1991] is unique in that it represents interracial love in a complex manner.... It insists that love alone would not enable one to transcend difference if the person in power—in this case the wealthy white man—does not shift his ways of thinking ... learn to understand, appreciate, and value her world. Mutual give-and-take enables their relationship to work—not the stuff of romantic fantasy. (1994, pp. 53–54)

Many of Kristin's children knew about two films that do feature interracial romance: *Dragon: The Bruce Lee Story* (DeLaurentis & Cohen, 1993) and *Jungle Fever* (Lee, 1991). (In the first, love seems to overcome difference and, in the second, love has little to do with what seems an essentially tragic and superficial relationship.) Moreover, the only composing-time texts in which race figured into the main storyline were four texts seemingly linked to these media productions.[4] In the children's stories, though, race was not named as an issue but implicated through the positioning of named characters—fictional or nonfictional—known in the classroom community.

The children's use of this strategy was not necessarily a means of deliberately circumventing the issue of race. Children's appropriation and transformation of adult material that names race into child material that names names seems consistent with the history and the symbolic resources of Author's

Theater. Naming was an important child means of identity declaration and transformation (see Chapter 6, Note 14).

Two of the children's romance stories began on the same January day, rooted in a class brainstorming discussion about possible characters and settings for children's "fictional" stories, a word explicitly used in that discussion. Melissa had suggested Bruce Lee as a lead character, which led to Tina's proposal of Chinatown as a possible setting and, then, to animated talk among many children about Bruce Lee, his martial arts expertise, and the premature deaths of Lee and his son. It was in the midst of this discussion that Lettrice asked if there was an Africatown and, then, stated her intention to invent one when she grew up. Moreover, Lettrice began writing a story, not about Bruce Lee, but about Spike Lee, a story intertextually linked to *Jungle Fever*.[5]

In her story, Lettrice placed "Spike Lee" in the central role of an unsuccessful husband, a role played by Wesley Snipes in the film. (Lena and Thomas also referred to "Spike Lee" as if he were the Wesley Snipes character.) In the film, this troubled husband has only one wife, named Drew, only one child, named Ming, and just one affair (with an Italian-American woman named Angie). In Lettrice's story, however, he is much more prolific—he has *three* wives and *nine* children. Lettrice began her story by naming Spike Lee and, then, naming his wives after her classmates Makeda, Sarah, and Rhonda. She explicitly described Spike's life as "pretty good" before, and "better" after, his encounter with his second wife, Sarah, his only White wife.

> Once there was a man named Spike Lee. And he got mared 3 times and had 9 kids and here we go. The first wifes name was Makeda [African American] and she loved Spike Lee. And then she had 3 kids. . . . And then they got daverst [divorced] and the kids had so much fun at the Foan Foam [Funny Farm]. Spike Lee had a pretty good life until he met someone else. . . . And her name was Sarah [European American]. They went out a lot and then he proposed to her they got married and had three kids. And he took them to toon town [in Disneyland]. And then they got divorced. Sarah toled him not to take them to toon town but he took them anyway. Spike's life went better then the life he had with his second wife. One day he met some [one] and her name was Rhonda [African American]. She loved children. So Spike asked her out. So they went to dinner. And they ate spagetti, garlic bread and salad. And then he papasted [proposed] to her and then they got married and had three children and thir names were Tina, Makeda, and Demario. And Spike stayed with that wife. (In the film, the Wesley Snipes character [Flipper] shares an Italian meal with his Italian-American lover, but he does not share her desire to

have children together; in the end, the husband returns, at least emotionally, to his African-American wife and child, but it is not clear that the wife will accept him back.)

The child Lettrice had written a childlike story, more conventional than Spike Lee's in its moral and narrative structure. In her story, people marry and have children rather than affairs. Her characters may fight about children—but not, as in the film, about the fate of anticipated "mixed" children; indeed, in her story, Spike Lee seems to have a good time with all his children. Moreover, Lettrice's Spike Lee eventually finds a home rather than ambiguity; he meets Rhonda, who "loved children."[6]

Still, like the original movie, Lettrice's story of romance (and, perhaps more aptly, family love) seems to be a response to her racialized world. Lettrice's appropriation of Spike Lee was consistent with—and another example of— her articulation of herself as a Black child in the classroom community. For example, Lettrice chose to read books about African-American historical figures and reacted strongly to racial exclusion. It was, as readers may recall, Lettrice who, along with Aloyse and Holly, had reacted immediately to the explicit denial of April's role to girls of color and, as reiterated earlier, it was also Lettrice who reacted to a class discussion of *Bruce* Lee and Chinatown with a stated plan to found an Africatown—and with the textual action of writing a story about *Spike* Lee.

Like Lettrice, Melissa invented a story that featured a figure from popular culture. And like Lettrice's story, Melissa's story did not name race as an issue, but her juxtaposition of characters served to link it to a racialized world. Moreover, also like Lettrice's—and like most films about interracial romance, Melissa's story suggested the societal uneasiness with romantic relations across racial lines, an uneasiness with complex roots, among them historical racism, including miscegenation laws, and ideologies of female desirability (very evident in this classroom drama in the figures of April, Emily, and Venus).[7]

But Melissa's text was situated quite differently from Lettrice's in the intertextual dialogue about race and romance. Lettrice, an African-American child, appropriated a cultural figure, Spike Lee, who shared her self-identified racial and cultural group. Her decision to appropriate that figure seemed tied to her reaction to the absence of a named urban neighborhood featuring African culture. Moreover, Lettrice seemed to structure racial relations in her story in ways similar to that of the Spike Lee film (i.e., she embedded racial relations in romantic and family ones).

Melissa, a European-American child, appropriated a cultural figure, Bruce Lee, with whom she did not share racial and cultural membership. Her decision to appropriate that figure had no identifiable link to classroom dialogues about race. Moreover, she did not structure racial relations as they were in the film about Bruce Lee's life. Consistent with her classroom stance on violence and fighting, Melissa did not mention Bruce Lee's expertise in Chinese martial arts, nor his conflicts (physical and otherwise) with Chinese-American martial artists. Rather, she wrote a story about a male search for love, one that resulted in more ideologically conventional relations than those of Bruce Lee's own life.

In Melissa's story, Bruce Lee has a friend named Bruce Wayne (who is, as she knew, Batman). Melissa did not name the race of these well-known figures. She did, however, name the race of his wife. In the film, Bruce Lee meets his wife Lynda, a White woman, on a college campus. In Melissa's story, Bruce Lee and Bruce Wayne meet Lynda, a *Chinese* woman, during a visit to Chinatown.

> The problem was they both liked her! But then Bruce Lee found
> another Chinese woman named Christy. And so they both got married.
> And then they both had four children.

In her story, Bruce Lee does not die, but Lynda does. After the funeral, "a couple of weeks later Bruce Lee found another Chinese woman." (This is an error, because, in *her* story, Bruce Wayne is the one who marries Lynda.)

Melissa's story features a racially homogenous marriage and one between a dominant group male and a subordinate group female (a common pattern in our society, except in the Black community [Spickard, 1989], where the reverse pattern is more common). Melissa had neither planned nor attempted to write a true-to-life story about Bruce Lee. She was writing a "fictional" story. Her authorial actions seemed shaped by her ideological common sense, her taken-for-granted assumptions about how a made-up story about Bruce Lee would "naturally" be constructed (Fairclough, 1992; Gilbert, 1994; Luke, 1995).[8]

Those ideological assumptions, however, were not mere abstractions, nor were they governing principles. They were discourses (Foucault, 1981)— webs of categories and definitions articulated as utterances, as responses to the particularities of the immediate social situation (Bakhtin, 1981). It was the immediate social situation and unexpected confrontations with others that led children to question such taken-for-granted ideologies. And this is what happened—and yet, what did not happen—when Lena and Melissa collaborated on a story ostensibly about interracial romance.

As illustrated in the following, in that collaboration, the girls explicitly separated the descriptor of race from the name of a character. And they exploited the classroom rule about equal access to roles (i.e., the rule that any child can play any desired role, without regard to race or sex) in order to attempt to circumvent the potentially divisive issue of race in the classroom community.

CIRCUMVENTING LOVERS' IDENTITIES

Both Lettrice and Melissa worked hard on their stories of Spike Lee and Bruce Lee over the course of the spring semester, since each had chosen their love story for eventual classroom publication. Lettrice wrote no other romance stories, but Melissa continued her interest in texts about love. One real-life object of Melissa's affections was Jason, a college student who volunteered regularly in Kristin's classroom. She even wrote a poem about him in her writing book. Among her descriptors of Jason were "young and *cute*," "really nice," "really silly too!" and "loves Amber." Amber was Jason's girlfriend, who sometimes came with him to Kristin's classroom. A portrait of Jason and Amber, from Liliana's writing book, is presented in Figure 7.1.

Although Melissa was particularly effusive about Jason, everybody in the class greeted that young man with great enthusiasm when he entered the room. Boys and girls alike gave him grand hugs. Jason helped the children with their schoolwork and, also, organized playground games for them. In addition, he talked with the whole class about his cultural identity as a Black man.

A light-skinned African American, Jason had lived as a child in an urban neighborhood much like that of the African-American children in Kristin's class—a neighborhood regarded with affection by the children but, also, a neighborhood with evident problems of poverty and crime. During adolescence, his life changed dramatically; he and his mother lived in Africa with

Figure 7.1. *Liliana's portrait of Jason and Amber.*

his new stepfather, who was a diplomat there. Jason formally shared with the class maps and cultural artifacts from his African experiences.

Despite this emphasis on his African-American identity and his strong sense of connection with Africa, Jason's racial identity became problematic during a composing event in which Lena wrote a story featuring Amber, his blond European-American girlfriend. Lena's story is unusual among the texts referencing romance, because, like Tina's about Bebe the baby bat, Lena made a female the most active character. Although Amber is not lethal, she is not innocent either, as is evident in the following text.

> Once there was a girl named Amber. She had a baby named Kristin. She had a boy friend. His name was Jason. But she had another boyfriend. His name was Matt. Matt was at her house. The telephone rang. Matt answered it. Then Lily said, "Hello, is Amber there?" "No but I'm her boy friend." "You don't sound like Jason." "Who is Jason?" "Um um um good bye." And then Lily said to Linda, "Amber is cheating on Jason. And his name is Matt." Then they ran to her house. But they were too late. They [Matt and Amber] were yelling at each other. Then Amber cried. Then they went in the house. Then Linda and Lily said, "Stop yelling at each other. Sit down." Then Lily asked Amber, "Who do you love more?" "Jason, but I love Matt too." Linda said, "Why are you cheating on Jason?" "Because I like Matt too." Then Matt said, "I don't want to be your boy friend." He went out of the house and slammed the door. And Amber started to cry. Amber went out the back door and went to Jason's house. . . . . (*Spelling and punctuation corrected for ease of reading.*)

Amber and Jason do get married. However, "they got divorced in '92 and they did not see each other until '94 but the mother had the baby."

Lena's decision to write about these characters may have been influenced by her identification with Jason; they were both, as she said, "part from Africa"—both of their families had lived in Africa and in America. Moreover, Lena had written about romance before; she had composed a brief text about Spike Lee, like Lettrice, portraying him as an unhappy husband who "hated everyone." (Interestingly, in *Jungle Fever*, as in Lena's story, the White woman has two boyfriends, one of whom is the married "Spike Lee.") When Lena explained her planned story to the very interested Melissa, she emphasized the romantic intrigue of Amber cheating on Jason.

Melissa's interest, on the other hand, seemed rooted partially in her attraction for the very "cute," "really nice" Jason. This attraction, though, seemed to contradict her inferred ideological uneasiness about interracial romance, as suggested by her Bruce Lee story. This uneasiness, in fact, became explicit in the course of her interactions with Lena.

Melissa, delighted with Lena's story idea, sat next to her peer as the latter child wrote, announcing Lena's topic with great pleasure to whomever happened by: "Lena's writing about Jason! Lena's writing about Jason!" Melissa asked for—and was granted—the role of Amber, and she even suggested the name of Amber's second boyfriend, Matt. The girls giggled happily as the story unfolded. They were affiliating with each other through their common interest in a good love story. Soon, however, the ideological ramifications of that love story fractured their relationship as girls and highlighted their differences in racial identity, as illustrated in the following.

> *(Melissa has just asked Lena if Radha [who is light-skinned and an Indian American] can be Jason.[9] Lena replies that she already promised the role to Victor [who is dark-skinned and of Mexican and African heritage]; Radha can have the part if Victor is absent. Melissa then suggests Kevin [who is White] for Matt. But Lena already promised the role of the "other man" to Demario [who is Black]).*

LENA: I do not want Kevin. I do not want Kevin. I'll take Demario. Demario will not fool around [on the stage].

MELISSA: 'Cause Amber's <u>White</u>.

LENA: Yeah. But Jason's not White. He's Black.

MELISSA: Yeah. But he's pretty White.

LENA: He's mixed. *(Lena later explains to me that she said Jason was "mixed" because he is from both Africa and America.) (The children continue to disagree on who should play Matt. Melissa is adamant; Matt plans "to marry Amber," she says. Lena finally agrees to Melissa's request, but refers to the official class policy that anyone can play any role, whatever the character's sex or race.)*

LENA: OK [Matt and Jason can be White], but I'm not going to say they're White. They'll [the actors] act like theirselves. They're not even going to know they're White.

MELISSA: OK.

Lena had imagined a romance story much more complex than the one Patricia Williams worried about in the opening scene. Amber was no "Barbie hunkered down in her Barbie Dream House waiting bravely for Ken" (1995, p. 133). Amber was a more complex woman, one more akin to Spike Lee's Angie than to the toy doll Barbie. Amber had conflicting emotions and was unsure of what to do; in the end, she and Jason do not live happily ever after. Melissa, however, could not pair a White Amber with a Black Jason. In fact, she erased Jason's color, despite his own strong declaration of himself as a Black man.

Lena had no problem imagining an interracial pair; after all, "Jason's not White. He's Black." Her use of Jason's and Amber's names implicated race; her planned choice of actors would reinforce those implications. But since, as Lena said, "it [race] mattered" so much to Melissa, Lena exploited her authority—her decision-making powers as author—to negotiate their tense encounter. That negotiation resulted, not in textual explicitness, but textual silence; she decided not to include the descriptive detail of race.[10]

In effect, Lena agreed to Melissa's interpretation: Amber's name would implicate Whiteness, as would Jason's. But Lena would not "say" that. She would be evasive on the issue of race, a time-honored strategy for "foreclosing open debate" in our society (Morrison, 1992, p. 10). In fact, Lena's decision not to name race *did* foreclose open debate in the public forum. But it did not foreclose angry words.

Lena's Author's Theater turn arrived on the last day of the project. As she prepared for her presentation, Lena called her actors to the front of the rug. Melissa was named Amber, as promised, and Melissa's friends Sarah and Susan were given their promised roles as Amber's two friends Lily and Linda. Radha was given Jason's role, since Victor decided that he did not want it.

"Who wants to be Matt?" asked Lena, a routine question asked by authors even when an actor had already been chosen.

Ordinarily, boys tended to avoid romantic roles. But the role of Matt was different; it allowed one to be in Jason's world. Indeed, many boys raised their hands, among them Demario, Thomas, Aloyse, and Sammy, all African American. Two girls, Tina and Lynn, raised their hands as well. But before Lena could respond, Melissa leaned over and whispered in her ear. Lena then chose, *not* Demario, the child promised the role, but Lynn, a White girl.

The Author's Theater performance went smoothly, although Demario and Thomas mumbled throughout the performance. Indeed, in the discussion that followed, the two boys seemed to continue to speak in muffled voice.

> *(Lena has finished her performance and asked for questions and comments. Thomas cannot contain himself, so anxious is he to comment.)*
>
> THOMAS: I didn't know Lynn was gay.
> KRISTIN: No. She was playing a man.
> THOMAS: The boys—they had their hand up. She [Lena] didn't pick nobody.
> DEMARIO: I know. Melissa told her to pick somebody else. She didn't say my name!
>
> . . .

KRISTIN: But you started out making a comment about Lynn that had
             nothing to do with it. Lynn was playing a man.... There are
             people who are gay. But playing a part doesn't mean that.... [11]
THOMAS: Look. But Melissa <u>told</u> Lena who to pick.
KRISTIN: You need to tell Melissa that.
THOMAS: *(to Melissa)* [I'm] <u>mad</u>. 'Cause me, Aloyse, Demario—we all
             had our hands up but nobody pick us.

                        . . .

LENA: Because I wanted a girl to play a boy. I didn't pick Demario
             because sometimes he plays around. *(This is exactly the rea-
             son Lena originally gave Melissa for rejecting* Kevin *and
             choosing Demario. Moreover, in singling out Demario from
             Thomas' list of boys, Lena indicates her particular responsi-
             bility to that child.)*
THOMAS: No no. <u>Look</u>—
LENA: <u>Sometimes</u> [he plays around], I said. I didn't say all the time.
THOMAS: But Melissa told her [Lena] to pick Lynn.

                        . . .

MELISSA: Thomas, the reason why I picked Lynn—I <u>told</u> Lena when I
             was whispering to her that—I said, if you want, you should
             pick Lynn because she hardly ever gets to play a boy's part and
             she likes acting, and she doesn't care if it's a boy or a girl....
             *(Note Melissa's opening self-corrections, which distance her
             from the actual decision ["if you want"].)*
DEMARIO: When she be playing outside, she be playing boys' parts. <u>Yes,
             ma'am</u>!
             *(Demario is disputing the claim that Lynn does not regularly
             play boys' roles; she does in fact regularly play male roles in
             superhero dramas. At the same time, he is, seemingly inad-
             vertently, pointing out that a girl playing a male role has not
             been an issue this school year.)*
KRISTIN: I'm just really confused, Demario and Thomas, why it's caus-
             ing such trouble. Thomas, I understand that you're upset that
             Melissa said she should pick Lynn. Is that your only problem?
THOMAS: Yes. 'Cause it was Lena's choice.
KRISTIN: Demario, I don't understand why you're so upset. Can you
             help us figure it out?
DEMARIO: No.

It would have been very difficult indeed for Demario to sort out the complicated social scene that had just evolved. Kristin did not know that Demario
had been promised the role. Nor did she know about the *representational* issue

involved, an issue mediated by a silent text. The children went on to discuss the issue of acting. They reaffirmed the long-standing class rules about the author's right to choose actors, and the actor's right to play any role without regard to sex or race.[12] The latter rule had, in fact, been central to Lena's original rationale for allowing Demario unwittingly to play the role of a White man.

But, in the class discussion, the issue of participation was not linked to the issue of textual representation. The comments about sexuality and about Melissa's infringement on Lena's right to choose seemed camouflages for unarticulated comments about race. Lena and Melissa could agree that the characters themselves would be White, but they could not dictate how others would "see" these characters. Moreover, they could temporarily agree that the *actors'* race did not matter, but, in the end, race did matter to Melissa. And the intensity of Thomas' and Demario's distress suggested that race mattered to them too. The children had just enacted what was (or seemed to be) a rare story inspired by an African-American man—and there were no African Americans in the production.[13]

It was just this sort of exclusion from a desired role that had led Tina and Holly to resist and, in fact, to write their own stories in which they named names, especially that of the X-man Rogue. In so doing, they stretched female roles in classroom superhero stories beyond love object to include teammate, warrior, and friend.

But "girls" had been explicitly and publicly identified as the issue in superhero stories. In a similar, but less public event, identifying "Whiteness" as an issue in the case of a goddess paved the way for Venus Tina. Perhaps, if Jason had been written explicitly as White, resulting ideological tensions would have paved the way for other textual visions of that popular young man. At the very least, such tensions may have given new meaning to the common school theme of the "different kinds of families" in "our" community and of the different choices people make in and out of texts.[14] But Melissa and Lena weren't "saying" anything—and the classroom rules about equal access to roles prevented Thomas and Demario from saying anything as well.

And, as it happened, time itself was an accomplice in the closing of Kristin's children's conversations. Lena's presentation was over; it was time for lunch. And Author's Theater itself was over now too. The school year had come to an end.

CODA: ON ENDINGS AND OPENINGS

The curtain comes down here too on this book's presentation of the children's drama. It is, I know, a textual ending that will leave no satisfied sense of closure in readers' minds, and absolutely none is intended. There *is* no end—the suggestions of the children's growing awareness of romance and sexuality suggest changes in their intertextual worlds to come. Indeed, the children's texts collectively comprise a kind of *Bildungsroman* (Bakhtin, 1986), a story of the children's "becoming" as they move along "the path from childhood through youth" (p. 22). As the children continue to move along this path— as the social configurations of their daily lives change and as their own bodies change, there will be new issues to consider. Thus, their grappling with the themes and plots of life in and out of texts will continue to need adult guidance and symbolic materials with which to work.

In the presented drama, this grappling was mediated through child composers' use of the popular figures of commercial culture and, in this chapter, popular figures from everyday life as well. These heroes served as shared symbols for the good guy or the bad guy, the nice lady or the man-in-search-of wife. Thus, as writers, Kristin's children were learning to manipulate more than words. They were manipulating ideological symbols of power and weakness, love and hostility, good and evil, and, at the very same time, they were manipulating their social relations with classroom companions.

When children brought their work to the public forum, ideological gaps— differences in interpretations—became audible. With Kristin's guidance, those gaps could become moments for collective consideration of text fairness and goodness and, also, for individual play with newly salient aspects of text (e.g., the qualities of certain characters and actions). One reason this guided focus on text could support the elaboration of child writing *and* the deepening of community was, in fact, the very focus on a specific world. Decisions about what's powerful and good, what's fair and worthy cannot be determined by universal law but by principled consideration of each case (Williams, 1991).

Thus Kristin and the children wrestled with the nature of power, the possibilities of female and male action, the relevance of race, not as abstractions but as realized details of specific plots and actions, engaged in by particular characters with motivations and constraints. In the process, children's appropriated heroes, embued with societal ideologies, could become open, subject to children's transforming imaginations. In Bakhtin's terms, the heroes became "dialogized," permeated with a "certain semantic open-endedness, a living contact with unfinished, still-evolving contemporary reality" (1981, p. 7).

This dialogic process continually gives rise to new potential issues, new potential gaps. In this chapter, Tina's story featured two couples, parents and teenage lovers, engaged in similar actions (working, disciplining, loving); but that story was enacted and dialogized by improvising actors who constructed gender differences (the mother taking her daughter to a beauty parlor, the father giving his daughter Barbie dolls, the boyfriend participating in football). Most dramatically, Lena and Melissa clashed on the racial identity of a well-known classroom figure; in the mediation of their conflict, Jason's racial identity was erased or at least muted into a "pretty white" gray zone.[15]

Thus, textual reconsideration and social reconsideration were linked in the details of specific plots and actions, created and enacted by specific children, whose own actions were linked. In this dialogic process, community considerations became a guiding influence on individual author's deliberations. This sensitivity to the micropolitics of the classroom community gave rise to Tina's sometimes superheroic moments; she was not afraid to name names and provide details that articulated a world different from the expected. On the other hand, this sensitivity also gave rise to Lena's decision to circumvent a detail. Without that detail—without a written word to contest—it was hard for Thomas and Demario to respond, to untangle the complexities of identity and community.

Both Melissa and Lena were children with a strong sense of fair play, children who were not afraid to speak up if they thought someone or something was amiss. But, on that day, in that social relationship, they chose silence, not realizing, being so inexperienced in these matters, that the denial of identity leads to precisely what they wanted to avoid—social discord. In Patricia Williams' words:

> It's a kind of heresy, I know, to suggest that the storybook desire to marry a Capulet and live happily ever after might be oppressive.... I personally believe that the streets of Verona will never be calm until there's a little more love between us. But what concerns me is, again, that the *West Side Story* solution ... obscures the possibility that simple cantankerous coexistence may be what we should be aiming for in a democracy based on live-and-let-live.... [And yet] it is genuinely hard, in these times, to come up with images [of people who are Black, White, Latino, Asian ...] that might suggest a model of hybridity that is fluid rather than static, a model of value that does not substitute a facile sociobiology for the actuality of culture. (1995, p. 192)

In this book, culture—shared ways of interpreting symbols, based on shared experiences—was audible and visible in the children's enacted patterns of textual choices and responses; those patterns declared them as "we girls," "we boys," "we African-American children," "we children of the economically comfortable," "we children of limited means...." And the fluidity was there too, in the instability of the patterns, in the children's shifting group alliances and in their unpredictability as individuals. Who, for example, would have predicted that Sammy, a consistent fan of powerful fighting men, would choose as a hero Rosa Parks? Who would have thought that Tina, the consistent advocate of strong women, would write a story about girls crying for Batman, or about an avenging, love-crazed baby bat?

In this book I have foregrounded the children themselves—and the complex social and ideological dynamics of their social lives—as a potential source of individual and collective growth. And yet, the children's grappling with the social, ideological, and textual dimensions of writing was linked to the grappling of their teacher, Kristin. The children, after all, were participating in and forming a social and historical childhood that the adults around them had not experienced and, moreover, they were trying to talk about and amidst differences, a discourse challenge that adults find daunting (Smith, 1993; Williams, 1995).

How often, I wonder, will the children find teachers like Kristin in their futures, teachers willing to engage with the issues of children's lives that we as adults may choose not to see (Derman-Sparks, 1995). Such teachers will require a comfort with their own identities (Sleeter, 1993) and an understanding of our pluralistic roots as a society (Takaki, 1993). They will need as well a depth of disciplinary knowledge and pedagogic skill that can support their efforts to pursue academic ends in ways that serve human ends consistent with democratic values. Those values include an active inclusiveness, a respect for the dignity of the individual, and a joint responsibility for the common good (Lagemann, 1994). These values undergirded Kristin's decisions to allow children to bring their heroes into the classroom, whatever their source, and to provide children with diverse symbolic avenues—writing, performing, and talking—for negotiating their vision of a good life.

Further, such teachers will require the support of their schools and communities, their own forums within which to explore the complexities and contradictions they themselves may feel about their children's words and worlds. In the tense, pressured atmosphere of many big city schools, there is little time for teachers to discuss and develop their ideas with each other, to themselves become a community respectful of differences, aware of their common principles. Those trying new ways can feel isolated, as did Kristin.

During the second year of the project, Kristin found support as a member of a study group composed of experienced urban educators. The teachers gathered together every other week to talk about contemporary teaching in city schools (Dyson, 1997). In the next chapter, Kristin and her colleagues will enter the dramatic spotlight, as I explore their reflections on popular culture, sociocultural differences, and the challenge of freeing the children to write.

▼ 8 ▼
▼

The Negotiating Teachers:
On Freeing the Children to Write

[W]hen I wished my children to have contact with wildness [around our Sonoran Desert home], I sent them "out," to climb high upon ridges and to absorb the grand vistas. . . . [I] later hear[d] them burst out of the brush across the road from the house, where a densely vegetated wash meanders not fifty yards away.

"Papa!" Laura crie[d]. "Come over and see the hideout we made beneath a tree over there. See if you can walk down the wash and find us. I bet you won't even be able to figure out where we are!"

G. P. Nabhan, *A Child's Sense of Wildness*, 1994, pp. 6–7

Nature lovers, like Gary Nabhan, desire freedom from urban denseness and distractions and freedom for reflection and imagination. So they gather their families and head toward the wild. As adults, they may find the desired sense of freedom when they view wide-open vistas. But their children may sense it in hidden crannies in the rocks and hiding places in the bushes, places within which to play—and to keep a look out for adults and other giants of the earth.

This difference in ways of experiencing freedom seems relevant to the drama of Tina, Sammy, and their peers and, more broadly, to the pedagogical complexities educators face in "freeing" children to write. As teacher, Kristin wanted her students to express themselves during the daily "free" writing time. When she turned them loose, so to speak, they took refuge in stories that may strike adult educators as not only constraining (i.e., unimaginative, derivative) but downright dangerous (i.e., filled with the complexities of power and identity, of gender and race).

"Innocent" children, adults may feel, should be free from such complexities, free to play on playground and paper. But children's imaginative play is all about freedom from their status as powerless children. Tales about good guys and bad ones, rescuers and victims, boyfriends and girlfriends allow children to fashion worlds in which *they* make decisions about characters and plots, actors and actions. Thus, for children, as for adults, freedom is a verb, a becoming; it is experienced as an expanded sense of agency, of possibility for choice and action.

Adults, then, cannot "give" children freedom by turning them loose with paper and pencil, any more than they can by turning them loose in the wild. But they can challenge children, helping them sense social and textual possibilities beyond their current borders. As critical pedagogists (most inspired by Freire, 1970) and educational philosophers (Dewey, 1931; Greene, 1995) argue, freedom must be continually renewed, or shelters become cages. This renewal occurs through "conscious and mindful transaction with what surrounds" (Greene, 1995, p. 178). Each of us is constrained by, and given possibilities for action within, a larger whole; and that whole (e.g., ecological system, political system, social system) only becomes visible as we interact with others (Dewey, 1931).

Bakhtin, whose dialogic theory undergirds this book, also talked about individuals beginning in an enclosed space and about their experiencing freedom as they move beyond that space. In his view, that moving beyond is dependent on becoming aware of diversity and, more specifically, of different languages linked to different social worlds (e.g., "the language and world of prayer, . . . of song, . . . of labor and everyday life, of local authorities, . . . of the workers freshly immigrated to the city [and so on; Bakhtin, 1981, p. 296]). For Bakhtin, then, freedom comes with understanding differences and making choices.

> Only by remaining in a closed environment . . . completely off the maps of socioideological becoming, could a man [or a woman or a child] fail to sense this activity of selecting a language and rest assured in the inviolability of his own language [i.e., his own world]. . . . (1981, p. 295)

In her classroom, Kristin's role was both to help children construct shelters within which to experience some control over the challenges of literacy, and, at the same time, to help them envision a world beyond their own borders. She allowed them familiar social goals (e.g., social affiliation), familiar symbolic tools (e.g., talking, drawing, dramatic action), and familiar storylines, as they grappled with the newer medium of writing.

Just as the Nabhan children's ecological niche and resources—the vegetation, their companionship, their capacity for speech, for construction, and, above all, for imagination—would shape their journey into the wider world, so too would the diverse sociocultural positions and particular resources of Kristin's children shape their own journey outward. Their symbolic resources—their use of talk and dramatic action—influenced the challenges they faced in gaining control of the written medium (e.g., in differentiating players from authors, actors from characters, written details from improvised ones). Similarly, their chosen stories—and the ways those stories reflected and refracted their social worlds—influenced the challenges they faced in negotiating a wider sense of community (e.g., in becoming aware of depicted human relations and of plot actions as authorial choices).

Thus, the specific nature of the challenges experienced by Kristin and her children cannot be generalized beyond her class. However, the sociocultural diversity evident in her classroom exists in many contemporary urban schools. In this last chapter, then, I situate Kristin's experiences within those reported by her teacher study group on literacy and diversity. In so doing, I aim, first, to amplify those experiences, illustrating that sociocultural diversity is a potentially powerful pedagogical resource for many urban teachers, just as it is a potentially powerful learning resource for urban children. Second, I aim to clarify the particular insight Kristin's experiences offer on how to exploit that diversity. Kristin, like her children, had to negotiate ideological tensions, as well as social borders, and, sometimes, become a superhero herself, able to move beyond taken-for-granted worlds (Greene, 1994).

Kristin's multiethnic study group, which met during her second year with her class, included 10 East Bay primary school teachers, all experienced in urban schools. I served as the group's chair person, organizing the meetings and preparing analytic summaries of the talk for the group's review.[1] (A full report of the study group's history, procedures, and reflections is available in Dyson [1997], which contains extended excerpts from the teachers' talk; samples of that talk are included in this chapter.)

In the first section to follow, I describe the study group's reflections on their experiences with sociocultural variation and the challenges that variation posed for them as teachers. I then summarize the group's consensus about inclusive ways of teaching writing that allowed all children to feel comfortable (i.e., couched within familiar social practices and able to use familiar media) and, therefore, more able to take up the challenging tool of writing.

In the second section, I focus on an important but sometimes unsettling aspect of those literacy shelters—popular culture. In the study group's talk, the content of children's media-based play and stories became a mediational tool for adults' own identity work. In response to the heroes and plot lines of these ideologically charged stories, study group members voiced their sometimes contradictory, sometimes conflicting responses as women, advocates of nonviolence, social activists, and writing teachers, among other such stances; in so doing, they articulated their individual and collective values and beliefs. I then discuss how Kristin's *children* similarly used the play and the stories to articulate their individual and collective values and beliefs—with her assistance.

That use suggests that it is within the ideological dimension of child writing that *sociocultural* variation emerges most powerfully as pedagogical resource (rather than *individual* variation in social and symbolic resources [e.g., artistic skills, leadership qualities, discussion skills, independent reading ability, and on and on]). In a pluralistic society, texts may reverberate in ways unanticipated by authors. But those reverberations may reveal new possibilities for textual action and social engagement. And, then, in their next dialogic turn, authors may have new choices to make—new responsibilities but, also, new possibilities. In the last section of this chapter, I consider the basic qualities that would seem to characterize any literacy pedagogy that aims to support children in the never-ending process of becoming free to write.

TEACHING AND LEARNING AMID SOCIOCULTURAL DIVERSITY

The classrooms of Kristin and her teacher colleagues evidenced rich sociocultural differences among children (e.g., in first language, in cultural styles of communication, in familial structure, and, of course, gender). These are differences that influence individual children's sense of who they are in school—their identities—and, moreover, differences that provide the classroom collective with diverse perspectives on the meaning of words, the appeal of a hero, the transformative possibilities of a storyline.

However, in our society in general—and the institutions of schools in particular—these differences are seldom viewed as "resources." They are primarily viewed as "problems" that more affluent (and homogeneous) schools do not have. The study group grappled with this societal discomfort with difference and its particular manifestations in the human complexities and institutional structures of their schools.

The Salience of Sociocultural Difference

In the teachers' classrooms, where one adult and as many as 30 children spent many hours in a constrained space, sociocultural differences often became salient as individual children negotiated their social identities and their social relations with both teacher and peers. All of the teachers noted children's tendency to join together within racial, ethnic, and linguistic groups, a phenomenon that seemed to increase as children moved through the grades.

Children's identification of significant groups in the classroom were sometimes revealed in moments of classroom tension, when remarks like "Hey, you are just calling" on the "other" kids revealed children's sense of being in competition with those others for teachers' attention and affection. As readers may recall, Kristin had experienced such tensions in her class on her very first days with her second graders (see Chapter 2). In the study group, Kristin learned that her colleagues, who had more teaching experience than she had, all experienced similar social tensions. In the following, Louise, Andrea, and Carol, each of whom has approximately 20 years of urban teaching experience, offer their comments.

> LOUISE: You run into that, I most ran into it in third grade, that . . . angst, which is "You only like the White kids," or "You only like the Black kids."
> ANDREA: Or you only talk to the Spanish children. . . .
> CAROL: I see that a lot . . . I have kids who are student helpers who get to call on kids for recess and I have kids who will say, "Hey, you are just calling on all the White kids or the Black kids.". . . They are really concerned about issues of fairness.

Moreover, the teachers also noted children's sensitivity to (and overgeneralization of) variations in cultural patterns in communication (e.g., the pace and volume of group talk among friends, the nature of interactional games) and to the way in which such variations were sanctioned by the school. For example, when Kristin asked her second graders for individual exemplars of "peaceful" children, they interpreted this as a child who "didn't move around a lot," in Demario's words, and who "talked quiet," in Lettrice's. All children, seemingly responding to stereotypes, tended to choose European-American children as exemplars (see Chapter 4, Note 4). Andrea offered the group her insights on such phenomena.

> ANDREA: Sometimes we get upset with the noise level, and playing the dozens [mutual insulting, especially of one's mother] that [some African American students] play all the time. . . . But they're not fighting. It's just a cultural thing. . . . But . . . when you're sitting there with someone from another culture, it's like the kids [who are not African American] sometimes sit like this *(gaping)*, just looking at them, like "What is *wrong?*" . . . And it may be like we're saying, just cultural awareness, to understand. . . .

Further, just as Kristin's children sometimes wrestled with the complexity of identity, its resistance to neat categorization, so too did other teachers' children. Lena's and Melissa's grappling with the notions of "pretty White" and "Mixed" had intertextual links with the reported words of other children. Consider, for example, Carolyn's report of her first graders' talk and Carol's reflections on her experiences as a dual-heritage child.

CAROLYN: Today [in my first grade] ... Shannon was saying, to Eric, "You're not Black." Eric was just sitting there. Somebody else was saying, "He is [so] Black." It was almost like Eric didn't really know whether he was or not.... Then when I sat down, they pulled me in and Shannon said, "Hey Mrs. McBride, is Eric Black?" I said, "Well, he's part African American, yes." Then she said, "Oh." Then Megan said, "Well, I'm White." Megan is blond hair, blue eyes. Then Shannon said, "You're not; you are just fair skinned."....

    ...

CAROL: I know with double heritage—I'm Native American and African American, and there are times when you are younger, and you're pitting one against the other, and you are just [thinking], "I'm just me."

In addition to differences associated with race, ethnicity, and ethnic culture, the study group also discussed their sensitivity to socioeconomic differences. For most teachers, variation in neighborhood wealth (rather than individual child wealth) seemed to figure most strongly into their daily experiences. As both Carolyn and Andrea had experienced, in schools serving more affluent neighborhoods, parent groups raised money for school supplies and many mothers (who did not work outside the home) volunteered in classrooms. In contrast, study group members felt that, in their low-income schools, they were often de facto administrators of poorly organized social services, sending home sometimes invasive forms for one program or another, but having little, if any, scheduled time for getting to know parents and neighborhoods.

In Kristin's school, socioeconomic differences *within* the classrooms themselves were unusually large, and those differences were interrelated with racial and ethnic ones. In her experience, a small group of middle-class parents were involved in her classroom but, also, concerned about the degree of pedagogical and curricular attention their children received. They wondered if the public school offered a sufficiently challenging education. (For an examination of parents' perspectives on schooling at this study site, see Conrad, 1994.)

In all of the teachers' experiences, then, sociocultural diversity was constructed by the actions and reflections of the children themselves, as well as by their parents. In response to that diversity, the teachers worked to develop inclusive literacy curricula, in which the broad spectrum of children could participate.

An Inclusive Writing Curriculum

The teachers in the study group did not worry about the children finding comfort with familiar faces and voices, with their tendency to have close friendships with neighborhood children. But they did worry about the establishment of productive classroom communities where children supported each other's learning, and they took steps to decrease social distance.

In so doing, the group evidenced an ethic of inclusion (i.e., of building on the knowledge and experiences of all children) and a sensitivity to collective exclusion (i.e., to the ways in which the knowledge and experiences of groups of Americans have been left out of our school curricula). For example, they included books featuring Americans of diverse heritages in their curricula, including the "forgotten heroes," to quote Carol, "the stories of women, Native Americans, others who have been left out of the traditional histories. . . . "

However, the teachers were also sensitive to the contradictory curricula pressures on teachers serving socioculturally diverse children (Scott, 1997). On the one hand, recent literature on "multicultural" education has urged them to make classroom space for the diverse sorts of experiences and knowledge children bring to school. On the other hand, the more politically influential "accountability" movement has urged teachers to narrow the curriculum and to concentrate on "basics" like phonics and spelling (Haberman, 1996; Walters, 1995).[2]

Urvashi Sahni, then a graduate student at the University of California, struck a chord with Kristin and other study group members when she came to talk with them about her experiences as a researcher and teacher in a rural Indian school (Sahni, 1994). Urvashi too knew that the appearance of veering away from teaching the basics caused unease among teachers and parents alike. Urvashi's students loved acting out stories and collectively (and, eventually, independently) composing their own. They even enjoyed copying the words of well-known songs and poems off the board so that they could have them to take home. (Books were rare items in their homes.) But, as she explained:

> URVASHI: When I would tell [the teacher] to tell stories, she would say, "Look. This is the village. Stop this story thing. No one is going to like stories. They [her supervisors] said teach them the letters and that's what I have to teach them.". . . [So] I told them the stories. . . . And I said, "I did it, and this is what happened. So what do you think?" I found that really helped.

Although she worked in an area quite different from the East Bay (in a village with a homogeneous population of the very poor), Urvashi's experiences were familiar ones, as Linda and Kristin noted in their comments to her.

LINDA: The playhouse, for instance, for [kindergartner] Kesha, has been a beauty parlor, a restaurant, a hospital. There's been a lot of writing that's gone on in there—making menus, making signs, all those kinds of things. That's why I was trying to explain to her mother ... [that being in the playhouse] doesn't mean that they're "just" playing dolls or something.

URVASHI: I think that the whole problem is that everything's valued only on the page.... [But] all of this [talking and dramatic play] is so valuable that you wouldn't have anything on the page if it didn't happen.

KRISTIN: I was struggling with some parents [the small group earlier noted] over those same issues, and I was trying to explain to them all the different things that were going on. ...

The study group teachers reflected on how they negotiated these conflicting pressures, aiming to make visible children's competence and to acknowledge the breadth of language, symbolic, and problem-posing and solving skills needed in our world—without abandoning the need to help children learn traditional school knowledge and skills. In their talk particularly about teaching writing, the basic question seemed to be, as stated by Carolyn, "When we're talking about literacy, is it just the ABCs or can we have a new definition?"

None of the teachers motivated children to write by stressing their civic duty to learn "the basics" and, thereby, to save their country from economic and moral demise (which seems to be a major theme of the popular media for adults). Moreover, although the teachers emphasized child choice in writing, they also had children who experienced a seemingly wide-open landscape of possibilities—like "draw and write whatever or however you want"— as a scary void: They would refuse to write. Thus, all mentioned literacy activities that, in my terms, were social practices energized by familiar social goals, including play (with friends and with language) and public performance. Within such activities, there was room for children to exploit familiar symbolic tools (e.g., talk, drawing, dramatic action) and to stretch their decision-making powers for new ends.

For example, Jill explained how her second graders engaged in an activity based on *Frog and Toad Are Friends* (Lobel, 1970). In this activity, the children paired up with chosen partners, imagined themselves Frog and Toad, improvised a Frog and Toad scene, wrote (and rewrote it), and then made puppets and presented their "play." During the writing process they generated dialogue, "fought about spelling," talked "about how you can mix fact and fiction," studied books to see how to format dialogue, and watched the clock so that they didn't "squabble" over whose turn it was to type.

Thus, the "new definition" of literacy that emerged in group talk was compatible with a sociolinguistic emphasis on literacy as a social event, one involving a wealth of knowledge and skills, a diversity of symbolic tools, and a range of possible social ends (see also The New London Group, 1996). Teachers reported activities that, like Jill's, involved diverse means of participation, among them, oral conversation and use of literary language, spelling and content planning, book consulting and time telling, formatting and social negotiating, drawing and dramatizing, and, in K–1 classrooms especially, various strategies for encoding (e.g., dictating, copying words, or "inventing" spellings), and, in bilingual or multilingual rooms, different language choices as well. There are many ways to enter into school literacy and, once engaged, to begin increasingly more complex decisions about, and constructions with, print itself.

Kristin's free writing period, with its Author's Theater event, was consistent with her colleagues' expressed approach to literacy activities. In her classroom, story and play were also important and, for some of her children, like Sammy, there was initially little "on the page" until these activities happened. Over time, her children made more and more complex decisions about text.

However, Kristin's children did not necessarily come together in their enjoyment of a familiar story. Rather, stories served to generate ideological tensions and, potentially, to mediate them as well. Her children's more complex decision-making about text was related, not only to their experience in socially sensible and interactive activities, but also to their experience with diversity in world view—to their "socioideological becoming" (Bakhtin, 1981, p. 295). It is here, with children's engagement with the ideologies of power and love, on the one hand, and of gender, race, and class on the other, that Kristin's drama, and the popular media it featured, makes its particular contribution to the understanding of teaching and learning to write.

TEACHING AND LEARNING AMID
CHILDREN'S "COMMON CULTURE"

The Study Group: Social Possibilities and Ideological Uneasiness

As evident in the preceding, the teacher study group emphasized the social dimension of learning—and students' engagement in familiar social practices—in organizing and stretching children's resources. Some of these familiar practices involved the genres of popular media. Louise, for example, referred to her video library of the children's dramatized fairy tales (made by taping over promotapes given away by Blockbuster Video). Linda discussed her children's enjoyment of making menus and taking orders for "Sizzler" play (the name of a popular restaurant chain in the school's neighborhood). And Carolyn talked about an interview activity, in which her media-experienced children readily adopted the role of the note-taking interviewer (and understood the role of the interviewee); they interviewed adult relatives and friends about their Halloween experiences.

The genres associated with commercial media (e.g., videos, advertisements, and television interview shows) did not, in and of themselves, cause any ideological uneasiness. But the *content* of media forms could. In Judy's classroom, some of her 6- and 7-year-olds reproduced symbols that reflected the importance of older siblings in their lives and, also, the children's interest in the youth culture of those siblings. The symbols (e.g., religious ones, like Our Lady of Guadalupe, and scenes from Spanish-language soap operas) "were part of the children's world," said Judy, and she was quite interested in them all. But she was very concerned about the barely dressed women draped over cars in the *Lowrider* magazine some boys brought to school. Judy told the boys that "'I'm a woman too, and I don't like to see pictures of women used like this.'" Judy did not allow the magazine in her classroom— but she did buy an alternative magazine, *HotRodder,* which did not depict women in that manner, and, in other ways, took advantage of the interest in cars (e.g., a child-organized survey on car preferences, a child-produced picture book on kinds of cars).

Judy responded in thoughtful and thought-provoking ways to her children's use of the material of contemporary culture, material that was "common" or shared by her children. That common culture was influenced by the children's ethnic culture (e.g., the dominant religion and the native language of their neighborhood), but it was also influenced by the materials provided by commercial culture (e.g., the car magazines). Judy wanted to open up her classroom to children's resources, and she recognized the social practices and the text knowledge those resources suggested. On the other hand, she was not always delighted with the symbolic stuff the children brought into the classroom.

Judy's response exemplified the way in which study group members positioned themselves relative to the symbolic substance children brought to school. In that response, Judy articulated her own identity and her perception of that of her children. The symbols were "part of the children's world," but because "I'm a woman too," aspects of those symbols were troubling (i.e., the use of women as decorative objects). Children's common symbolic materials could both reflect and refract study group members' visions of responsible, respectful human relations; through those ideological processes, cultural materials generated discussion of teachers' values and beliefs about the kind of world they wanted to live in and the kind of community they wanted to share with their children.

Certainly, the commercial media were not the only source of images perceived as pleasurable for at least some children and troubling for teachers. As noted earlier in this book, and as the study group members also noted, there are children's books that seem to constrain women's possibilities as well as those of people of color (e.g., readers may recall Carol's comments on history books), and there is also sanctioned children's literature that depicts violent resolutions to conflicts (e.g., some teachers were troubled by the ending of the well-known children's book *Millions of Cats* [Gag, 1977]).

But the media, unlike these latter sources, have no established role in the school world; their very commonness makes them of little cultural distinction (Bourdieu, 1984). Moreover, the commercial media emphasized in this book—television shows and films marketed for children—tend to portray human relations and actions in ways that are ideologically most dominant, most marketable, and thus most susceptible to criticism.

In response to children's appropriation of troubling images, group members, like Judy, referred to discussing their objections with the children, censoring material, and, particularly during composing activities, urging alternative characters and plot lines.[3] Thus, when Carolyn's children, influenced by the televised horror film *Leprechaun* (Amin & Jones, 1992), wrote unexpectedly violent St. Patrick's Day stories, Carolyn tried to "counteract," to provide an alternative image. She invited a fourth-grade class, who had studied Irish lore, to come talk to her children and to read them their stories. And she explicitly talked with her children about why the stories troubled her, including the fact that "this was a part of [Irish people's] culture, and they know how they feel about things that are important to their family and who they are." And, when her children wrote "cop" stories for the neighborhood officer, stories that featured violence against women, Carolyn pondered when she should intervene and say, "No, she can't die," or "Why can't the woman do something to the man?"

Kristin faced these same dilemmas and used these same strategies. She was forthcoming with the children about her own beliefs; she did not censor characters or plot lines, but she did not allow offensive name-calling in or out of texts; and she talked with the children about the choices they could make as authors.[4] But Kristin's enacted relationship to the symbolic media her children brought to school was more complex than that articulated in the study group. The complexity of this relationship was implicated, however. In response to Carolyn's comments about children rewriting stories, Kristin agreed and offered an elaboration—having children rewrite stories based on the popular media was not so easy to do, she said, and the difficulty did not *only* have to do with the media itself.

KRISTIN: It seems harder to challenge them to take control of [popular media stories than shared literature, for example].... I guess because there's a lot of status connected to [those stories] in my class. But I agree that allowing them to [rewrite stories], or encouraging them to do that, is important. I'm still trying to free them.... We've been talking a lot about, "Does it have to be violent? Can you think of a different way for them to interact?"....

CAROLYN: But it's kind of hard ... if that's how [the Power Rangers] solve their problems is through fighting.

KRISTIN: That's what I mean. We're talking about Power Rangers and how could the Power Rangers—or how could the X-People— solve "the problem" without having to fight? Maybe we do [those alternative ways] in our own [classroom conflicts].... "Why did they have to fight?" [I ask] ... "Because he's the bad guy," [they say]. "Why is he the bad guy? What did he do to be the bad guy?" "He was born a bad guy." So we had a talk about that. "Are people born bad guys?" *(emphasis added)*

In the study group, talk was primarily about the symbolic material itself and teachers' responses to that material. In the enacted classroom drama, Kristin's relationship was not directly to the symbolic material but, rather, to the "social work" (Dyson, 1993, p. 11) the children were doing through that material. That work involved issues of belonging, of "status," as Kristin said, or social power. As teacher, it is hard to intervene in a social world in which one's own power is limited (i.e., in the unofficial social world of children).

Thus, from the position of her own values and beliefs, Kristin tried to free her children from taken-for-granted characters and plots by negotiating—talking—with them. In fact, her notion of "freeing" children—of critical pedagogy—through composing crystallized in response to the children themselves.[5] Kristin's initial valuing of the media-based stories emphasized the social dimension of child writing; that is, how these stories contributed to children's engagement with each other through composing. However, the stories themselves generated ideological tensions, and thus the ideological dimension of child writing emerged as important to children's participation in both writing and community.

Kristin's reference to *X-people* was an echo of a term first introduced the year before, by second grader Sammy, as he responded to classroom issues about female roles in superhero stories. In Kristin's room, the ideological uneasiness was shared by the children themselves ... and so was the responsibility for addressing it.

Kristin's Children: Social Possibilities and Ideological Uneasiness

During her visit to the study group, in May of Kristin's year with the third grade, Urvashi commented on children's culture, as distinct from adult culture—as a social world with its particular construction of shared values and symbols—and on how children are not often heard from in discussions of culturally appropriate curriculum. This comment sparked a response from Kristin.

> KRISTIN: I keep thinking of the writing that the kids in my class are doing.... We've done a lot with African-American literature. In [free] writing my kids write what they want to write, and they're writing all these stories about superheroes.... And I was just thinking how even though they're not writing African fairy tales or anything like that, but what they're doing is [when] they're writing these stories they have power.... Basically, my kids are showing their power.
>
> URVASHI: They're negotiating differences [in power] with this. And they do it in their own way.... Inequality is the important difference, and that's the one they want to bridge.
>
> KRISTIN: And you know, I have people say, "Oh ... that Power Rangers stuff." ... And even though [some of the children] are writing a lot with that theme, it seems like there's so much more to it....

In Kristin's classroom, that "so much more" had to do, not with the "Power Rangers" in and of themselves, but with the social, ideological, and, ultimately, textual processes mediated by that "stuff." The drama that unfolded in her room illustrated how sociocultural diversity—evident in all her colleagues' classrooms—became manifest in the children's use of their so-called "common" culture in the classroom context.[6] In orienting themselves to particular cultural material, children were, at the same time, orienting themselves to each other; their ways of using, or avoiding, particular cultural heroes (e.g., Gambit, Rogue, or Nancy Drew) were associated with their membership in particular peer social groups, and those groups themselves were marked by the interplay of gender, race, and class.

Consider, for example, the comfortable shelters in which Sarah and Tina approached "free writing." The two girls had played together in kindergarten (according to both Tina and Sarah), but by third grade, not only did they play in different social circles, their classroom selections from the "image store" (Warner, 1994) were different as well. Out on the playground, Sarah played *Jaws* (Zanuck & Spielberg, 1975) and *Jurassic Park* (Kennedy, Molen, & Spielberg, 1993), but most of her classroom free writing was based on books. She and

Susan did write a "superhero" series about "Weaving Women" (inspired by a class study unit on weaving)—but they never got to the "superhero" part. Sarah's choice for a classroom-published book was her own version of *The Secret Garden,* which was originally a children's book (Burnett, 1962) and, then, a film (Lanning & Grint, 1992). In contrast, Tina drew often on the symbolic stuff of popular culture for her free writing, and, moreover, her published book was about a team of heroes whom Sarah was not allowed to watch—the X-Men.

"Too violent," Sarah's mother had told her child, so Sarah just watched the commercials for *X-Men.* Although Sarah's mother was talking only to her own child, she was also enacting a class-related stance toward the commercial media. "No girls" on my X-Men team, the composing boys had told Tina, but those boys were enacting gender-related assumptions that privileged romantic relations over collegial ones between women and men. "You can be Emily" in our *Three Ninjas* story (Chang & Turteltaub, 1992), the boys consistently told Sarah or Melissa, but they were implicating race-related ideologies of beauty.

Like all of us, children and adults, Kristin's children (and their parents) acted contingently in local circumstances—they responded to their children, their peers, their friends, for example. But, in the larger socioeconomic and political systems, they were all connected. Through affiliating with their friends in pleasurable, imagined worlds, children could assume powerful roles, garner some respect, and have a little fun. But those familiar, manageable child worlds contained within them complex ideological links to the larger society. Thus, societal "inequalities," to use Urvashi's words—and the means for bridging them—were experienced in child terms: Who imagines—and who gets to play—what sort of role with whom and for what effect (i.e., for what sort of response)?

Ideological tensions, revealed during free writing and Author's Theater, helped children problematize and, in fact, conceive of their choices of roles and plots as matters of authorial choice. Because sensitivity to textual decisions was linked to sensitivity to community response (e.g., along lines of gender or race), learning to write became linked to socioideological awareness and community participation—and bridge building. In this way, composing and, more particularly, the social and ideological dynamics that undergirded it, helped children learn about their interconnectedness as "fellow planeteers," to quote a child I once knew, even as that interconnectedness informed their learning to write.

This linking of literacy and community was detailed in the analytic narrative presented in this book. In the beginning of that narrative (in Chapter 3), many child composers seemed to view the source of their social power during "free" writing—their capacity to influence their peers—as residing in familiar media stories themselves. Sammy's variant of "I'm doing X-Men" was enough to secure the involvement of other fans, who wanted to be in his story. There was no need to specify characters or plots—these were common knowledge among fans. The text itself was simply a prop, a ticket to public play.

When planned or presented stories generated social conflict with ideological overtones (e.g., Tina's desire to play too), child authors could refer to the social power or, more accurately, the authority of the given media material (e.g., "That's how [ninja stories, X-Men, Streetfighters] are"), as well as to the authority of their own texts (e.g., "That's how my story is"). But individual child authors were not able to maintain singular authority over media material—many children felt free to play with, or pass judgment on, these stories, about which children have more expertise than do most adults.

In Chapter 4, for example, Holly and Tina used the culturally sanctioned tool of writing to reinforce their own agency over X-Men stories and to make others literally listen to their different selections of character roles and qualities, their different ideas about plots. Alternative stories and textual discussions did not permanently change classroom social divisions, nor did they yield some sort of communal solution to the complexities of human relations. But, as illustrated in Chapter 5, when taken-for-granted human relations had been explicitly and publicly questioned, they could no longer, in fact, be taken for granted.

As choices emerged, and as authors began to anticipate possible responses to their choices, texts became dialogic mediators of relations among community members. For example, in Chapter 6, Sammy's, Sarah's, and their peers' shared experiences with Greek gods and Power Rangers contributed to the complication of the too-simple idea that exercising physical power against others—violence—could be found only in the stories and play of the superhero fans or that a distaste for senseless violence belonged only to the superhero detractors. Authors could choose to venture forward into community dialogue, or remain silent (as in Chapter 7), but, whatever their choice, they were responsible both for, and through, their texts.

A PEDAGOGY OF RESPONSIBILITY

The vision of composing pedagogy that arises from studying both children and teachers is one that both extends and, in certain respects, contradicts the one developed in the 1970s and 1980s. Like the earlier pedagogy, in this one too a prime instructional goal is for children to conceive of themselves as authors who engage in planning, drafting, revising, and editing (Hansen & Graves, 1983). But the earlier pedagogy stopped, in a sense, with the concept of ownership—individual children would learn to write if they felt they owned their text and its meaning (Graves, 1983). This is what "real" authors do.

In contrast, what emerges here is a pedagogy of responsibility.[7] As the cases of Sammy and Tina dramatically suggest, it is not ownership that fuels the use of the written medium—or any other medium, for that matter. It is the desire to participate in a particular community, to have a say. As authors, children must learn that, no matter how much they revise and edit their texts (and despite the importance of those tasks), they can never "own" meaning, because meaning only exists in the *meeting* of voices. So authors never have the last word, just (hopefully) a good turn that furthers or deepens an ongoing conversation.

A pedagogy that links literacy and community learning would not necessarily involve a composing period and an Author's Theater structured like Kristin's. Nor would it necessarily yield the same ideological issues Kristin's children confronted. But any such pedagogy would necessarily involve certain classroom social structures: open-ended composing activities; regular classroom sharing of children's texts; and class discussions of those shared texts. Most importantly, those structures would be energized by two teaching qualities that were central to the study group's deliberations and, also, made more complex by the project in Kristin's room: an ethic of inclusion and a sensitivity to collective exclusion.

Making Curricular Space for a Diversity of Cultural Resources

The study group teachers all stressed structuring literacy activities for inclusion, for accessing young children's knowledge, experiences, and their capacity for emotional and intellectual engagement. In helping children become writers, teachers must begin with whatever is familiar and comfortable to their children, in terms of supportive symbolic media, like drawing or dramatic play, supportive social structures, like writing with friends, and familiar content, whatever its source. It was this latter aspect of familiarity—and, particularly, the ideological nature of content—that was distinctly highlighted by the project in Kristin's room.

As one of a range of classroom writing opportunities, open-ended composing activities, like free writing, are potentially valuable sources of information about children's experiences in families, day-care centers, and neighborhoods and about the cultural symbols that are important to them, including symbols like the X-Men. Recognizing child-chosen symbols does not mean that teachers abandon their responsibility to make judgments about good literature for the young, nor does it mean that they adopt a vacuous cultural relativism.

There is more than ample reason for concern, not only about children's popular media (see Levin & Carlsson-Paige, 1994), but also about the general influence of the market economy on children's lives (see Kline, 1993).

Moreover, as Seiter comments, "different children have different things to win or lose when they take pleasure in a peer-oriented mass culture" (1993, p. 234). Middle-class children play with cultural material from the popular media, as do low-income and working-class children. But the former children's out-of-school lives are more likely to involve other cultural materials highly valued by schools (e.g., those available in theaters, museums, book stores, and libraries).[8] Further, in official classroom activities, middle-class children may "define their own class position," their own difference from others, by being critical about the very television programs or films they watch (Buckingham, 1993, p. 145).

Despite these realities, children's unofficial use of diverse cultural materials *can* provide substance for official engagement and reflection—for critical resistance and thoughtful negotiation. To this end, the literacy curricula teachers negotiate with children must be undergirded by an inclusive vision of cultural art forms as fluid and fuzzy, intertwined in complex, dialogic relationships (Bakhtin, 1981): The historicism of folk traditions, the immediacy of popular art, and the endurance of classic productions all intermingle in our cultural conversations. What is "popular" can become enduring and universal (Levine, 1988); what is "universal" can be reinterpreted as a biased fiction of its immediate time (e.g., Harris, 1992; Sims, 1982; Taxel, 1992).

In addition, such a curricula must be undergirded by a belief that meaning is found, not in artifacts themselves, but in the social events through which those artifacts are produced and used. Children have agency in the construction of their own imaginations—not unlimited, unstructured agency, but, nonetheless, agency: They appropriate cultural material to participate in and explore their worlds, especially through narrative play and story. Their attraction to particular media programs and films suggests that they find in that material compelling and powerful images. If official curricula make no space for this agency, then schools risk reinforcing societal divisions in children's orientations to each other, to cultural art forms, and, to school itself.

In Kristin's room, children's imaginative stories and dramatic play, whatever their source, were about the human condition, about good and evil, about power and love of varied sorts. However, those grand themes were embedded in their play and their stories, rather than explicit in their talk, as were their assumptions about the nature of human relations in and out of texts. The children needed the assistance of the official curriculum, with its structures and teacher guidance, to reflect on those themes, as well as on the literacy knowledge implicit in their media use (e.g., knowledge about genre, literary elements, and dramatic language). Providing that assistance is related to an additional quality of a pedagogy for responsibility—not only being sensitive to but, moreover, exploiting diversity.

Inviting Children Beyond the Familiar: Human Diversity as Community Resource

The study group teachers all felt strongly about explicitly acknowledging the diverse ethnic cultures present in their classrooms and, in addition, about helping children become aware of—and appreciative of—those cultures. This importance was reflected in their discussions of multicultural children's literature, of projects that helped children learn about others (e.g., Carolyn's response to the children's St. Patrick's Day stories), and of activities that brought children together across racial, ethnic, or linguistic lines (e.g., Kristin's field trip to Elise's Chinatown classroom [see Chapter 5]).[9]

In addition, all stressed the importance of developing a *classroom* culture in which children listen respectfully to each other. In Jill's words, "before [children] can even write [about important matters] they need to have this voice in the classroom.... [My children] know that they're not going to be put down for what they say, because what they say is important. Someone else can feed off of that."

In Kristin's classroom, children's respect for each other as individuals and as members of significant groups merged in the classroom forum created through composing time, with its Author's Theater and its lively discussions. In that forum, children's diverse cultures were not so much shared practices (e.g., communicative patterns or rituals) as shared contexts for interpreting the world and its symbols (Geertz, 1983). Moreover, that context was neither fixed nor static but articulated in individuals' responses to someone else's words, to someone's story. Children could speak from their position as a "girl" or "boy," "African American," "European American," or other ethnic membership— even as a "writer" or an "actor," among other possibilities.[10]

As in the well-known practice of Author's Chair (Hansen & Graves, 1983), the children responded to story presentations with questions and comments. But their responses had to do with more than clarifying each other's textual sense, the focus of the pedagogical practice popularized in the 1980s.[11] They also had to do, in part, with what Vivian Paley refers to as young children's "3 Rs" ("the realms of fantasy, fairness, and friendship where each child [has] ... a deep wellspring of opinions and images" (1987, p. 80). The children's willingness to share their opinions in the forum was supported by the presence of images rooted in popular culture, images that the *children* had expertise in.[12] (The children *never* asked Kristin for information about or for her opinions about these images—although she sometimes offered her views.)

In any such classroom forum, the teacher's role is to monitor the proceedings, summarize points of connection and difference, and supply clarifying assertions. In Kristin's forum, those threads of connection and difference could involve many levels of language use, including those not emphasized herein (spelling strategies, grammar, editing). Most relevant for this project, issues of fairness and goodness linked with textual elements (e.g., action and details), literary ones (e.g., character motivation and purpose, the logic of the plot), genres (e.g., superhero stories, love stories, Greek myths, video game texts, essays), and ideology itself (i.e., assumptions about characters' relations).

Thus, in Kristin's forum, Paley's "3 Rs" were mediated by the more traditional "Rs." Kristin helped the children compare their symbolic worlds and discussed ways of constructing and reconstructing those worlds. It was possible to imagine a story—a world—where Gambit (and thus Sammy) was on the same team as Wolverine (Jonathan), where Rogue (and thus Tina) had a greater role in the X-Men's action, where Psyche (and thus Sarah) might venture from the hearth and join the battle.

Certain transformations adults might hope for (e.g., the Power Rangers and Rita deciding to just "talk it out") were not possible within the given genre (e.g., superhero stories). But Kristin could draw on heroes and on themes from across the curriculum and from different kinds of genres. Especially important in this project was the connection between the heroes and themes of children's fantasies and those studied in the social studies curriculum. Without that connection, neither Kristin nor her children would have had available sufficient images—and sufficient language—for articulating their points of view. Listen, one last time, to Kristin and her children.

> *(An old issue, that of the relative strength of boys and girls, has once again been raised in response to a superhero story. The dominant response is that "some girls are stronger than some boys." Kristin decides to comment on this response, but the children are talking so furiously that she finds it hard to intervene. Demario and Makeda come to her rescue.)*
>
> DEMARIO: Let the teacher talk.
> MAKEDA: Be quiet! I want to hear her point.
> DEMARIO: She gives <u>us</u> lots of respect.
> KRISTIN: *(able now to speak)* I was going to say that I believe that there are some women who are stronger than some men.... [Kristin then notes that she herself is not that physically strong.] But I think I have strengths that don't involve using my fists.... Maybe it's through talking, maybe it's just through my presence, the way I can stand and look confident.... We talked about Gandhi [whom Radha had researched for his peacemaker essay] and about how ... [England had] control of India. And if you've ever seen pictures of him, he was a very very thin, small man.... But he was able to get all these people to follow him.

DEMARIO: He was strong, but except with words.
KRISTIN: Aloyse, think about Haile Salase [whom he researched]. Is he
           strong?
ALOYSE: No.
KRISTIN: Do you think about him as being a strong person? If you
           think about strong inside, is he strong?
ALOYSE: Yeah.

Thus, in the forum, teachers may exploit not only the diverse perspectives and stories of the children themselves, but also those the teachers themselves feel are important.

In sum, I have argued for a pedagogical approach in which teachers—and administrators, parents, and the public—are sensitive to the ideological as well as the social dimension of literacy and, moreover, one in which teachers respond to and build on what the children know and can do but, also, help the children respond to and build on what *each other knows* and can do. In such an approach, teachers who work amid sociocultural diversity have a distinct advantage over those who do not. That diversity is their key pedagogical resource for helping children to move beyond the familiar and to become more conscious of their authorial choices and of the rhetorical *and* the social consequences of what they choose to say.

It was just such skills with words and social worlds that Bruner seemed to have in mind in the quote that opened this book's Introduction. The new generation, he said, would need to know how "to prevent the world from dissolving into chaos"; it would need to know that "many worlds are possible, . . . [and] that negotiation is the art of constructing new meanings," new ways to come out of our familiar worlds and construct new ones that can contain us all.

A CLASSROOM OF SUPERHEROES

In the drama presented in this book, stories and heroes intermingled in a classroom forum, yielding surprising twists in and out of texts. Media stories with well-known plots and heroes with clear identities had been superb material for negotiating play: Good guys fight bad ones, superheroes rescue the weak, girls marry boys and tend to babies. But then, in the forum, those identities were less sure, and there was new negotiating to do. Some children dismissed both superheroes and their arch-enemies as quite bad, and others thought that the plum role of a superhero's girlfriend was just plain boring. And fear of romance—and the teasing it inspired—seemed to be behind the powerful superheroes' refusal to let Rogue on the team.

Moreover, Zeus showed up in a Power Rangers story. A grown-up Emily waited at home as her husband Batman met his doom at the hands (or more accurately, the teeth) of the baby bat Bebe (transformed from *The Sideways Stories*)—and some children thought Emily should have gotten to the lab and done a little saving of her own. And what about this woman, Rosa Parks, who fought back by sitting down, or this thin Gandhi, who helped wrestle India from England. "Power," as it happens, is a matter of perspective, of the kind of story—the kind of situation—one is in. And so, perhaps, was "love," another powerful theme on the children's horizon, one awaiting more serious consideration, and one the children seemed to be both approaching and avoiding.

Neither the children nor their stories were quite what they might seem, as they engaged in play with cultural material that would not end up on anyone's "recommended list." But the "so much more to it," as Kristin said, came because the children were not able to stay in their seemingly safe shelters, playing with familiar stories and familiar others. And, for this, they had each other and Kristin to thank. They all had their superheroic moments.

In his book on language, culture, and identity, Michael Agar (1994) argues that imagining different worlds requires "a kind of courage." When we are exposed to information, to details, that are other than what we expect and, moreover, when those details challenge our sense of self, it can be hard to open up to their possibilities. But, if we do open up, we can change. "The old 'self,' the one in your heart and mind and soul, mutates as it comes into relationships with others. The self stretches to comprehend them all" (p. 28). Thus, we become like X-Men, superheroes of a special kind.

For children to display this sort of courage requires teachers of courage, teachers like Kristin, who are not afraid of children's worlds and children's concerns, who are interested in their ideas and, also, in challenging and extending those ideas. Those with such courage, whatever their age, may be rewarded by a life, not of "being," as Agar (1994) writes, but of "becoming. You turn into a sailor and immigrant for as long as you live" (p. 28), a participant in the continual process of reinventing, rewriting, one's world.

Coda
▼ ▼ ▼

On Writing "Good Guys"

God is no saint, strange to say.

J. Miles, *God: A Biography*, 1995, p. 6

In his Pulitzer-prize–winning book, Jack Miles argues for the complexity of God as a literary character. Having made humans in his own image, God did not always like what he saw. As written by man, God is a contradictory character—a powerful warrior, a jealous father, as well as a generous creator and a kindly savior. He learns about himself as he interacts with the mere mortals he has made. The ambiguity of life—and the nature of inner struggles among conflicting desires and tendencies—may be, in Miles' view, one of the great lessons of the great book.

This was a part of my own lesson in the story that opened this book, the story of me as a small child, listening to the angels sing. In applauding the angels, I applauded those who could hear them and dismissed those without the good sense to listen up. When the angels were not so obvious, it was also not so obvious how to divide the informed from the ignorant ... nor, of course, how to situate myself among the "us" and the "them."

And so it was for Kristin's children. In making use of popular cultural symbols (including the tough but good guy), the children situated themselves within, and constructed, their social lives. In the classroom forum, they came together in a public place to play out the imagined encounters of appealing heroes and, in the process, the children encountered each other. With Kristin's guidance, they turned around, listened, discussed. In so doing, they reworked their relationships with each other by reworking their relationships to cultural symbols. In their talk, the good guys and the bad guys— and, more particularly, the words that gave them life—had to be considered and reconsidered; the "guys," whether female or male, were characters with motivations, purposes, constraints, and possibilities.

Such deliberation is a hallmark of language development in a socioideological sense, argued Bakhtin. Given the opportunity—a diversity of others to know—we learn simultaneously about words and social worlds, about ourselves and others. We learn to choose more carefully, more deliberately, the words that situate us among others.

In a recent *New Yorker* cartoon, a young girl, a look of distress on her face, watches a bird pull an earthworm from the ground. Her father, standing beside her, watching too, offers some commentary: "Earthworms are good guys, and birds are good guys. That's just life, honey." (Miller, 1995, p. 53)

The child, it is implied, wanted to know who was the good guy and who was the bad guy. She wanted to know who to root for, so to speak, who to identify with: the worm or the bird. Unfortunately, as her father told her, worms and birds do not have clear roles in a story of good and evil and of "us" and "them." The world is more complicated—more ambivalent—than that.

It is not only children, however, who look for good guys and bad guys. Adults look too. They find them in commercial media, in "traditional" teachers or "progressive" ones, in "proper" parents or "improper" ones, and on and on. This book about Tina, Sammy, and their peers underscores both the pleasures and the limits of the search for such a fixed world. We can play good guys and revel in moral assurity and might that's right, and we might even play bad guys and enjoy the pleasures of violating all the rules and of might that's raw. And we can look to cultural heroes (or superheroes) for guidance as we choose our roles. But, alas, our heroes are not always what they seem. Ultimately, we have to look to each other to negotiate the common good (and the common evil) and, in this way, jointly construct our future.

Appendix A
▼ ▼ ▼

TABLES

TABLE AI. *Conventions Used in the Presentation of Transcripts*

(abc)	Parentheses enclosing text contain notes, usually about contextual and nonverbal information (e.g., laughs, points at her).
( )	Empty parentheses, on the other hand, indicate unintelligible words or phrases, e.g.,

> MICHAEL: Soon as Tina try to punch me ( ), I go in back of her.

[abc]	Brackets contain explanatory information inserted into quotations by me, rather than by the speaker.
A-B-C	Capitalized letters separated by hyphens indicate that letters were spoken or words were spelled aloud by the speaker.
ABC	A capitalized word or phrase indicates increased volume.
<u>abc</u>	An underlined word indicates a stressed word.
/c/	Parallel slashed lines indicate that the speaker made the sound of the enclosed letter or letters.
/c:/	A colon inserted into word or sentence indicates that the sound of the previous letter was elongated.
. . .	Ellipsis points indicate omitted data; when they are inserted in the beginning of a line, they indicate omitted speaking turn(s), e.g.,

> TINA: When I went to the funeral [as the Mother Wolf], and the pigs were teasing me, I felt like eating them.
>
>   . . .
>
> MAKEDA: I liked the story—when we ate the wolf, and the mama was coming to the funeral, and we was laughing.

Conventional punctuation marks are used to indicate ends of utterances or sentences, usually indicated by slight pauses on the audiotape. Commas refer to pauses within words or word phrases. Dashes [—] indicate interrupted utterances.

TABLE A2. *Ethnicity and Sex of Second-Grade Children*

Ethnicity	Male	Female	Total
African American	6	7	13
African American/European American	1	1	2
Asian American	2	0	2
Asian American/European American	1	0	1
European American	3	7	10
Total	*13*	*15*	*28*

TABLE A3. *Ethnicity and Sex of Third-Grade Children*

Ethnicity	Male	Female	Total
African American	6	5	11
Asian American	2	0	2
Asian American/European American	1	0	1
European American	3	5	8
Mexican American	2	0	2
Total	*14*	*10*	*24*

TABLE A4. *Sex and Ethnicity of Kristin's Children*

Sex	Grade Level(s)	Ethnicity
FEMALE		
Holly	2	African American/European American
Johnetta	2	African American
LaShanda	2	African American/Native American
Lena	3	Eritrean American
Lettrice	2,3	African American
Liliana[a]	2,3	European American
Lynn[a]	2,3	European American
Margaret[a]	2	European American
Makeda	2,3	African American
Melissa[a]	2,3	European American
Monique	2	African American
Rhonda	2,3	African American
Susan[a]	2,3	European American
Sarah[a]	2,3	European American
Tamara	2	European American
Tina	2,3	African American
MALE		
Adam	3	European American
Aloyse	2,3	Ethiopian American (immigrant)
Bryant	3	African American
Demario	3	African American
Edward	3	Mexican American
James	2,3	Korean American
Jonathan[a]	2,3	European American/Chinese American[b]
Kevin	2,3	European American
Lawrence	2	African American/European American
Michael	2,3	African American
Nyem	2	African American
Patrick	2,3	European American
Radha	2,3	Indian (Asian) American
Ricky	2	African American
Sammy	2,3	African American
Seth[a]	2	European American
Thomas	2,3	African American
Victor	3	Mexican American

[a]Children from homes in which at least one parent had a middle-class, white-collar job.

[b]Jonathan was partially of Chinese heritage. However, he looked Caucasian and his racial identity as Chinese did not seem salient to the children, unlike that of James and Rahda, the other Asian-American children. (For example, Melissa included James and Rahda as potential leads for her Bruce Lee story because of "their hair." She did not consider blond Jonathan.) In the product analyses, Jonathan's work was grouped with the European-American children.

TABLE A5. *Data Analysis Categories*

SOCIAL GOAL

Affiliating: Children refer to common knowledge, common pleasures, or common miseries or injustices, thereby emphasizing similarity to others in a particular group. (For example, boys often built conversations about the media by individually displaying their knowledge about a group-valued media program; "oh yeah," each boy would say after each contribution, implying his own prior knowledge of the shared scene before adding his own recollections.)

Soliciting: Children seek others' desire to be included in their own plans. (For example, children often announced their desire to write about a commonly valued character or story [an implicit assumption of affiliation] in order to solicit others' requests for a part in their story; sometimes children directly requested others' involvement or inquired about their desires: "You wanta be in it [my story]?")

Allowing or Denying: Children allow or deny desiring others to be included in their own plans. (For example, children could agree to give others their desired roles: "You could be a good guy" or other requested role. Usually the allowed requests had been indirectly solicited [e.g., by an announcement that one was writing about a popular character]. But sometimes unanticipated others solicited roles. Denying desiring others could have clear ideological echoes: "You're not no bad guy. You a lady.")

Controlling: Children direct others to comply with their own plans and/or anticipate how others will have to comply with their own words. (For example, children directed others to act out their words during Authors' Theater events; sometimes children anticipated what their words would make others do: "Jonathan's gonna hafta kiss Melissa [when they act out my story]!")

Complying or Resisting: Children comply with or resist others' plans. (For example, children could voice dissatisfaction with others' planned roles and actions. Like denying, resisting could have clear ideological echoes: "Amber's White," so her boyfriend in a child's romance story should not be Black.)

Distancing: Children disassociate themselves from others' chosen characters or actions. (For example, children could distance themselves from superhero stories by proclaiming them "not original" or full of "too much fighting.")

Negotiation: Children attempt to interact in ways that involve mutual accommodation between two or more participants, each seeking some control. (For example, child authors could agree to include character roles desired by another in their own texts, if that other would return the favor.)

TEXTUAL FUNCTIONS

Text as Ticket: The written text functions to allow children to have a turn directing or controlling their peers; the paper is thus both a ticket allowing access to, and a prop for the child enacting the role of, the author—the authority—in an Author's Theater event. (For example, sometimes children's texts were invisible, as it were—they pretended to read texts that were not actually written.)

Text as Memory Support: The written text functions to help children remember information relevant to their stories or the stories themselves. (For example, children often jotted down names of story characters, matched with names of child actors, even when they used an "invisible" text.)

Text as Representation: The written text functions to represent valued characters, relations among characters, and actions. (For example, boys often chose superhero thematic material, which marked their maleness in this class.)

Text as Authority (the "Reified" Text): The written text functions to reinforce the control of the author. (For example, when girls complained that boys did not include female characters in their stories, the boys often replied by repeating their complaint but without any sense of personal responsibility [i.e., with a variant of "Yes, there are no girls in this story"]; that is, they implied that the matter was out of their hands as authors—the texts were set.)

Text as Dialogic: The written text functions fully as a mediator of relationships among author, actors, and audience members. Its mediational role is not only inter-personal but also ideological. (For example, in response to the objections of others, the author might change the written relationship between males and females; most often, such changes occurred in a forthcoming text, not in the one under criticism.)

TABLE A6. *Percentage of Children's Products Based on Commercial Media*

	Media Superheroes		Total Commercial Media	
	2nd Grade	3rd Grade	2nd Grade	3rd Grade
BOYS				
African American	51% (18/35)[a]	59% (33/56)	51% (18/35)	96% (54/56)
European American	65% (11/17)	19% (9/47)	65% (11/17)	43% (20/47)
Other[b]	33% (5/15)	61% (46/76)	87% (13/15)	82% (62/76)
Total	*51% (34/67)*	*49% (88/179)*	*63% (42/67)*	*76% (136/179)*
GIRLS				
African American	11% (3/28)	22% (11/49)	21% (6/28)	35% (17/49)
European American	0% (0/29)	1% (1/74)	14% (4/29)	5% (4/74)
Total	*5% (3/57)*	*10% (12/123)*	*18% (10/57)*	*17% (21/123)*

Note: In addition to Superhero stories, Commercial Media Sources included Fantasy stories (e.g., varied Disney films), Video Games (e.g., "Streetfighter"), Other Television Shows (besides those featuring superheroes), and Other Movies (e.g., besides those featuring superheroes or fantasy characters).

[a]Numbers in parentheses indicate proportion of products. Individual child products that were revised for classroom publication were only counted once.

[b]Includes James, Lawrence, and Radha in the second grade, and James, Radha, Victor, and Edward in the third grade.

Appendix B

▼ ▼ ▼

MEDIA SUMMARIES

MOVIES

*Aladdin (animated)
Musker, J., Clements, R. (Producers & Directors). (1992). Burbank, CA: Walt Disney Pictures.

Characters

Aladdin is young, athletic, and dashing despite his ragged clothes. Always accompanied by his loyal but mischievous monkey, **Abu**, the main character and romantic male lead is a poor yet bright street urchin surviving the only way he knows how—through trickery and thievery, the Robin Hood of Arabia. **Jasmine** is a princess with long, dark hair, big eyes, and curves. Although she has spent her life protected inside palace walls, with **Raja**, her pet tiger, as her only friend, Jasmine is smart enough to voice her desires and even makes an attempt to run away to discover what the world is about. The big, blue, amorphous, omnipotent (yet humble) **Genie** is capable of taking on many shapes and personalities, from animals to Arsenio Hall. Aladdin, Jasmine, and the Genie are assisted in their adventures by a **Magic Carpet** with a personality, an animated rug from the Cave of Wonders. **Jafar** is the tall, gaunt, angular sultan's advisor. He has slanted eyes, a spidery mustache, and a sneer that turns into an obsequious simper when manipulating the sultan. Jafar is the quintessential Disney villain, purely evil, motivated by nothing more than sheer greed, lust for power, monstrous ego, and just plain badness. The **Sultan**, Jasmine's father, is a rolypoly childlike character who is harmless and ineffectual, in contrast to his strong-willed daughter. He is a foolish ruler, letting Jafar push him around and worrying about his daughter only because she does not like being a princess.

Asterisks (*) indicate longer, more detailed summaries; these are the media programs that were used extensively by Kristin's children and/or central to key classroom episodes analyzed in the book. Summaries are provided for movies, television programs, and video games, in that order.

Media summaries were prepared by Gwen Larsen, Sheila Shea, Elizabeth Scarboro, and Wanda Brooks, with additional assistance provided by Michael Ford.

Plot Summary

Set in the mystical times of princes and princesses, flying carpets and genies, Aladdin is a noble thief whose wish is to live as a rich prince, wealth being the key to his happiness. The story is adapted from the traditional *Arabian Nights* version, complete with an all-powerful genie and three wishes to the owner of the lamp. After Aladdin's chance meeting with the beautiful and brave Jasmine, they fall in love, and he discovers that, despite her wealth, she feels just as trapped and powerless in her world as he does in his. Disney has altered the villain, Jafar, from a vagrant magician to the Grand Vizier of the Sultan, whose evil scheming to snatch the lamp, marry Jasmine, and become ruler of Agrabah, is foiled by Aladdin in the end. Jafar is tricked into wishing himself a genie for the sake of power and is enslaved in the lamp for a thousand years. Aladdin uses his last wish to set Genie free; he is then transformed into a pauper again and, thus, unable to marry the princess. The Sultan, however, decides that the law will be changed: Jasmine may marry whomever she desires.

A brief, opening scene of this film is highlighted in Chapter 5 of this text: Aladdin and Abu have just settled down with their stolen breakfast when Aladdin catches sight of some starving children digging through the garbage. He sacrifices his breakfast to them, and, after a moment of selfishness, so does Abu.

Notes on Stereotypes

Although Disney apparently attempted to "Arabicize" the characters, Aladdin and Jasmine appear quite Western; the evil Jafar's features are the most clearly Asian. Disney also seemed to allow Jasmine some female independence and power, but, in the final scenes, she is shown as a scantily clad handmaiden to Jafar; her only power lies in her sexual appeal. Even after being released from Jafar's prison, she winds up in the traditional role of (Aladdin's) bride-to-be (after all that talk of independence!).

Batman Returns

Guber, P., Melniker, B., Peters, J., Uslan, M. (Producers), & Burton, T. (Director). (1992). Burbank, CA: Warner Brothers.

Characters and Brief Plot Summary

Bruce Wayne, alias, **Batman**, must (again) save Gotham from the evil **Penguin** and **Catwoman,** who have teamed up with corrupt megacorporation owner Max Schreck to destroy the hero and his city. Both the events that led to Penguin's existence in the city sewers and the dual personality of Catwoman (alias, Max Schrek's secretary **Serena Kyle**) parallel Batman's own dark past and his present dual identity. In the end, Penguin is killed by the backfire of his own maniacal plans, and Catwoman, who is secretly in love with Batman, sacrifices the eighth of her nine lives to save Batman and kill her former boss, Max Schrek.

Beauty and the Beast (animated)
Hahn, D. (Producer), & Wise, K., Trousdale, G. (Directors). (1991). Burbank, CA: Walt Disney Pictures.

Characters and Brief Plot Summary
This Disney remake of the classic tale features an independent and strong-willed girl named **Belle** and the fearsome prince-turned-**Beast**. As a beautiful intellectual, Belle is wooed by the chauvinistic village machoman, **Gaston,** but much prefers the escapism of her books. When her father loses his way home and is held prisoner at the Beast's castle, Belle agrees to remain with the Beast in exchange for her father's freedom. While in the castle, the unlikely couple eventually learn to appreciate and love one another, despite their obvious differences.

The Bodyguard
Kasden, L., Costner, K., Wilson, J. (Producers), & Jackson, M. (Director). (1992). Burbank, CA: Warner Brothers.

Characters and Brief Plot Summary
Rachel Marron (Whitney Houston) is a Black superstar of film and song. Passionate, impulsive, and spoiled, she is everything **Frank Farmer** (Kevin Costner), her White bodyguard, is not. He is disciplined, stoic, and unimpressed with her celebrity status. He is hired to protect her when she starts receiving death threats from a fanatical fan. Despite their differences, they fall in love and catch the stalker. He even takes a bullet for her (and lives). Alas, their relationship is fated to end, since he never accepts a permanent position. They kiss farewell as the refrain of her hit song, "I will always love you," plays in the background.

*Dragon, The Bruce Lee Story
DeLaurentis, R. (Producer), & Cohen, R. (Director). (1993). Universal City, CA: Universal Pictures.

Characters
Bruce Lee is the legendary martial arts hero, a Chinese man who is strong, determined, ambitious, and courageous. He is also stubborn enough to sacrifice his family life for a career in the movies. **Lynda Lee** is the White woman who loves him enough to marry him despite strong objections from her family and society at the time (circa 1960s). She is tough, determined, and a dedicated mother and wife. She puts up with Bruce Lee's familial neglect to help his career.

Plot Summary
Bruce comes to the United States after being driven out of China for fighting with the local ganglords. By working in a Chinese restaurant and washing dishes, he puts himself through college and sets up his own martial arts studio. Here he faces discrimination from both sides—Chinese and White—in his teaching practices. He shows his stubbornness in dating and marrying Lynda, despite the disapproving eye of society. Bruce meets Lynda when she attends a kung-fu class demonstration, in which she is his only female student. While demonstrating a flip, Lynda flips and pins *him*. She hints that, were he to ask her out on a date, she would not say "no." He asks her out that night.

Lynda sneaks out of her house to see him. That night, at the restaurant, Bruce and Lynda wait for a table, although the White host immediately seats several White couples who arrive after them. They leave indignantly, and Bruce takes her to a Chinese restaurant. Their romance follows a pattern of Lynda sneaking out of her house to meet Bruce, who is anxious to confront her mother with their relationship so that they can get married.

On meeting Bruce, Lynda's mom tries to be polite, but her racist views are apparent. She lectures Lynda in front of Bruce on the dangers of interracial dating, let alone interracial marriage. "What about your children?" she pleads. When Lynda is forced to choose on the spot between her family and Bruce, she chooses Bruce. They mount his motorcycle and race off to start their new life together.

With Lynda, Bruce Lee starts a family and continues to disobey the orders of the Chinese martial arts association, who warn him to stop teaching kung-fu to the "White man." His ambition and devotion to "open the White man's eyes to the world and possibilities of martial arts" lead him to the movies. Lee becomes a star in Hong Kong and China and a cult figure in the United States, where he battles against the discriminatory Hollywood policies of having White people play Chinese heroes. Eventually he produces and stars in his own martial arts movies. Bruce Lee dies mysteriously at a young age, fulfilling the prophesy of the Chinese elders who claim he was cursed for exposing their cultural secrets to Western society.

Notes on Stereotypes

The movie simply presents an interracial relationship that is only stereotypical in the reactions it provokes in the White society—fear, distrust, suspicion. It makes little attempt to explore the interplay of race and gender beyond the superficial problems that arise with a mixed couple. The movie focuses on Bruce Lee's professional struggle against stereotypes in the Western media.

Jaws

Zanuck, R. (Producer), & Spielberg, S. (Director). (1975). Universal City, CA: Universal Pictures.

Characters and Brief Plot Summary

A small East coast town is terrorized by great white sharks. Although the mayor refuses to believe the stories, fearing threatened tourism, the police chief, **Martin Brody,** convinces him otherwise. With the help of Quint, a daring shark hunter, and **Matt Hooper,** a marine biologist, Brody ventures off to the high seas to extinguish the ominous creature.

*Jungle Fever

Lee, S. with 40 Acres and a Mule Productions (Producer), & Lee, S. (Director). (1991) Universal City, CA: Universal Pictures.

Characters

Flip, one of the central characters, is an African-American man in his late thirties, the only African-American architect in his firm. He and his wife, **Drew,** a woman of mixed descent (African American/White), live with their young daughter, **Ming,** in an upper-middle-class neighborhood in New York. **Angie,** an Italian woman in her mid-twenties, lives in a working-class neighborhood (Bensonhurst) with her two brothers and father. She is hired to work as Flip's temporary secretary. **Paulie,** also Italian, has been dating Angie for a long time. He runs the family newspaper shop, which is home to a group of neighborhood men and boys.

Plot Summary

Flip, Drew, and their young daughter are a happy family until the hiring of Angie, Flip's new Italian-American secretary. Although furious at his employers for denying him an African-American secretary, Flip quickly develops an attraction for Angie, with whom he soon has an affair. Abandoned by their families, Flip and Angie rent an apartment together. Although they clearly have feelings for one another, they are continually harassed by family, friends, and strangers who object to their interracial relationship.

Soon their relationship deteriorates when the two discuss their future. Although Angie hopes to have children, Flip objects to the idea of "mixed babies." After Angie leaves Flip, he tells her that the reason they were together was because of "Jungle Fever"—they were mutually "curious" about dating someone of another race. In the end, the future of Flip and Drew is uncertain, and the relationship between Paulie and Angie is bleak, since Paulie develops a fondness for an African-American customer and friend.

Notes on Stereotypes

With the exception of Gator, Flip's coke-addicted brother who is constantly stealing and begging for money, there are no stereotypical roles based on gender or race in this film. Rather, it explores beliefs about interracial relationships, particularly in the context of romance. While the two main characters are romantically involved, others, like Drew's female friends, Flip's and Angie's respective families, and Paulie's neighborhood friends, are quite adamant about their objections to interracial dating.

Jurassic Park

Kennedy, K., Molen, G. (Producers), & Spielberg, S. (Director). (1993). Universal City, CA: Universal Pictures.

Characters and Brief Plot Summary

Based on the novel by Michael Crichton, this film features a dinosaur theme park gone awry when the genetically cloned dinosaurs (created by using prehistoric DNA) break free of their cages and exhibit unusual signs of intelligence. The struggle to escape from the carnivorous dinosaurs on a remote island is heightened as they continually feast on their victims.

Leprechaun

Amin, M. (Producer), & Jones, M. (Director). (1992). Burbank, CA: Trimark Pictures.

Characters and Brief Plot Summary

A demonic and bloodthirsty **leprechaun** uses his tricks and magic to terrorize **Tori** and her friends after they steal his bag of gold coins. Their only hope for survival is to find a magical four-leaf clover.

The Mighty Ducks
Avnet, J., Kerner, J. (Producers), & Herek, S. (Director). (1992). Burbank, CA: Walt Disney Pictures.

Characters and Brief Plot Summary

Gordon Bombay is the reluctant coach of this motley team of inner-city hockey players, the **Mighty Ducks.** In the process Gordon learns some lessons about being a good coach and father figure to these unfortunate kids. With the help and advice of his own mentor and father figure, **Hans** the skate-maker, the Ducks make it to the play-offs to face down Gordon's old team, the **Hawks,** and Gordon's ruthless old **Coach Riley.** The team includes the typical inner-city toughs: **Aberman** the joker, **Jessie** the punk, **Peter** the runt, **Connie** the tomboy, **Fulton** the bully, and **Charlie** the sensitive one, who encourages Gordon to romance Casey, his pretty divorced mother. Although the movie is set in the urban streets of a large Midwestern city, the only member of the Ducks who is not White is Jessie, who is African American.

The Secret Garden
Lanning, S. (Producer), & Grint, A. (Director). (1992). Los Angeles, CA: Republic Pictures Corporation.

Characters and Brief Plot Summary

Based on the children's book of the same name by Francis Hodgson Burnett, *The Secret Garden* is the story of a young English girl, **Mary Lennox,** who leaves India, where her parents have died of the plague, and moves to a gloomy English manor in Yorkshire to live with her father's friend, **Mr. Archibald Craven,** an eccentric and mysterious old man. There she discovers a secret garden and befriends the old man's invalid son, **Colin Craven.** With the help of a local boy, **Dicken,** who can speak to animals and make things grow, Mary and Colin transform the secret garden into a place where Colin regains his strength and Mary finds friends she never had. By the end of the movie, Mary manages to reunite the estranged father and son and bring springtime back into the hearts of the people of Misslethwait Manor.

Star Wars
Kurtz, G. (Producer), & Lucas, G. (Director). (1977). Burbank, CA: Twentieth Century Fox.

Characters and Brief Plot Summary

In this space odyssey, young **Luke Skywalker,** unwitting savior of the galaxy, is swept from his childhood home planet into an adventure that leads him to the rescue of the beautiful rebel leader, **Princess Leia,** and into the jaws of the evil overlord of the Empire, **Darth Vader.** With advice from the wise old Jedi knight, **Obi Wan Kanobi,** and the help of a motley duo of space smugglers, **Han Solo** and **Chewbacca,** Luke manages to destroy the Death Star, a war machine of awesome destructive power that would have left the galaxy at the mercy of the Empire.

*Teenage Mutant Ninja Turtles
Dawson, K., Fields, S., Chan, D. (Producers), & Barron, S. (Director). (1990). Burbank, CA: Limelight Productions.

Characters
The "good guys" are man-sized mutant ninja turtles—**Raphael, Donatello, Michaelangelo,** and **Leonardo**—under the tutelage of a giant ninja rat named Splinter, whose Japanese ninja training has given him the air of ancient wisdom. Together, the Teenage Mutant Ninja Turtles and Splinter fight against the forces of evil in the form of the **Foot Klan,** a band of teenage delinquent boys who steal and wreak havoc under the direction of **Shredder,** an old arch-enemy of Splinter. The Turtles routinely admire and rescue **April O'Neil,** the White female news reporter. Her exposés on police corruption put her in deep trouble with her boss, **Charles,** who is under pressure from the police to fire April. Charles' son, **Danny,** is the troubled adolescent, whose estrangement from his father leads him to the Foot Klan for a sense of belonging. The turtles also are assisted by **Casey Jones,** the only humanoid-hero, an older White man, who also pursues April and wins the kiss in the end.

Plot Summary
The city is experiencing a rise in crime and violence owing to the antics of the Foot Klan and the laxity of a corrupt police force. Reporter April O'Neil, assigned to this mysterious trend, is herself a victim of the Klan's attacks until she is rescued by the Teenage Mutant Ninja Turtles. While the Turtles party with April, their old master is kidnapped by the Klan and taken away to be tortured. On discovery of this, Raphael storms off on his own, without the other Turtles; he is jumped and beaten badly by the Foot Klan until a mysterious stranger named Casey Jones comes to the rescue. Meanwhile, the Klan has burned April's house to the ground; this is the final straw, and the Turtles and Casey retire to April's country home to plot revenge.

While the final battle is being set up, a parallel story involves Danny, the troubled adolescent, and his search for a family. He finds one with the Foot Klan after running away from his father, but he comes to doubt his actions as he witnesses the torture of Splinter, the Turtles' captive teacher, by the cruel Foot Klan. As Danny experiences a revelation and runs to the Turtles' old lair to fight, this time for the forces of good, the Turtles prepare themselves for battle at April's house. Throughout this plotting, April flirts with Casey and leaves the plotting to the men.

The battle begins as the Turtles storm the city and successfully fight an army of Foot Klansmen. Danny finds a father figure in Casey Jones, who is fighting alongside the Turtles, and they all go to capture the evil Shredder. The battle ends as the Turtles defeat Shredder, and the police race onto the scene to arrest the defeated Klan. Danny's father shows up to embrace his son and give April back her job. She goes on the air "live" to report the story but not before rewarding her hero, Casey, with a big kiss. The Turtles cheer on in the background.

Notes on Stereotypes
April's role is stereotypically that of the victim to be rescued and of the female prize to be won. She is depicted as pretty and feminine, in contrast to the cruder and more violent Turtles. Although she is introduced as a tough, smart woman to be reckoned with, her role is gradually marginalized to that of a cheerleader on the side-

lines, or objectified to that of someone to be seen and not heard; she becomes more provocative with each passing scene. Finally, it is the Turtles' ability to use force, rather than April's shrewd reporting skills, that end the crime in the city.

*Three Ninjas
Chang, M. with Global Venture Hollywood (Producer), & Turteltaub, J. (Director). (1992). Burbank, CA: Touchstone Pictures.

Characters
The protagonists in this movie are three brothers named Rocky, Colt, and TumTum, cute White ninja fighters. **Rocky,** the eldest brother, is more responsible than his younger brothers and also tends to be preoccupied with an attractive girl, **Emily,** the blonde schoolmate who occasionally needs "rescuing." **Colt,** the middle brother, is hot-headed, but the most talented ninja, whereas **TumTum,** the youngest brother, is preoccupied with eating and teasing Rocky about his romantic encounters. Throughout the film, both Colt and TumTum constantly chant "Rock-y loves, Em-i-ly." **Grandpa (Maurie),** possessing a slight accent, was raised in Japan, where he developed the ninja skills that he is now passing on to his grandsons. The father (**Sam**), an FBI agent, is less understanding than the mother, but he tolerates his sons' ninja training. **Snyder,** trained by Maurie in martial arts, is the leader of an organized crime ring and is determined to get the FBI "off his back."

Plot Summary
The movie introduces the three boys and their grandfather, who devotes much of his time to training his grandsons in ninja skills. The boys' father is investigating an organized crime ring, led by Snyder. After a failed attempt by the FBI to capture him, Snyder realizes that the agent after him is in fact Sam, Maurie's son-in-law. Snyder then decides to threaten the grandfather about his son-in-law's involvement. Prior to the confrontation between Snyder and Maurie, the boys fend off several of Snyder's men, also ninja fighters.

One scene (referenced in Chapter 5) deals with Emily and her stolen bicycle. When the boys ride to school, taking the path through an abandoned lot, Emily chooses to take the paved one instead. Along the way, Emily comes across several school bullies and is forced to give them her bicycle. After hearing Emily yell "Rocky!" several times, Rocky finally locates his helpless friend, only to find her angry at his "showing off" while she had been left alone with the school bullies. Feeling guilty, Rocky tells her that he will somehow get her bike back.

At school, Rocky and Colt themselves face the bullies when both sides agree to a basketball game that will settle who will keep Emily's bicycle. Rather than being content that her "hero" Rocky will retrieve her bicycle, Emily at first is frustrated that Rocky must again "show off" but later cheers excitedly as she stands on the sidelines holding his baseball cap. This time Rocky does not fail her. Instead he and Colt manage to triumph over the bullies with a spectacular display of high-flying dunks and incredible jumps.

The plot develops as Snyder's three clumsy morons attempt to kidnap the ninjas from their home. The babysitter is trapped in a closet by the intruding morons after they smash her in the face with a pepperoni pizza. Although they elude the moronic kidnappers by setting a series of "traps" in their home, the boys eventually are captured by Snyder's men and taken to his hideout, where Maurie defeats Snyder in a gruesome duel. Unable to take defeat, Snyder pulls out a gun, only to be stopped by a timely appearance by the FBI.

Notes on Stereotypes

The film portrays Emily as a somewhat independent female, but one who is occasionally helpless without Rocky or the boys at her side. To the boys' surprise, Emily manages to knock one of the kidnappers to the floor, with a kick to the shin and a swift right punch. In addition, throughout the movie, she is unimpressed with Rocky's "showing off," thereby somewhat relinquishing the typical "damsel in distress" role. However, she remains helpless when the bullies take her bike and clearly is disappointed when she is not "rescued" in time.

TELEVISION

Barney
Leach, S. (1988). Texas: Lyons Group.

Characters and Brief Plot Summary

This educational program for young children contains no "good" guys or "bad" guys; rather, it stars a jolly purple dinosaur named **Barney.** The classroom is the main setting of this daily show, in which children of various racial groups, both female and male, join Barney for a half-hour episode that combines singing, sharing stories, and rhyming as they learn about the day's featured alphabet letter, number, and color. At the end of the show, Barney's friends, always cheery and animated, accompany Barney in singing his theme song: "I love you. You love me. . . . We're a great big happy family."

Biker Mice From Mars (animated)
Unger, R. (1994). Los Angeles, CA: Genesis Entertainment.

Characters and Brief Plot Summary

The "good guys" are three really "cool," motorcycle-riding Martian mice who have come to Earth to save it from the same destruction that their own planet suffered at the hands of the evil **Plutarkians. Vinnie** is their leader, the Don Juan of them all, who uses lots of snappy one-liners to flirt with **Charlie,** the only female character in the series, a tough woman and a skilled mechanic. **Throttle** is the rational mouse, and **Modo** is the biggest, toughest one. Charlie helps the Biker Mice by fixing their bikes, but she also gets rescued by them. Although Charlie pulls her own weight in a fight, the Biker Mice usually leave her in their dust when they go to battle, or else they bring her along in order to exploit her obvious sex appeal to distract the enemy while they set up a sneak attack. Together, they try to stop the leader of the Plutarkians, the alien **Limburger.** Under his command are the monster-creating mad scientist, **Dr. Carbuncle,** and **Grease-Pit,** the thug who works in the same garage as Charlie. The Mice must stop the Plutarkians from draining the Earth's natural resources and turning Chicago into an industrial wasteland.

The Cosby Show
Weinberger, E., Leeson, M., Cosby Jr., W. Ed.D. (Creator). (1984). Carsey-Werner Productions. New York: Kaufman-Astoria Studios.

Characters and Brief Plot Summary
The Cosby Show centers around an upper-middle-class African-American family consisting of two loving parents and their five children. The father, **Cliff Huxtable,** played by Cosby, is a successful obstetrician who operates his practice out of his home, whereas his wife, **Claire Huxtable,** is an equally capable attorney. Sondra, a graduate of Princeton, is the level-headed eldest daughter, who eventually marries another Princeton alum. **Denise,** the second eldest, is also intelligent but is portrayed as more zany and free-spirited in her dress and mannerisms. Eventually Denise's character moves out of the house to attend a fictitious Black college. **Theo,** the only son, suffers academically, not because he is incompetent but because he doesn't apply himself, as his father suggests; he is the typical music-loving, junk-food-eating, sports-fanatic teenager. **Vanessa,** the second youngest daughter, who is often jealous of her older sisters' freedom, is a bright teenager who attempts to look or act older than she is. The youngest sibling is **Rudy,** the adorable "baby" in the family who is sometimes neglected and gets in her fair share of trouble, often with her multiracial friends from school.

Notes on Stereotypes
This show has been applauded for its absence of negative stereotypes and caricatures of African Americans but, at the same time, has suffered criticisms of being "white-washed" owing to its upper-middle-class setting.

Lois and Clark: The New Adventures of Superman
Levine, D. J. (Creator). (1993). Burbank, CA: Warner Brothers Studios.

Characters and Brief Plot Summary
The legendary comic book hero, **Superman,** a.k.a. **Clark Kent,** has been updated in this modern-day television series. Although he still works for the Daily Planet newspaper, the 1990s series portrays a more intelligent, courageous, and yet still sexy **Lois Lane;** she is not only his girlfriend but his cohort, who shares in much of the detective work as they work together in an attempt to rid society of evil villains such as the notorious and unstoppable **Lex Luthor.**

Martin
Barnett, W. (Producer). (1992). You Go Boy Productions. Universal City, CA: Universal Studios.

Characters and Brief Plot Summary
This weekly comedy features standup comedian **Martin Lawrence** as a wisecracking radio talk show host recently turned television talk show producer. Among Martin's cohorts are his wife **Gina,** a marketing executive, **Pam,** Gina's friend who is always ridiculing Martin and whom Martin despises, and **Tommy** and Cole, friends of Martin, who are always dropping by the apartment of the newly married couple. The sitcom focuses on Martin's relationship with his wife and his friends, who all live and work

in New York. Martin is the outspoken, macho boyfriend/husband, whereas Gina is the loving girlfriend/wife who somehow manages to put up with Martin's sexist comments. The entire cast is African American with the exception of Shawn, the White handyman at Martin's previous radio station.

Martin also plays several minor characters, caricatures of both male and female stereotypes. The most notorious is **Sheneneh**, the loud, sexually aggressive bimbo who lives in Martin's apartment building and who apparently has the "hots" for Martin.

*The Mighty Morphin' Power Rangers
(original cast, 1993–1994)
Saban, H. (1993). New York: Saban Entertainment.

Characters
The **Power Rangers** are a multiracial group of five high school students who are picked by **Zordon,** a benevolent alien being, and his robot servant **Alpha 2,** to regularly save the Earth from destruction by the evil aliens, **Lord Zed, Rita Repulsa,** and their Earth-minions, the **Putties.** The teens are granted the ability to transform into karate-kicking superheroes, each with a specific color and a **dino-zord,** a robotic dinosaur that they summon to defeat the monsters that Rita creates.

In their daily lives, the Power Rangers are normal high school students who hang out together. They all happen to know karate as well. Although their superhero identities are a secret, at school they wear their Ranger colors anyway; for example, Trini (the Yellow Ranger) wears yellow, Kimberly (the Pink Ranger) wears pink, and Jason (the Red Ranger) wears red. **Jason** is the "leader" of the team, the one contacted by Zordon; he alerts the others of an impending battle. He is a White male who also runs the school's Karate Club. During the course of data collection, Jason was joined as leader by **Tommy** (the Green Ranger). Tommy, also white, is portrayed as "cute" (Kimberly has a crush on him). Unfortunately, Tommy is sometimes controlled by the evil Rita Repulsa. **Billy** (the Blue Ranger), another white male, is the "smart" one, always portrayed as slightly nerdy, working on some scientific gadget for the Rangers' secret hideout. **Zack** (the Black Ranger) is African American and runs the school's "Hip-Hop Dance Club." **Trini** (the Yellow Ranger) and **Kimberly** (the Pink Ranger) are the only females on the team. Trini is Asian American and runs the Volleyball Club; Kimberly is White and runs the Gardening Club. At school, there are two peripheral but ever-present characters who serve as the witless, bumbling school bullies; they taunt the Rangers and cause problems that need to be resolved by the end of an episode. They are named **Bulk** and **Skull,** both White; they cause trouble just because they are bad-tempered and stupid.

General Plot
The plots, which are nearly identical in each episode, are simple, with little development of motive or character. Rita sends a monster to kill the Rangers because they give her a hard time. The monsters and the Putties appear, everyone fights, the Rangers call in their dino-zords, the Rangers win, and the episode ends with a moral delivered by Tommy or Jason about the value of teamwork.

Notes on Stereotypes

While in their Rangers uniforms, the team fights the Putties and the monsters equally, male alongside female. But when they are portrayed as average high school students, gender stereotyping is rampant. The girls usually are portrayed with stereotypically female interests, like shopping, gardening, and boys, whereas the boys are more interested in fighting and are more cerebral and less emotionally preoccupied. But this gender stereotyping pales in light of the racial stereotyping in terms of the colors they wear: Zack wears black, Trini wears yellow, Kimberly wears pink.

Since the original cast was replaced in 1994 (after the end of our data collection periods), the colors have switched so that the African-American Ranger no longer wears black, and the Asian-American Ranger no longer wears yellow; however, gender roles remain highly stereotyped, and plot structure is still simple.

Sonic the Hedgehog (animated)

Bohbot Entertainment (Producer). (1993). Redwood City, CA: SEGA of America Inc.

Characters and Brief Plot Summary

Sonic is a hedgehog who lives on the planet Mobius. Sonic's main ability is a Tazmanian devil-like whirling that can propel him at high speeds through just about anything. He lives with his young friend, **Miles Tails,** a male fox with two tails that he whirls around propeller-style to fly. Together, Sonic and Miles outwit the evil **Dr. Robotnik** and his two mechanical henchmen, **Scratch,** a robot chicken and the smarter of the two, and **Grounder,** the "stupid one." Sometimes Sonic and Miles have the help of **Hacker,** a mole whose computer genius foils all the mechanics of Robotnik's schemes. Dr. Robotnik sets traps for Sonic or kidnaps Miles, but Sonic stops him from turning the planet into a huge, evil, robot factory.

Star Trek, The Next Generation

Roddenberry, G. (Executive Producer). (1986). California: Paramount Pictures.

Characters and Brief Plot Summary

Captain Jean-Luc Picard has taken over where James T. Kirk left off in the sci-fi 1960s TV show. He is captain of the Federation Starship U.S.S. Enterprise on a mission of scientific discovery through the galaxy. *The Next Generation* still features alien encounters, but the plots are more cerebral, dealing with the moral and ethical dilemmas of two worlds in contact, alongside the usual dangers of hostile natives. His humanoid support team includes **Dr. Beverly Crusher** and her son **Wesley, Second Officer William Riker, Deanna Troi,** the ship's counselor, and **Data,** the android who longs to be human. These main figures are White. The non-White crew include **Lieutenant Worf,** the ship's chief of security and a Klingon by birth, **Commander Geordi LaForge,** the ship's chief engineer, and **Guinan,** the ship's bartender.

*The Uncanny X-Men (animated)
Lee, S. (Author & Illustrator). (1963). New York: Marvel Entertainment Group.

Characters

During the project's data collection period, the X-Men, who have populated comic books since the 1960s, began to make their way into the mainstream through their popular television cartoon show. They are an army of multiracial male and female mutants. After being orphaned or exiled for their strange "gifts," they were taken under the direction and care of **Professor Xavier,** himself an outcast who has overcome the paralysis in his legs through development of his powerful telepathy. Professor X acts as a benevolent father figure, who trains his students (the X-Men) to control their powers; under his influence, the X-Men fight for peace and justice in a world where they are feared and despised by the very humans they protect and defend.

The major players are both male and female mutants. **Rogue** and **Storm** are central female action figures in the X-Men team. These women fight alongside the men with superhuman strength and specialized powers. (Rogue can drain the energy from anything she touches, and Storm can command the forces of nature.) These women rush to rescue their male colleagues as often as they need to be rescued themselves; both are highly developed characters through episodes that feature them. Storm is of royal African blood, which explains her serious, almost regal manner. Rogue had a Southern-belle upbringing; despite her coquettishness, she despairs because of her inability to ever touch anyone with love, lest she drain him of all life and thus destroy him. **Jubilee** and **Jean Grey** are less physically involved women than Rogue or Storm. Jubilee is the teenage mutant whose impulsive explosive powers are still "in-training." Jean Grey is Professor X's protege (and the first woman, also known as "Marvel Girl," in the original comic books series); she is a powerful telepath whose battleground is her mind, so she need not get her hands dirty physically fighting.

Of the male characters, there is **Cyclops,** a mutant whose ability to harness and redirect solar energy with his eyes gave him his name. Cyclops is a team leader, usually ordering the other, more undisciplined male X-Men around. He and Jean Grey are romantically involved and eventually get married, much to the despair of **Wolverine,** the rebel X-Man, who also "loves" Jean Grey. Wolverine's name comes from the deadly steel claws he obtained through a medical accident. He is unhappy with his powers and burdened with his place as an outcast in human society. He is less of a team player, preferring to be solitary, rash, and stubborn. He is also one of the strongest X-Men. The brilliant **Beast** is an admired member of the team, despite his brutish physical characteristics. Often found hanging upside down from the ceiling, his strength lies in his powers of incredible speed, agility, and acrobatic talents. **Gambit** is the Cajun mutant whose deck of magic cards and ability to gamble make him a roguish, but amiable character. Gambit's Southern charm and sense of humor are similar to Rogue's, and they carry on a playful flirtation throughout their episodes. **Morph's** specialty is his ability to transform, or "morph," into any other person or robot. In one episode, Morph is killed off; he later returns as an evil mutant.

On the side of evil are a shifting band of mutants who, for one reason or another, have lost faith in their eventual peace and acceptance in the world of humans. Every "good" X-Man is paired with an archvillain of the same gender and of similar physical and mental abilities. Even Professor X has his nemesis in **Magneto,** the leader

and most powerful of the evil mutants. A popular pairing is Wolverine's arch nemesis **Sabertooth**, a ferocious beastman whose animal-like powers almost defeat Wolverine
in every fight. **Juggernaut** is another popular villain, a man-machine of superhuman
strength and below-human intelligence, whereas **Blob,** another mutant of low intelligence, is so massive that he is virtually immovable and impenetrable. Foes of all mutants
alike are the **Sentinels,** an army of robots spawned by the anti-mutant paranoia that
Professor X has battled his entire life. The Sentinels are programmed by humans to
kill all mutants regardless of allegiance. The X-Men regularly face destruction at the
hands of these machines.

There are numerous other mutants, less central to the television show during the
project's data collection periods; among the mutants mentioned by the children were
the seductive and telepathic **Black Queen** and **White Queen**, both evil; **Bishop,**
Nightcrawler, and **Colossus,** all good; and **Archangel,** who has had both good and
bad phases.

General Plot
The episodes usually feature an X-Men character, delving into the person's history and how she or he became a mutant, then pairing the character up with an arch-
enemy and allowing the X-Men and the "bad guys" to "tag-team" themselves into a
battle that becomes a full-scale war between good and evil. Good triumphs, of course,
but not without a reminder, usually from the cerebral Professor Xavier, that the victory is only minor in the great scope of things; the X-Men have bigger battles to fight
in terms of being accepted as "different" in the human world, and in coming to self-
acceptance and awareness as mutants. There are several episodes in which Professor
X himself is in need of rescue from his team of mutants, and many episodes in which
alliances shift back and forth between good and evil, as one X-Man gives in to the
"evil within us all" and must be stopped by her or his more secure friends.

Notes on Stereotypes
This is the least stereotypical representation of persons of different gender and
race in our analysis of children's television shows. The X-Men have roughly equal
powers and roles. Although the women and most of the men have gorgeous bodies
outlined in Spandex costumes, each character is a distinctive personality with a complex history.

VIDEO GAMES (ALL ANIMATED)

Mortal Kombat II
Tobias, J., Boon, E. (Creators). (1993). San Diego, CA: Midway Games.

This game has minimal plot behind the fighting; the characters are given some
history as assassins or henchman of some evil warlord or another. The fighting is graphically bloody, and the settings are mystical, varying from exotic island-like locations
to dungeons. The players chose their "fighters" from a cast of sinister-looking men
and women, most dressed like ninjas. Each character in Mortal Kombat has a special
way to kill his or her opponent. At the end of the winning round, the screen flashes
the words "Finish him!" and the winner gets the opportunity to blow torch, flay

alive, or dismember the loser. The two boys who wrote stories based on Mortal Kombat featured the characters **Scorpion, Sub-Zero, Liu Kang,** and **Kano** (all men).

Sonic the Hedgehog
Bobbot Entertainment (Producer). (1993). Redwood City, CA: SEGA of America Inc.

Sonic started as a home game for the Nintendo. **Sonic** is a hedgehog of remarkable agility who dodges, jumps, and climbs his way through several levels of an elaborate maze going from level to level until he is "killed." He is sometimes accompanied by his friend **Miles "Tails."** The premise is that an evil scientist has turned all the fuzzy animals of the forest into dangerous robot-like creatures. Sonic "frees" these animals by jumping on them or rolling into them, after which they turn back into bunnies or turtles.

Street Fighter
Capcom Games (Producer). (1991). Sunnyvale, CA: Capcom.

Street Fighter is less gory than Mortal Kombat. (There is even a warning of sorts in the display before the game starts: "life-like violence-mild.") The premise for the fighting is in the title: These fights are more like boxing matches than vendettas or revenge fights. The settings range from old temple ruins with cracking Buddhas, to barbed-wire fight rings on a dirty city street. Almost always, there are bystanders depicted, both males and females of various ages, who are watching and cheering the fighters on or wandering through the scene. The players have the opportunity to chose male or female characters with which to fight. Collectively, the six boys who wrote stories based on Street Fighter featured the characters **Chun-Li** (a woman), **Ken, Ryu, Guile, M. Bison, Vega, E. Honda, Sagit,** and **Zangif.**

Note: More boys chose to write stories featuring characters from Street Fighter than characters from Mortal Kombat. The two boys who wrote about Mortal Kombat also wrote about Street Fighter. In the stories of three boys, Chun Li, a woman, was a principal fighter. In the Berkeley campus arcade where Larsen and Shea observed the games being played on three different afternoons, they saw more players choose a female fighter in Street Fighter—Chun Li—than did so in Mortal Kombat.

The arcade itself contained approximately the same number of Mortal Kombat games as Street Fighter games. Both games seemed equally popular among the approximately 16- to 21-year-old students in the arcade (30–40 present on each visit, all males). An especially good player would attract a flock of admirers huddled around the screen. The X-Men game, with its inferior graphics and tame violence, was ignored.

Appendix C

▼ ▼ ▼

ANNOTATED LIST OF FIGURES FROM THE GREEK MYTHS

The following annotated list includes, in bold, the names of the major gods and goddesses referred to in this book. The entries are organized alphabetically by the figures' Roman names, which were used more often by Kristin's children than were the Greek names. (The Greek names are given in parentheses.) Individual entries include the names, also in bold, of family members and other creatures associated with the god or goddess by Kristin's children. Certain figures were interesting in and of themselves, outside any familial or narrative relationship to the gods and goddesses, and are listed separately.

APOLLO (APOLLO): The god of light, music, and reason. He is the son of Jupiter (Zeus) and Leto and twin brother to Diana (Artemis).

BELLEROPHON: A mortal and a fine horse tamer. He tamed **Pegasus,** the winged horse and, on this flying horse, he slew the **Chimera,** a fire-breathing beast who was part lion, part goat, and part serpent. Bellerphon tried to ride to Olympus, but he fell to the ground and, thus, wandered the Earth for the rest of his days as a lame beggar.

CERES (Demeter): The goddess of the harvest. As a result of her grief when Pluto (Hades) stole her daughter, **Proserpine** (Persephone), she plunged the Earth into a wintry sleep so that none of the crops would grow. To appease her, Jupiter (Zeus) made his brother give her back to her mother for half the year, and so the Earth rejoices and spring and summer bring harvests to the mortals.

CUPID (EROS): The mischievous son of Venus (Aphrodite), who shoots his arrows of love into unwitting mortals and immortals for the fun of it. He had a taste of his own medicine one day when he accidentally wounded himself with his own arrow and fell in love with the beautiful Earthly maiden, **Psyche.** (The children in Kristin's classroom gave Cupid and Psyche two children, **Callisto** and **Bliss.**)

HERACLES (HERCULES): The son of Jupiter (Zeus), half god and half mortal. He is the strongest man on Earth. He performed the 12 impossible tasks set forth by the King of Mycenae.

This annotated list of Greek beings was prepared by Gwen Larsen.

Juno (HERA): The sister Jupiter chose to marry. She is known for being insanely jealous, very powerful, and vindictive; she does horrible things to the mortals with whom Jupiter has affairs.

JUPITER (ZEUS): Deemed the father of all the gods and goddesses in the pantheon. The most powerful god of them all, he is the god of thunder and lightening and often is pictured with a thunderbolt in his hand. He is well known for his lechery with women, both mortal and immortal. He tricked his father into throwing up his swallowed brothers and sisters, who rule beside him. His siblings include: Juno (Hera), also his wife, Ceres (Demeter), Neptune (Poseidon), Vesta (Hestia), and Pluto (Hades).

MARS (ARES): The god of war and, also, son of Jupiter (Zeus) and Juno (Hera). He is bold, reckless, and merciless. He is disliked by most of the gods, especially his half-sister, Minerva (Athena).

MERCURY (HERMES): The god of shepherds, travelers, thieves, and all those who live by their wits. He is the most mischievous god of them all. He is the son of Jupiter (Zeus) and another titan, Maia, and only escaped Juno's wrath by tricking a herd of cows to cover his footprints. Mercury is the god with winged feet, who guides the dead down to the underworld.

MINERVA (ATHENA): The goddess of wisdom and the favorite child of Jupiter (Zeus), since she sprang, fully grown, out of his skull. She watches over the righteous and favors the just armies in battles. She is accompanied by Nike, the spirit of victory. Minerva is the goddess who was angered by **Arachne**, the boastful and disrespectful mortal girl who claimed to weave better then Minerva. In a contest Arachne made fun of the gods and was turned into a spider for her attitude.

MINOTAUR: A monster—half bull and half man—who ate nothing but humans until he was slain by the mortal hero Theseus.

NARCISSUS: A beautiful youth who fell in love with his own image; he wasted away pining after himself.

PLUTO (HADES): The god of the underworld, who presides over mortals' souls, both good and evil. He is the one who stole the goddess Proserpine (Persephone) from her mother Demeter (Ceres), the goddess of the harvest.

VENUS (APHRODITE): The only goddess who is not related in some way to Jupiter (Zeus). She simply appeared one day, floating on a clam shell in the sea and was deemed the beautiful goddess of love. She is attended by the Three Graces, also goddesses of beauty. She admires Mars (Ares), the reckless and handsome god of war, but is married to Vulcan (Hephaestus), who makes her jewelry.

VULCAN (HEPHAESTUS): The son of Jupiter (Zeus) and Juno (Hera) and the god of smiths and fire. He works in the forges making magical weapons and jewels. He is gentle and peace loving; he even dared try to calm his father who crippled him for life for getting in his way. To apologize, Jupiter gave him a beautiful goddess for a wife, Venus (Aphrodite).

Notes
▼ ▼ ▼

CHAPTER 1

1. I am not using the word *ideology* pejoratively to refer to a kind of "false consciousness" (Williams, 1983, p. 156). Rather, I am using it to refer to a "set of ideas" that arise from a particular historical and material circumstance (p. 156). It is this latter meaning that underlies Bakhtin's use of the term. There is no meaning outside some governing ideology. Thus the Bakhtinian sense of *ideology* is similar to that of the poststructuralist's *discourse*.

2. Although Vygotsky defined the creation of an imaginary situation as the essence of play, he saw young children's play (e.g., with its implicit rules about how mothers and babies behave) as leading to older children's and adults' games (e.g., with their explicit rules about how chess pieces can be moved). This project, with its emphasis on children's play with cultural expectations, does not fit comfortably within such a trajectory. As Franklin (1983) notes, given that play involves improvisation based on, not simply reproduction of, everyday life—that play is "creative rather than codified"—it "would seem to have much more in common with mythmaking, literary works, and even scientific theory-building than with conventionalized rule-governed games" (p. 217).

3. In contemporary times, the social worlds that children interactively construct with other children—their "folk" worlds, so to speak—are heavily influenced by commercial culture (Sutton-Smith, 1975). Indeed, the folklorist Sylvia Grider (1981) has coined a term for children's oral retellings of stories from the commercial media: "media narraforms." Although Grider is referring specifically to stories about the supernatural, her description of the qualities of these narraforms—their tendency to be communally and collaboratively performed, their descriptive stringing of episodes, their minimal development of characters—would apply also to children's retold superhero stories. In this project, the commercial media are viewed as providing semiotic material for children's construction of their shared symbols and stories, that is, for their construction of an unofficial (child-governed) social world.

4. Buckingham (1993) demonstrated how children used talk about the media to distance themselves from popular culture and, simultaneously, to affiliate themselves with the official school world. In his study of 7- to 12-year-old British children's talk about television, older, middle-class children (in contrast to working-class children) tended to confidently display their critiques of television shows. In Buckingham's words, "to commit yourself to liking anything—with

the exception of documentaries . . . —would be to run the risk of aligning your-self with the mass of viewers who are stupid enough" to accept such material (p. 72). Buckingham argues that this behavior was not related in any direct way to social class but, rather, to complex relationships between school, home, and peer cultures; for middle-class children, in the context of what seemed to be an "educational" discussion, the appropriate behavior was to align oneself with the school and the home against popular culture. This is consistent with anthropo-logical studies that suggest that, although children from all sociocultural back-grounds participate in the unofficial school sphere, the intensity of that work is influenced by societal structures, including families' perceptions about the ulti-mate worth of school (D'Amato, 1987, 1988; Ogbu, 1987).

In Kristin's class, however, social class and race were interrelated. Moreover, there was clear interplay between participation in ethnic and popular cultures. For example, the African-American children tended to be very knowledgeable about certain media productions that featured African-American actors (although they thought the actor Wesley Snipes in *Jungle Fever* was named "Spike Lee"). Similar associations between children's participation in common and ethnic cul-ture have been noted by others (e.g., Lee, 1995; Smitherman, 1986). Thus, I will offer no conclusions about class-related patterns in children's media use; but I will offer insights into the social and ideological dynamics that undergirded particu-lar children's social and authorial actions in particular contexts.

5. In our society, by age three or four, children are aware of racial differences (Ramsey, 1987). However, in Derman-Sparks' words (1995, p. 19), "bias [does not] come from noticing differences, [but] rather than from institutional and interpersonal behaviors that rank differences for economic, political, and social purposes." In their preschool and kindergarten years, children seem more socially concerned with gender than race in choosing playmates in racially diverse school settings. Moreover, they tend to play with other children who are situated phys-ically close to them (Fishbein & Imai, 1993; Holmes, 1995). But as they grow older, racial differences increasingly influence children's choices (Finkelstein & Haskins, 1983; Schofield, 1979).

Many factors influence children's crossing of both gender and racial bound-aries in their play and friendship patterns, among them, the racial composition of the school and the classroom (Hallinan & Smith, 1985), gender differences in activity preferences (e.g., boys' preferences for more inclusive team games [Russell, 1986]), cultural differences in interactional styles (Corsaro & Rosier, 1992), and variations in classroom instructional designs (e.g., an emphasis on potentially more inclusive cooperative learning groups as opposed to more hier-archical individually competitive tasks [Slavin, 1983]). It should be noted, how-ever, that children's preferences for playing with those they view as like them-selves, those with whom they may feel most comfortable, does not automatically imply that they have hostility for those outside their groups. And, whatever chil-dren's behavior in unofficial contexts, in official ones, it is the responsibility of educators to meet "the national goal of preparing all children for first- not sec-ond-class citizenship in a multicultural, multiracial democracy" (Perry & Fraser,

1993, p. 17). The concern in this book is not with children's interpersonal relationships per se but with their understanding of the social and political (i.e., power) consequences of constructed words and, more particularly, of stories.

6. Vygotsky (1978) did view learning to play as a critically important step in children's literacy development. As already discussed, in imaginary play children learn to assume more deliberate control over themselves and their environment: They do not bow to the literal meaning of actions and objects but, rather, use their own volition to imbue actions and objects with new meanings. In this way, writing—as the deliberate manipulation of meaning—builds on play's symbolic and communicative functions. Writing serves these functions through more abstract means: It involves using, not objects and actions, but one symbol system (graphic marks) to represent another system (oral language), which itself represents meanings. Although Vygotsky did discuss the developmental value of play, he did not discuss the particular value of players' *social* decision making (i.e., about who plays what role) and any subsequent ideological conflicts for written language growth.

7. The children's minimal use of print per se in "literacy" events was consistent with that of other observed children (e.g., Dyson, 1981, 1989a,b). Children tend to depend on other available symbolic media (e.g., drawing and/or speech) to accomplish their representational, reflective, and social ends. Over time, functional shifts occur, and the written medium itself realizes more of child authors' intentions. Accomplishing such functional shifts in media narraforms may be particularly challenging, since much of the original meaning of those stories is conveyed through background music and visual effects (Grider, 1981).

8. The notion of tracing relational appropriations and transformations was informed by the work of Babcock (1993) and Tsing (1993). Both are scholars concerned with the interplay of gender, culture, and story. And both have studied, in Tsing's (1993, p. 101) words, how, "in writing [or, in Babcock's case, pottery], women incorporate dominant conventions at the same time as they invert them, resist them, and transform them."

CHAPTER 2

1. Abrahams (1969, p. 97) includes a 1938 citation of the Macy's chant and presents the chant itself as follows:

> I won't go to Macy's anymore, more, more,
> There's a big fat policeman at the door, door, door,
> He takes me by the collar, and makes me pay a dollar.
> So I won't go to Macy's anymore, more, more.

2. It is important to note that Sammy was a temporarily unattached child, not a rejected (Asher & Coie, 1990) or "omega" one (Garnica, 1981). As a contrasting case, here I briefly introduce Tamara.

Tamara was a slight, blue-eyed blonde. Like other children in the class (including Sammy and Tina), she was from a low-income family and, also like others, she struggled with the official school agenda. However, she seemed to have a set role outside the children's play groups. Her social distance may have been aggravated by her stylistic distance. Instead of the usual variants of blue jeans and t-shirts, Tamara wore tired dresses with raggedy sleeves and uneven hems. No beat-up sneakers for her, but old patent-leather shoes worn with no socks. Her appearance was considered "ugly" by some children, and her social awkwardness and lack of knowledge about popular culture undoubtedly added to her isolation. Despite the efforts of Kristin to engineer cooperative learning groups throughout the day—and the efforts of Sarah's mom, who encouraged Sarah and her friends to play with Tamara, she remained on the outside.

Tamara did not return in the third grade. Lettrice, writing in her journal on the topic of prejudice, recalled second-grader Tamara's social place in the classroom:

> Here is something that everybody should have on their papers [about prejudice] that was here in second grade that should know what I am going to write. Do you know that when Tamara was here everybody hated her and I really hated her and once I had to work with her and everybody teased me and I got my feelings hurt and when LaShonda was here she loved to beat up on Tamara and in 1994 Tamara didn't come to our school anymore. *(Spelling corrected for ease of reading.)*

Tamara did have a hidden strength however. Near the end of school year, she volunteered for Author's Theater. She had no written story, but she told a well-structured tale about a family who goes on a picnic, becomes separated, and, in the end, joyously reunites. Tina, Holly, and Liliana, chosen as sisters, "had fun," as Tina said, acting out the involving story, and Tamara was warmly praised by all concerned.

3. Like Tamara, Patrick was another child who challenged any simplistic rendering of the children's social world into neat divisions of gender, race, or class. Patrick, who was European American, had attended the school since kindergarten. Although he was not allowed to watch superhero stories, he happily joined in on any such dramatic play. He struggled with reading and writing, but he was not resistant to those tasks.

Patrick was not a social isolate, like Tamara. He was a very quiet child, though. He did not participate in the competitive verbal gaming that occupied many of the boys (e.g., who knew the most about popular superhero figures, who could draw the best, who could, if need be, beat up whom). And he seemed to like Sammy very much, another child who enjoyed dramatic play and early on displayed no talent for verbal gaming. Although Sammy never considered Patrick his best friend (Aloyse would come to fill that role), the two were good companions. And, on the last day of third grade, when Patrick wrote in his journal about leaving his old K–3 school, the only child he mentioned was Sammy, whom, he said, he would miss.

4. Consistent with both my own earlier studies (especially Dyson, 1989a,b) and, more broadly, with Vygotskian theory (Vygotsky, 1987), the children's understandings of the functional possibilities for writing shifted over time. For example, as already noted, initially many children used writing primarily as a ticket to play; they actually wrote very little. Participation in composing activities and, more particularly, in their organized social relations, made salient new functional possibilities for writing or, to rephrase, motivated children to attend to their written texts in new ways.

5. A number of researchers have documented the tendency of young boys in particular in our society—whatever their social class or ethnic background—to appropriate material from popular culture for their oral and written stories (e.g., Nicolopoulou, Scales, & Weintraub, 1994; Paley, 1984; Sutton-Smith, 1975).

6. Penny, who was African American and in her thirties, was a school instructional aide, who assisted Kristin in the mornings during the second grade. Penny was a particularly artful and dramatic oral reader; she often read poems for the children to act out.

7. Although sometimes children did suspect or even notice that someone had not actually *written* a story, no one criticized anyone on this score. Makeda once read a long, unwritten, and very involving and involved story about "five girls and three dogs [played by boys]" who went out for a walk and were caught in a tornado, among other unfolding disasters. When Kristin asked her if she was near the end, Makeda replied, "Not yet ... there's more on the back," and she turned over her invisible story and kept reading.

Holly seemed quite surprised by this comment and remarked, "I thought you didn't really have no writing. But you did."

"Yes," said Makeda. And no one said anything else.

8. There are possible cultural influences on the observed oral storytelling during Author's Theater. With the exception of Tamara (discussed earlier), no European-American child engaged in extensive oral elaboration of a text—even when, as in Kevin's Author's Theater event (presented in this chapter), Kristin explicitly encouraged a child to do so. Educational ethnographers and sociolinguists have documented that middle-class children in our society may be socialized into a "print-reliant approach to knowledge, entertainment, mental stimulation, and everyday social interactions and transactions" (Schieffelin & Cochran-Smith, 1984, p. 5). Others have documented the language traditions of African-American communities, which traditions include oral and stylized elaborations of written texts, for example, in church services (e.g., Davis, 1985; Foster, 1992; Heath, 1983; Moss, 1994; Smitherman, 1977).

9. Despite Splinter's status as the master of the ninjas, Splinter was not a coveted role (i.e., it was not a role children asked for first). Splinter is depicted as much older and frailer than the fun-loving, physically lively ninja turtles; in

fact, in the ninja turtle film, Splinter is a victim in need of saving. In a related way, Professor Xavier, the leader of the X-Men, was not a popular role—in fact, he was rarely included as a central character in a child's story. The professor's mutant powers do not involve physical strength but telepathy. He too is sometimes in need of rescuing. The desired roles in superhero stories were those involving the most action—and the most physically experienced power.

10. Both boys and girls were aware of the most popular characters, especially those shown on television (X-Men and, in the third grade, Power Rangers). Extensive knowledge of these characters was class- and, thus, race-related, at least in part because the middle-class parents generally did not encourage this form of entertainment (as reported by children and verified in parent interactions by Kristin).

11. The performative quality of being tough was earlier documented at this site (Dyson, 1993). This observed quality is consistent with the observations of James (1993) on British playgrounds of 3- to 9-year-old children. For a detailed sociolinguistic analysis of the performative qualities of talking tough through forms of conversational storytelling, see Goodwin (1990), who studied preadolescents in an urban Black neighborhood. Both James and Goodwin see verbal challenges and counterchallenges as male pursuits; in this class, this was not always the case, as Tina illustrates.

12. In her valuing of both nurturing and being tough and in her sense of her own physical possibilities and vulnerabilities, Tina defied simplistic, dualistic gender relations in ways characteristic of other urban, working-class girls (e.g., Anyon, 1984; Connell, Ashenden, Kessler, & Dowsett, 1982; Fordham, 1994; Miller, 1982). Some playground observers (particularly British observers, like Grugeon [1993] and the Opies [e.g., 1959]) illustrate how—outside the confines of the classroom—young girls can be decidedly unladylike; even their chanting, rhyming, and clapping can become tools for cooperatively constructed but decidedly rowdy and sometimes raw talk about teachers, boys, and school itself.

13. In this, the spring of the Rodney King episode in Los Angeles, racism and racial tensions were both on display, and this display may have contributed to the reported voicing of racial tensions. However, the East Bay teacher study group, of which Kristin was a member, reported that many primary school children reveal their sensitivity to racial, ethnic, and gender divisions in their classrooms and, moreover, voice a sense of being in competition with children in other groups for classroom attention and affection (Dyson, 1997).

14. Tina had not yet been retained, nor was she during the course of this study. Although the principal felt it might be best to do so, Tina's mother did not want her child retained.

15. The children had journals, in which they might choose to record their daily experiences and feelings and in which they sometimes were assigned to record responses to certain class topics and experiences (e.g., the topic of prejudice, the experience of visiting Chinatown). Journal writing took place separately from the writing that occurred during the formal composing period.

CHAPTER 3

1. As the folklorist Rosemary Zumwalt notes, children may play with cultural ideals in their texts, even as their own "actions—both in the performance of the folklore [or other texts] and in their daily lives—show me how it *really* is" (1995, pp. 39–40, building on Malinowski, 1922). In displaying stereotypical male–female relations, Sammy and other children played with cultural ideals; and the tension between these ideals and their daily realities as boys-and-girls together revealed "an area of cultural stress, of shifting cultural values" in the society as a whole (Zumwalt, 1995, p. 40).

2. George Lewis argues that April is "probably the most fully realized [liberated female figure in popular culture]" (1991, p. 39). The vision of April put forward by Lewis—an adult male sociologist—differs strikingly from that which emerged in the children's talk, stories, and play. Their April was *not* liberated. She was a "cute" girl who often "needed some help." Carlsson-Paige and Levin (1991) report similar teacher observations of children's enactments of April. This discrepancy in visions suggests the limits of analyses of the nature and influence of "kid heroes," in Lewis' words (p. 31), when those analyses have little to do with "kids" themselves.

3. Lawrence's regular school playmates were African American and often included both girls and boys. Lawrence was making a specific statement about a specific story, and he seemed genuinely startled by the children's objections to his claim that April had to be White. Lawrence, I should add, did hear those objections. He offered Monique, a dark-skinned African-American child, the role of April in his next ninja production. Unfortunately, Lawrence never actually brought that text to the classroom stage.

4. In her illuminating study of Australian school children's use of television in their social interaction and play, Patricia Palmer (1986) reported that all superhero "good guys" were boys; "baddies" were imagined or played by younger sisters and girls.

5. The ninja turtles are more grown up superheroes than the ninja brothers. Perhaps for this reason, Sammy's ninja turtle stories, like his second-grade "X-Men" ones, were more straightforward encounters between the good guys and the bad guys.

6. The inherently problematic nature of a child superhero may have accounted for the girls' lack of interest in Jubilee, an X-Men girl with the power to emit plasma energy from her fingertips—but a child who has to be rescued even more often than Storm does. (Interestingly, a major source of varied forms of weakness displayed by X-Men characters lies in their childhood traumas. Indeed, for most X-Men, as for Jubilee, the approach of adolescence triggered the emergence of their mutant characteristics, which were a source of humiliation and discrimination as well as of power.)

7. In the third grade, Kristin set a nine-person limit on all Author's Theater performances. Large casts were difficult for children to control and, moreover, left few children to serve as an audience.

CHAPTER 4

1. In this book, consciousness about human relations—about the construction of stories—is both manifested in and furthered by "material expression (in the ideological material of word, a sign, drawing, colors, musical sound, etc.)" (Volosinov, 1973, p. 90). It is not a quality of individual mind but of social response, of authorial action. When fully expressed in the symbols and organizational structures of a particular life, consciousness becomes a social force in the world—and it also "exerts a powerful, reverse influence on experience; it begins to tie [an individual's] inner life together, giving it more definite and lasting expression" (p. 90). This reverse influence is evident in this chapter, particularly in the case of Tina; her successful public storytelling is dialectically linked with a stronger, more forthcoming public stance about gender roles.

2. The concept of "border" is based on the research of Fredrik Barth (1969). He studied how interaction across ethnic group boundaries may strengthen, rather than weaken, those boundaries. Barth's work influenced Barrie Thorne (1993). She developed the term "sexual borderwork": boys and girls can strengthen, rather than reduce, their sense of difference through particular kinds of interactions (e.g., boy–girl chase games, teasing when gender expectations are violated). The same phenomenon is described as "category-maintenance work" by Bronwyn Davies (1989).

3. Vygotsky described thoughts "unembodied in words" as vague, slippery "shadows" (1962, p. 153). Those shadows are not so much expressed as "completed" in words, that is, given a more definitive shape (1987, p. 250). Words thus are a dynamic unity of thinking and speech and the "key to the nature of human consciousness" (1962, p. 153).

In contrast, Bakhtin does not stress the completion of thoughts in spoken or written words. Rather, he stresses the completion of a speaking turn, of an utterance—that moment when the floor is relinquished to the other (Bakhtin, 1986, p. 72). An utterance can be as modest as an oral rejoinder in casual conversation or as bold as a published philosophical treatise. In any case, the key to human consciousness is the entrance of that utterance into a responsive (if tension-filled) relationship with others.

This distinction between completing words (i.e., a written text) and completing an utterance (i.e., the entire composing turn) is important herein. This distinction makes clear the ideological struggles facing Holly and Tina as they worked to bring their texts (completed or not) to the public's attention.

4. Holly designated as good kids Radha, Kevin, Seth, Liliana, Sarah, and Tina (who was sitting next to her). Holly designated as bad Patrick, James, and Monique. Like Holly, the children in this classroom tended to identify mainly European-American children as "good" or "peaceful," to use Kristin's term. (She sometimes asked if anyone had noticed someone being especially "peaceful" in their actions that day.) Kristin was aware of the children's apparent perceptions and talked with them about the difference between being "peaceful" and being "quiet."

The children's views may have been owing in part to schools' traditional valuing of displayed silence and compliance and because, culturally, middle-class European-American children—when compared to working-class African-American or Latino children—tend to seem quieter in their interactions with each other, engaging in fewer teasing and challenging behaviors (Heath, 1983; Rizzo & Corsaro, 1991; Smitherman, 1977). However, Holly's identified misbehavers—James, Patrick, and Monique—were all unusually quiet children (in my view and Kristin's), as quiet if not quieter than any of the children designated as behaving themselves. Perhaps those designated as behaving had acquired the official and unofficial status that made them particularly visible when one was looking for the usual "good" suspects.

5. Talk that seems "off task" can be a social byproduct of children's academic work and, potentially, a catalyst for that work. For a discussion of this potential, see "The Value of 'Time Off Task': Young Children's Spontaneous Talk and Deliberate Text" (Dyson, 1987).

CHAPTER 5

1. Contemporary children may learn about folk characters, as well as newly originated characters, through the television, film, and video (Grider, 1981; Sutton-Smith, 1975; Sutton-Smith, Mechling, Johnson, & McMahon, 1995; Tucker, 1992). Moreover, face-to-face folkloric processes may occur with commercial as well as folk material; that is, children may use cultural material, whatever its origin, to "work through and sustain their common tastes and identities" (Laba, 1986, p. 11; see also Spigel & Jenkins, 1991). Further, although the particular content of popular superhero stories may be faddish, like traditional folk tales, the stories involve magical transformations of characters (e.g., troubled adolescents become X-Men, suburban teenagers become Power Rangers, tiny turtles become adult-sized ninjas). Contemporary transformations, however, may involve teams, rather than singular heroes (Benton, 1993; Lewis, 1991).

2. Mukerji and Schudson (1991) have discussed the recent legitimation of the scholarly study of popular culture. In their words:

> As evidence grows that "authentic" folk traditions often have metropolitan or elite roots and that mass culture often is "authentically" incorporated into ordinary people's everyday lives, it becomes hazardous to make an invidious distinction between popular culture and high culture or a rigid separation of authentic, people-generated "folk" culture from unauthentic and degraded, commercially borne "mass" culture. (p. 3)

For extended illustrations of the "folklore-popular culture continuum," see Narvaez and Laba (1986).

3. During this discussion, Jonathan, whose Chinese heritage had not seemed salient in this class, volunteered his paternal grandmother as a potential classroom

visitor and resource about Chinatown. Moreover, Jonathan displayed his own knowledge about his Chinese heritage. He explained to the class that, "when the Chinese came to America they were sort of poor, and they were looking for a better life. And maybe they got sort of sick of the American life, and they wanted to go back home. But, a lot of times, they didn't have enough money to, to go back to China. So maybe they just built something like China up there [in Oakland]."

4. Although Sarah explicitly identified books as the source for her Nancy Drew stories, the character of Nancy Drew has also been featured in films and television. Similarly, Jonathan identified books as the source for his long story (told mainly through pictures) about the land of Narnia, but C.S. Lewis' tales have also been public television productions. Consistent with the comments in Note 2, there are multiple versions of stories available in multiple media.

5. When symbolic material from adult or popular culture is appropriated by children, changes occur that reflect children's attitudes and concerns. As McDowell, a folklorist, comments, "the child (and by extension, the human being) projected by this paradigm [of appropriation] is a much more interesting figure, one immersed in real-life contingencies, and not a mere cipher in a superorganic device" (1995, p. 62). This paradigm, illustrated by the work of many child folklorists (see especially Tucker, 1992, 1995), is consistent with that undergirding contemporary cultural studies (see especially Willis, 1990).

6. In June, four months after her last completed Aladdin story, Tina began another one. In this never-finished story, Aladdin is even more upset about being called a "street rat," and, moreover, the perpetrators of that act are named:

> There was a boy and his name was Aladdin
> and the rich called him a street rat
> and he creid [cried] and ran home
> and he cird to uboo the monkey.

7. For Tina, sharing pizza may have had a more immediate connection with friendship. Her good friend Makeda lived above a pizza parlor.

8. Since the third graders' stories were longer than they had been in the second grade, and since Author's Theater remained a popular activity, the children now had to sign up for an Author's Theater turn. For this reason, there could be a delay of a couple of weeks between text composing and performance, depending on whether or not a child chose to present their most recent story or an older one. For Tina, the delay could be longer, because of her frequent absences.

9. Typically, the children only revised the texts that they had chosen for publication. Kristin structured individual teacher–child and peer conferences on those texts, and, in some cases, children took their chosen texts home for parental help as well. The children corrected their texts for spelling and punctuation and, also, for sentence sense and plot clarity, sometimes adding sentences to explain character motivation. Outside the social structures provided for the publication activity, the children rarely revised.

10. Rosaldo, Lavie, and Narayan (1993) put forward a concept of originality that stresses just this process of selecting from and recombining culturally available meanings.

CHAPTER 6

1. The children's play was based on two popular movies, *Jaws* (Zanuck & Spielberg, 1975) and *Jurassic Park* (Kennedy, Molen, & Spielberg, 1993). In this play, the girls played horrified innocents, running from violent creatures.

2. *Star Trek: The Next Generation* (Roddenberry, 1986) and *Star Wars* (Kurtz & Lucas, 1977) are popular productions that are sometimes defended as a kind of "ersatz high culture" (Jenkins, 1992, p. 22). As Jenkins discusses, communities of adult fans have been generated and sustained by social talk about the symbolic material of these productions, particularly those episodes or scenes with serious themes and multilayered meanings. For this reason, these shows may be less apt to garner adult criticism than those shows that appeal primarily to communities of child fans.

3. Both Tina and Makeda seemed to view calling on their relationship to bigger and older peers (not bigger and older adults) as a part of sticking up for themselves. Thomas figured in differential ways into each child's way of doing this. Once Tina and Makeda had a particularly angry confrontation. After a collaborative science activity in which they were jointly drawing a fresh water scene, each child wrote her name on the drawing. However, Tina wrote "by Tina" instead of just "Tina," which made Makeda angry. Makeda saw Tina as marking her ownership of the whole drawing. Tina saw this as unreasonable "and so I told her to shut up." Each girl complained about the other to her girlfriends. In the midst of complaining to me, Tina reported that Makeda "said she gonna beat me up when Thomas wasn't here ... cause Thomas my cousin, and my mom told him to watch after me so that's why he ... say [to Makeda] ... 'I'll hurt you before you can even touch her.'" As was their pattern, however, Tina and Makeda made up the next day, joining each other for rounds of tricks on the metal bars. (Two weeks later, some older neighborhood boys jumped Thomas on his way to school and beat him up. The word among the children was that Makeda had arranged this for unspecified reasons.)

4. During the 1993–1994 television season, the Saturday morning *X-Men* cartoon did have a subplot in which the future death of all X-Men figured. Indeed, in one scene, the gravestones of the central X-Men characters were shown one-by-one under a darkened sky, as slow, mournful music emphasized the somber mood. A character from the future visited the present in order to prevent the sequence of events that led to that disastrous outcome. (He was, of course, successful.)

5. The very first documented objection to fighting was made by Johnetta in the second grade, who complained about Sammy's very brief X-Men story (see

Chapter 3). As an actor and player, Johnetta had not gotten to do "nothing good like talking . . . but we just fighted through the whole thing." However, Johnetta did watch X-Men, and she actively sought roles in superhero stories. In the third grade, objections to fighting became more frequent, more explicitly linked to textual detail (i.e., to the sense of the plot and the motivation of the characters), and, also, to the objectors' social affiliation (i.e., Melissa, Susan, Sarah, and Jonathan agreed with each other).

6. Lena, an African immigrant, was a new girl in the third grade. Initially, she played exclusively with the African-American girls. By the end of the year, Lena and, also, Liliana, were floaters; that is, they moved between the two major groups of girls (i.e., sometimes each girl played with Sarah, Melissa, Susan, and, when she wasn't playing with the boys, Lynn; sometimes each played with Tina, Makeda, Rhonda, and Lettrice). Still, Lena did not join the children on the rug writing about the Greek myths, and those children did not include Lena's character (Persephone) in the family portraits.

7. The inclusion of Radha, as Jupiter, among the family portraits is interesting. Radha, like Lena and Liliana, was a floater with no consistent social group, although his social circle was wider. For example, in the second grade, he had been the only child of color who had regularly sat with Seth and Jonathan; although no girl ever sat with these boys, Radha himself sometimes sat with groups of girls from diverse backgrounds. In the third grade, he talked and wrote about superheroes and played football on the playground, but he also often joined Jonathan, Patrick, James, Lynn, Sarah, Melissa, and Susan for dramatic play (especially for the games involving sharks and dinosaurs). Perhaps his longtime association with the children writing about Greek gods contributed to his inclusion, as may have the very fact that Jupiter was such a dominant figure in the Greek myths read to, and appropriated by, the children. The children referred to Jupiter as the father, the boss, and the king.

8. Sarah and Susan had earlier written an original superhero drama in which the powerful action never materialized on the paper. Inspired by a class unit on weaving, the girls decided to devise female superheroes named Weaving Woman and Weaver. However, in Sarah's words, they "never got to the part" where the women become heroes. Instead, Sarah and Susan wrote a detailed family epic in which the weaving women weave wonderful clothes, go to parties, get married, have babies, die, and then have their weaving responsibilities taken over by their children, and so on.

9. Since the completion of this project, "Hercules" has become the lead character in a television adventure show.

10. The preceding year, in the second grade, Sammy's written texts had become more coherent and detailed, as he had worked to please his peers through—and, moreover, to gain their company in—his Author's Theater performances. In the third grade, though, Sammy had to wait longer between Author's Theater turns (see Note 7, Chapter 5). In the long wait to present his "done" story, the concentration required to keep writing—to plan, encode, and

monitor his next written text—seemed to dissipate. When he *collaborated* on his writing, however, he did attend to it, as will be illustrated. In addition to his collaboration with Patrick, Sammy wrote with Radha and with Thomas.

11. The discussion of Sammy's and Patrick's Power Rangers story preceded the even more inclusive and complex one of Tina's story about Emily and Bebe (see Chapter 5). Unlike in that latter discussion, the authors—Patrick and Sammy— were quiet, although attentive, throughout the discussion, perhaps because the discussion was not so much about *their* story as about stories in general.

Nonetheless, as was characteristic of Sammy, his subsequent text actions were at least consistent with the tenor of the discussion. In Sammy's next and last superhero story of the school year, written alongside Thomas, he included action other than fighting, wrote dialogue as part of the fight scene, and spontaneously revised his text to clarify plot sequence and characters' feelings (although minimal, the deliberate inclusion of emotional motivations and consequences seems significant). These are all written actions consistent with articulated community values.

> 2:00 [time show will come on television]
> Once upon a time there were Power Rangers. Their names were Jason, Kimberly, Tommy, and Trini. The bad guys' names were Rita and Godar. The Power Rangers were eating ice cream. Then Zordon had beeped their watch. And Zordon said, "The bad guys is destroying [the world]."
> Morphin' time! They were Power Rangers. Jason said, "We need Dinosaur Power now!" The Dinosaur Power came. They started to fight the bad guys. Rita said, "Make the bad guys grow." The bad guys grow. Jason said, "We need Tommy." Tommy came. Tommy said, "Dragon sword!" His Dinosaur came and help[ed] the Power Rangers. They were winning.
> Tommy['s] Dinosaur Power <u>was fighting the bad guys too. Then he</u> blew up the bad guys <u>because he was mad</u>. The Power Rangers was happy because they won. Rita was very mad <u>because she lost</u>. The End *(Spelling and punctuation corrected for ease of reading; Sammy erased the last paragraph and, on rewriting it, added the underlined text.)*

12. Lena and Melissa both chose Persephone as their Greek character; Lettrice decided on Jupiter; Liliana, Makeda, and Tina all chose Venus; Lynn picked the Chimera; Rhonda picked Juno; and Sarah and Susan both chose Psyche.

Among the boys, Aloyse and Bryant both decided on Hercules; Demario, James, and Adam all chose Apollo; Edward picked Narcissus; Jonathan picked Cupid; Kevin, Patrick, and Radha all chose Jupiter; Michael and Victor decided on the Minotaur; Sammy chose Mars; and Thomas chose Bellerophon.

13. In her analysis of the history of fairy tales and their interrelationship with attitudes toward women, Warner (1994) details the way in which "the blonde" is a metaphor for luxuriance and fertility, perhaps because of a link with

the color of the harvest, that is, of corn and wheat. Nonetheless, as illustrated here, this "metaphor" has very literal ramifications in children's lives and, more particularly, in how little girls conceive of culturally valued beauty.

14. Tina's naming of her goddess as Venus Tina was an illustration of the tremendous importance many children place on the act of naming and the link between naming and identity. For example, Aloyse at one time rejected his own Ethiopian name and told everyone to call him by his "real" name, Mike. When Sammy's mother married his stepfather, Sammy began using that man's first name, writing "Robert," rather than Sammy, on all his papers. As a third grader, Tina wanted to change her name to Lisa Bonet, the good-looking, long-haired, culturally conscious, smart but somewhat flighty adolescent daughter on *The Cosby Show* (Weinberger, Leeson, & Cosby, 1984; a situation comedy featuring an African-American family, discussed by Turner, 1994). Tina explained herself to Lettrice:

> TINA: You know my real name is—No, it's not Tina. My mom said I
>   could change my name.
> LETTRICE: It's gonna take hecka money.
> TINA: No. My mom said I could change my name for free. I know this
>   guy who like my mom, and he told her, "If your child want to
>   change her name, she could change her name for free." So I can
>   change my name any time I want to. And guess what name I
>   want? Guess what it is? Lisa. Lisa Bonet. Cause I like Lisa Bonet.

CHAPTER 7

1. As discussed in Chapter 1, in this school the majority of children (76%) were from families who identified themselves as either "White" or "Black" (see Table A4), a racial difference underlined by class differences. Children whose families identified themselves in other ways (e.g., the 13% who were "mixed," and the small percentages of children from many different heritages) most often chose to associate with either the "White" children or the "Black" children. Both Edward and Victor, who were Mexican American, associated with, and were sought out as play partners by, children of color. These child groupings, however, were not based solely on skin color. Children's interests and interactional styles also figured into their associations.

2. Chapter 6 illustrated the third graders' turn toward greater realism, even in their retold stories. Readers may recall, for example, Susan's dutiful Daddy Cupid and Thomas' exercising Bellerophon. (Thomas, in fact, wrote a series of stories featuring each of the male Power Rangers engaged in a sometimes violent street encounter with another boy. His plots, carried by tough talk as much as by fighting ["You should know that when I get mad I do not play with people."], were much more realistic than the television series ever was.)

The children's personalization of stories may, in part, have been unconscious, as child authors embedded unfamiliar stories in familiar human situations (McDowell, 1995). However, there has also been evidence of at least some deliberateness in these transformations (as in the event leading to Tina's Venus story). Moreover, folklorists who study children's story retelling among their peers have consistently reported the tendency for early schoolage children in our society to personalize, rather than to attempt merely to retell, familiar stories, be they from oral, written, or multimedia sources (e.g., Grider, 1981; Tucker, 1980, 1981, 1992, 1995). In contrast, very young children may juxtapose figures from diverse sources, with no evident basis for their choices (e.g., Mama Bear, Superman, and the eensy weensy spider may all take turns falling down); and preschoolers may aim to retell quite accurately stories that they have heard repeatedly, particularly those with formulaic, repetitive structures (like "The Three Bears" and "The Three Pigs"). (For a thorough discussion, see Tucker, 1995.)

Although such folklorists, interestingly enough, tend to give few details about their methods, including the sociocultural background of their informants, their findings are relevant here. Early childhood teachers worry quite justifiably about the repetitive nature of children's media-based stories (see, e.g., Carlsson-Paige & Levin, 1991). However, the findings of this study of children's writing in the company of their peers are consistent with those of children's storytelling in the company of their peers. In the early school years, children seem at least as interested in personalizing stories as in simply retelling them.

3. Mario Barrera, Professor of Chicano Studies at the University of California-Berkeley, teaches a course on ethnic and racial identity as represented in film. Gwen Larsen, a graduate research assistant for this project on children's media use, also served as graduate instructor for Professor Barrera.

4. Race was explicitly discussed in many children's essays about nonviolent heroes (like Sammy's about Rosa Parks; see Chapter 6). The children also wrote assigned journal entries about their experience with "prejudice." They seemed to define prejudicial behavior as treating someone who is "different" from you in a mean way, especially by calling them "bad names" or excluding them from play. Most children's examples of such behavior included, but were not limited to, explicit references to race or ethnicity. Sammy and Victor, for example, wrote about "being prejudiced" against an autistic child who was mainstreamed in their classroom and who had serious difficulties controlling his behavior (e.g., he screamed a great deal). Lettrice and Kyle recalled how mean all the children had been to Tamara, who was "ugly." And Susan felt her cousins were prejudiced against her because she was from this particular East Bay city.

5. Lettrice planned to publish this story (i.e., to turn it into a book for the classroom library) and, also, to bring this story to the classroom community through Author's Theater. However, the school year ended before Lettrice accomplished these goals. She was slowed by a broken arm, a result of a fall from the hanging bars.

6. As with all of the children's media-based stories, I have no direct knowl-edge about whether or not Lettrice actually saw the original film. Children viewed questions about whether or not they had seen the particular film or pro-gram they were talking or writing about as an insult. As Tina said to Aloyse (who asked her if she watched X-Men), "That's a real stupid question. If I didn't watch the cartoon X-Men, I wouldn't be playing it [i.e., writing this story about it], if I didn't *really* watch it, OK::?" And, since no one responded to Lettrice's "Spike Lee" story with another version (perhaps because it was never presented), it was not possible to document transformations as "Spike Lee" was revoiced by dif-ferent class members, as had easily been the case with Rogue or Emily, for exam-ple. What matters, however, is that Lettrice made a decision to appropriate "Spike Lee," a known African-American cultural figure, for *her* production and for *her* audience; she associated this figure quite correctly with a plot about unhappy families and about interracial relations.

7. For an historical and psychological analysis of interracial marriage and ethnic identity in the United States during this century, see Spickard (1989).

8. Melissa published her Bruce Lee story, which she entitled "Some Things Change," and she also presented it to the class through Author's Theater. For her production, she chose James, who was Korean American, for the role of Bruce Lee, and she chose Radha, who was Indian American, for the role of Bruce Wayne. European-American Kristin played the role of Lynda, and African-American Lena played the role of Christy, the second Chinese wife, and Makeda, also African American, the third Chinese wife. (There were no girls of Asian her-itage in this class.) None of the children commented on Melissa's explicit descrip-tion of Lynda as "Chinese," perhaps because that character was played by the teacher (which the children found very amusing).

As will be illustrated, in *Lena's* story of interracial romance, actors seemed to be deliberately chosen to circumvent the issue of race. In *Melissa's* story, how-ever, there was no confirming evidence that this was the case. It is suggestive, though, that Melissa, who usually chose her friends Susan and Sarah to be in her stories, chose girls of color to play "Chinese women" (except for the character of Lynda).

9. Melissa had also written a poem about Radha, her choice to play the role of Jason.

10. Lena's authorial decision is developmentally quite sophisticated. As dis-cussed in Chapter 1, in this classroom, children's writing functioned as a major means for children's play. Thus, children were able to bring their symbolic resources as players to the writing task (i.e., their experiences manipulating oral words, dramatic actions, and each other). But developmental resources contain within them developmental challenges (Dyson, 1989b)—playing on paper is not the same as playing on the playground. As readers may recall, throughout the project, Kristin worked hard to help the children, including the audience mem-bers, differentiate between the actions of writers and of actors. In this instance, then, Lena has clearly differentiated her perspective—and prerogatives—as an

author from that of her actors and audience members. It is a developmentally sophisticated action, in the context of this study.

11. Kristin was particularly sensitive to children's potential use of sexuality as an insult because two of the children lived in families that included their mothers and their mothers' female partners.

12. In the discussion a number of boys pointed out that their right as boys to play girls' roles was not an issue because, in Michael's words, "boys never raise their hands for girl parts." "Never" is too strong a word, however, as Radha noted. Since Radha wanted to be a professional actor when he grew up, he "raise[d] [his] hand for every little part." Kristin reminded the class that, during ancient Greek times, "women were not allowed to act; men played those roles." Kristin then had the children act out the Rosa Parks story, having actors of different sexes and races play parts different from them. And Lynn concluded that, "You're not even being who you're acting, forget about being a girl or a boy. Demario wasn't Rosa Parks. Same color, but he's not Rosa Parks." In brief, the children discussed differentiating actor from character, an important concept, and, also, the important classroom principles of the authors' right to pick their actors, and the actors' right to play desired roles.

13. Williams (1995, p. 81) argues that actors' race and ethnicity do matter in a political sense in our society because historically actors of color have been restricted to their own "category." hooks (1994) makes a similar argument, but she emphasizes aesthetic sense as well. For example, she suggests that, because of the rarity of leading roles for Black women in popular films, the movie *The Bodyguard* (Kasden, Costner, Wilson, & Jackson, 1992) was about interracial romance, even though the movie did not in any explicit way have to do with race; the very selection of lead actors (i.e., Whitney Houston, an African-American performer, and Kevin Costner, a European-American one) made this a film about race.

A consideration of these complex interrelationships between the layers of meaning in any multimedia production (text, actors, setting, etc.) were beyond the scope of Kristin's goal for Author's Theater (to teach her young children to write), and beyond my goals as classroom researcher. Still, as the children, their media interests, and we adults as teachers and researchers continue to develop, these complexities will compel our attention (The New London Group, 1996).

14. One does not need to subscribe to the dubious and racist notion that complex differences can be married away (Spickard, 1989; Williams, 1995) to proscribe, as I do through this book, that classrooms be open to children's own lived realities. This was a school that included a substantial number of self-identified "mixed race" children and a classroom that included several children living in interracial families, even if they themselves were not mixed race.

15. Children's books provide many examples of adult authors who eliminated, rather than somehow confronted, potentially controversial issues. For example, Heilbrun (1995) discusses the evolution of Nancy Drew (Stratemeyer, 1930), the curious and courageous girl sleuth, into a *helpful* girl who herself often needs help (and who never operates outside the law). The racist stereotypes of the

early books have been eliminated in more recent productions—but so have any images of racial or ethnic heritages other than White (Dyer & Romalov, 1995). To further illustrate, Kohl (1994) uses examples of books about Rosa Parks to illustrate how African Americans' passionate, deliberate, and collective action against racism and segregation has been transformed into an individualistic and rather impulsive action of a single woman too tired to give up her seat on the bus. (Kohl, however, does not mention Greenfield's [1973/1995] award-winning book on Rosa Parks, which presents Parks as part of a much larger movement).

CHAPTER 8

1. The teacher study group was formed with the assistance of Alice Kawazoe, Director of Staff Development for Oakland Unified, who helped recruit a multiethnic group of experienced teachers, who were themselves working with children from diverse sociocultural backgrounds. The group participants all voiced an interest in reflecting on sociocultural diversity—on differences of race, ethnicity, culture, language, and socioeconomic status—and on how those differences figured into their teaching experiences.

2. In the 1990s, there has been political and legal action designed to highlight these narrow aspects of early grade curricula—precisely those aspects that have long dominated in inner city schools (for discussions, see Berliner & Biddle, 1995; Haberman, 1996). For example, in May 1995, the California legislature passed an "ABC" bill, which mandated that "phonics, spelling, and basic computation skills be emphasized" in the early grades (Giroux, 1995, p. 1).

3. The pedagogical value placed on child ownership and language expression seemed to make the teachers reluctant to "censor" the children's writing (cf., Lensmire, 1993, 1994). As a group, the teachers seemed more comfortable censoring children's dramatic play (i.e., banning guns, including "finger" guns) than they did censoring children's writing. As discussed, in response to child composing, a preferable strategy was helping children consider alternative possibilities for imagining stories.

4. Like her study group colleagues, Kristin provided a written avenue for children's direct expression of their feelings about each other. In their private journals, children, including both Sammy and Tina, wrote about being upset with (i.e., "hating") or having had fun with (or, in girls' journals, "loving") particular classmates. Other study group teachers provided children with diaries, memo forms (for writing messages to the offending child or to the teacher), or complaint boxes. The teachers of the older children had classroom rules about authors seeking peers' permission before including their names in stories to be shared.

The intensity of children's feelings can provide them with a powerful impetus to write (see especially O'Loughlin, Bierwiler, & Serra, 1996). However, on the public stage, written stories that name and embarrass or, worse, ridicule peers can pose ethical and pedagogical dilemmas for teachers (Lensmire, 1993, 1994).

Kristin's children did not do this, with the exception of a few texts based on the crazy mixed-up kids in *The Sideways Stories* (Sachar, 1985); when those stories were deemed "too real"—and not "turned around" enough, in Lynn's words—most children responded by branding the stories "mean." There were, of course, ideological issues that undergirded the children's public stories, and those hurt too. Hence this book and this chapter on pedagogy.

5. In a critical pedagogy, as influenced in particular by Freire (1970), teachers help students reflect on the social order of their everyday lives, on whose interests are served by that order, and on what they might do to help make a more equitable world. Australian researchers and educators have been particularly interested in how critical pedagogy might be enacted in primary grade literacy programs. See, for example, Comber (1994), Comber, Nixon, Badger, and Hill (1994), and Gilbert (1994). Greene (1988, 1995) has provided rich discussions of how narratives (both literary and historical) serve as mediators of critical reflection. And Derman-Sparks (1989) provides superb guidance for teachers who aim to base their critical pedagogy on careful observation of young children's daily interactions.

6. The very use of terms like "popular" or "common" culture (Willis, 1990) can mask the potential interplay between participation in ethnic and common culture. Ethnographic studies of children's use of commercial culture are themselves rare, and studies in socioculturally diverse settings are even rarer. However, Lee (1995) conducted small group writing sessions in a fourth–fifth grade classroom in the Bay Area serving Chinese and Vietnamese immigrant children. In combination with the study of Kristin's room, his work suggests the insight that could be gained from comparative classroom studies. During Lee's writing sessions, the boys' intense involvement with an Asian cartoon named *Dragonball Z* (Jiichan, 1993) surfaced in their talk and drawing, despite the classroom ban on that cartoon. Interestingly, like the talk of the younger children observed in my project, the talk of Lee's older boys was highly interactive and narrative. But the latter boys did not write stories; they wrote reports on cartoon characters, despite Lee's encouragement to try other genres. In addition, Lee examined the portrayal of gender and race relations in the cartoon (particularly relations involving characters with, on the one hand, physical features associated with African-heritage children and, on the other, those associated with European-heritage children); those portrayals were a potential resource for the children's own construction of their relations with children across gender and race lines. It was not surprising—and seemed to me quite reasonable—that the Asian-American girls Lee studied detested *Dragonball Z*.

7. In a thought-provoking paper, Lunsford (1995) discusses the complex issues of authority and ownership raised by our "literally electrified world" (p. 14). As she notes, there are many legal arguments about who "owns" information and who has the right to appropriate and use it. Although Lunsford situates her paper within (or at least plays against) the theories of Foucault, rather than Bakhtin, her reflections on composition teaching are well-suited to the latter's perspective.

For example, she suggests a pedagogical emphasis, not on text products themselves, but on the "response-ability" both teachers and students take for their relationship to their own and other people's products. Lunsford is speaking to college teachers, but her suggestion seems embodied in Kristin's "free writing" time.

8. Kristin's school had a parent-sponsored, afterschool arts program offering music, drawing, and drama activities, among other possibilities. This program was not free, nor was transportation provided. Kristin reported that the neighborhood, middle-class children participated in the program; the children from outside the immediate neighborhood—primarily the children from low-income and working-class homes—rarely did. But in their homes and day care centers, they had siblings, peers, and televisions—the stuff of everyday social play with media. It seems a reasonable inference that, well before Kristin ever entered this school, before the children had performed their first superhero story on an official stage, they were beginning to orient themselves to cultural material available for social fun and affiliation (for an extended discussion of this phenomenon with middle-school students, see Fisherkeller, 1995).

Thus, along with Seiter (1993, p. 234), I wish to argue that "parents and teachers should worry less about the debilitating effects on children ... of toys and television and worry more about ways to improve access to education *and* entertainment for children against whom the odds are already stacked." At the very least, educators can exploit children's pleasure in dramatic play and in narrative imagination across the curriculum (a recommendation consistent with the views of the study group teachers). In Willis' (1990) words:

> The real survival of any art form is in its being pulled—not pushed—into everyday forms of informal symbolic work and meaning, as these forms reach out from their own vitality, from their own internal life, for relevant and usable symbolic material. (p. 148)

9. When Kristin's children visited Elise's children in Chinatown, Sammy was quite nervous, as Kristin explained to the teacher study group.

KRISTIN: [Sammy] said, "Those kids aren't going to like me because I'm Black. They only like White kids."

JUDI: Oh my gosh.

KRISTIN: ... I went to Elise, and she picked out with great care a Black boy and his best friend, who is Chinese, and we walked him over, and I said, "Sammy, Elise has someone who she wants you to meet." And we introduced [Sammy to the other Black child]. And I saw Sammy's face! [Kristin beams.] ... And then I said, "And this is his best friend." And then he went over and sat down with them. And then afterwards, the next day, we wrote about the field trip ... and Sammy shared that he had at first been scared.

Kristin's and Elise's experience with Sammy is a clear illustration of the importance of teacher-organized and teacher-monitored opportunities for children to interact in pleasurable ways with those they regard as "different."

10. In their analysis of urban African-American children's talk during neighborhood play, Goodwin and Goodwin (1990) describe how an unfolding interaction can provide different social identities for participants. In the project in Kristin's room, that talk could provide different sociocultural identities as well. For example, in Chapter 7, Lena and Melissa were sitting together, enjoying the text about Jason and Amber. They were two girlfriends. But when their talk shifted to choosing the actors, they became a Black girl and a White girl. In socioculturally diverse settings, then, analysis of language use yields a "linguistics of contact ... that places at its center the workings of language across rather than within lines of social differentiation, of class, race, gender, age" (Pratt, 1987, p. 61). In educational settings in particular, such an analysis allows insight into how classroom practices support, or inhibit, children's learning of both literacy and community.

11. In Kristin's room, there were teacher–child and peer conferences, in which individual children received feedback about the clarity of their prose and about their mechanics (e.g., spelling, punctuation, usage).

12. Since this was an ethnographic study, I have examined the commercial material that the children used in the school setting. The boys' dominant use of such material, particularly material from superhero stories, was predictable. However, it was not *only* the boys who were interested in superheroes. Girls' interest, especially in the X-Men, could be interpreted as an indication of cultural change, or perhaps of the distinctive nature of the X-Men themselves. However, it is also possible that media critics have inaccurately assumed that girls are not interested in superhero stories.

As noted earlier, there is a dearth of ethnographic studies of children's use of commercial materials, not to mention the lack of attention to low-income and working-class children from diverse cultural backgrounds. In S. Willis' words (cited in Seiter, 1993, p. 192), "Barbie can slide down avalanches just as He-Man can become the inhabitant of a two-storey Victorian doll's house."

I did not grow up with the commercial media in the way that contemporary children do. But as a little girl in the 1950s, I spent hours playing war, with and without plastic soldiers (which technically belonged to my brother). In most of our exciting cultural stories, whether passed on through the media or not, males are featured (especially European-American males from [or on their way to achieving] economically comfortable homes). And yet, that does not mean girls have no interest in action and adventure, only that the commercial media (and, for that matter, book publishers [Gilbert, 1989]) have done a poor job of providing female heroes in action-packed stories. Luckily, the child drama presented in this book had Tina, a superb female superhero.

References

▼ ▼ ▼

Abrahams, R. D. (1969). *Jump-rope rhymes: A dictionary*. Austin, TX: University of Texas Press.

Agar, M. H. (1980). *The professional stranger: An informal introduction to ethnography*. New York: Academic Press.

Agar, M. H. (1994). *Language shock: Understanding the culture of conversation*. New York: William Morrow.

Ahlberg, J., & Ahlberg, A. (1986). *The jolly postman, or other people's letters*. Boston: Little, Brown.

Anderson, C. C. (1984). The Saturday morning survival kit. *Journal of Popular Culture, 17,* 155–161.

Angelou, M. (1991). Foreword. In Z. N. Hurston (Au.), *Dust tracks on a road* (pp. vii–xii). New York: Harper Perennial.

Anyon, J. (1984). Intersection of gender and class: Accommodation and resistance by working-class and affluent females to contradictory sex-role ideologies. *Journal of Education, 166,* 25–48.

Apple, M. (1993). *Official knowledge: Democratic education in a conservative age*. London: Routledge.

Asher, S. R., & Coie, J. D. (Eds.). (1990). *Peer rejection in childhood*. Cambridge, London: Cambridge University Press.

Babcock, B. (1993). At home, no women are storytellers: Ceramic creativity and the politics of discourse in Cochiti Pueblo. In S. Lavie, K. Narayan, & R. Rosaldo (Eds.), *Creativity/Anthropology* (pp. 70–99). Ithaca, NY: Cornell University Press.

Bakhtin, M. (1981). Discourse in the novel. In C. Emerson & M. Holquist (Eds.), *The dialogic imagination: Four essays by M. Bakhtin* (pp. 259–422). Austin: University of Texas Press.

Bakhtin, M. (1986). *Speech genres and other late essays*. Austin, TX: University of Texas Press.

Bakhtin, M. (1990). *Art and answerability: Early philosophical essays*. Austin, TX: University of Texas Press.

Barth, F. (1969). *Ethnic groups and boundaries: The social organization of cultural differences*. Boston: Little, Brown.

Bauman, R. (1977). *Verbal art as performance*. Rowley, MA: Newbury House.

Benton, M. (1993). *The comic book in America: An illustrated history*. Dallas, TX: Taylor Publishing.

See Appendix B for publishing information and summaries of movies, television programs, and video games mentioned in the book.

Berliner, D. C., & Biddle, B. J. (1995). *The manufactured crisis: Myths, fraud, and the attack on America's public schools.* Reading, MA: Addison-Wesley.

Boichel, B. (1991). Batman: Commodity as myth. In R. Pearson & W. Uricchio (Eds.), *The many lives of the Batman: Critical approaches to a superhero and his media* (pp. 4–17). New York: Routledge Publishing.

Booth, W. C. (1988). *The company we keep: An ethics of fiction.* Berkeley, CA: University of California Press.

Bottigheimer, R. B. (1987). *Grimms' bad girls and bold boys.* New Haven, CT: Yale University Press.

Boulton, M., & Smith, P. (1993). Ethnic, gender partner, and activity preferences in mixed-race schools in the U.K.: Playground observations. In C. Hart (Ed.), *Children on playgrounds: Research perspectives and applications* (pp. 210–237). Albany, NY: University of New York Press.

Bourdieu, P. (1973). Cultural reproduction and social reproduction. In R. Brown (Ed.), *Knowledge, education and cultural change* (pp. 71–112). London: Tavistock.

Bourdieu, P. (1984). *Distinction: A social critique of the judgment of taste* (R. Nice, Trans.). Cambridge, MA: Harvard University Press. (Original work published 1979)

Brown, A., & Palinscar, A. S. (1982). Inducing strategies for learning from texts by means of informed, self-control training. *Topics in Learning and Learning Disabilities, 2,* 1–17.

Bruner, E. (1993). Epilogue: Creative persona and the problem of authenticity. In S. Lavie, K. Narayan, & R. Rosaldo (Eds.), *Creativity/Anthropology* (pp. 321–334). Ithaca, NY: Cornell University Press.

Bruner, J. (1986). *Actual minds, possible worlds.* Cambridge, MA: Harvard University Press.

Buckingham, D. (1993). *Children talking television: The making of television literacy.* London: The Falmer Press.

Burnett, F. H. (1962). *The Secret Garden.* Illustrated by Tasha Tudor. Philadelphia: Lippincott.

Capote, T. (1956). *A Christmas Memory.* New York: Random House.

Carlsson-Paige, N., & Levin, D. E. (1991). The subversion of healthy development and play: Teachers' reactions to the Teen-age Mutant Ninja Turtles. *Day Care and Early Education, 19*(2), 14–20.

Chapman, M. L. (1994). The emergence of genres: Some findings from an examination of first-grade writing. *Written Communication, 11,* 348–380.

Charren, P., Szulc, P., & Tchaicha, J. (1995). A public policy perspective on televised violence and youth. *Harvard Educational Review, 65,* 282–291.

Children's Defense Fund. (1994). *Wasting America's future: The Children's Defense Fund report on the cost of child poverty.* Boston: Beacon Press.

Christian-Smith, L. K. (Ed.). (1993). *Texts of desire: Essays on fiction, femininity, and schooling* Washington D.C.: Falmer Press.

Clark, K., & Holquist, M. (1984). *Mikhail Bakhtin.* Cambridge, MA: Harvard University Press.

Cole, J. (1989). *Anna Banana: 101 Jump-rope rhymes.* New York: Morrow Junior Books.

Comber, B. (1994). Critical literacy: An introduction to Australian debates and perspectives. *Journal of Curriculum Studies, 26,* 655–668.

Comber, B., Nixon, H., Badger, L., & Hill, S. (Scriptwriters). (1994). *Literacy, diversity, and schooling* [Videotape]. Armadale, Victoria, Australia: Eleanor Curtain Publishing.

Connell, R. W. (1994). Poverty and education. *Harvard Educational Review, 64,* 125–149.

Connell, R., Ashenden, D. J., Kessler, S., & Dowsett, G. W. (1982*). Making the difference: Schools, families, and social division.* Sydney, Australia: Allen & Unwin.

Conrad, M. (1994). *Literacy at the knee: Parent and teacher perspectives on parent involvement and school achievement.* Unpublished doctoral dissertation, University of California, Berkeley.

Corsaro, W. (1985). *Friendship and peer culture in the early years.* Norwood, NJ: Ablex.

Corsaro, W. (1992). Interpretive reproduction in children's peer cultures. *Social Psychology Quarterly, 55,* 160–177.

Corsaro, W., & Miller, P. (Eds.). (1992). *Interpretive approaches to children's socialization.* San Francisco: Jossey-Bass.

Corsaro, W., & Rizzo, T. (1990). Disputes in the peer culture of American and Italian nursery-school children. In A. Grimshaw (Ed.), *Conflict talk: Sociolinguistic investigation of arguments in conversation.* Cambridge, London: Cambridge University Press.

Corsaro, W., & Rosier, K. B. (1992). Documenting productive reproduction processes in children's lives: Transition narratives of a Black family living in poverty. In W. A. Corsaro & P. J. Miller (Eds.), *Interpretive approaches to children's socialization* (pp. 67–92). San Francisco: Jossey-Bass.

Daiute, C. (1989). Play as thought: Thinking strategies of young writers. *Harvard Educational Review, 59,* 1–23.

Daiute, C. (Ed.). (1993). *The development of literacy through social interaction.* San Francisco: Jossey-Bass.

D'Amato, J. D. (1987). The belly of the beast: On cultural difference, castelike status and the politics of school. *Anthropology and Education Quarterly, 18,* 357–360.

D'Amato, J. D. (1988). "Acting": Hawaiian children's resistance to teachers. *The Elementary School Journal, 88,* 529–544.

D'Aulaire, I., & D'Aulaire, E. (1962). *Book of Greek myths.* New York: Bantam Doubleday Dell.

Davies, B. (1989). *Frogs and snails and feminist tales: Preschool children and gender.* Boston: Allen and Unwin.

Davis, H. G. (1985). *I got the word in me, and I can sing it, you know.* Philadelphia: University of Pennsylvania Press.

Derman-Sparks, L. (1989). *Anti-Bias curriculum: Tools for empowering young children.* Washington, D.C.: National Association for the Education of Young Children.

Derman-Sparks, L. (1995). How well are we nurturing racial and ethnic diversity? In D. Levine, R. Lowe, B. Peterson, & R. Tenorio (Eds.), *Rethinking schools: An agenda for change.* New York: The Free Press.

Derrida, J. (1978). *Writing and difference.* London: Routledge & Kegan Paul.

Dewey, J. (1931). *Philosophy and civilization.* New York: Minton, Balch, & Company.

Dixon, J., & Stratta, L. (1986). *Writing narrative—and beyond.* Ottawa, Canada: The Canadian Council of Teachers of English.

Douglas, S. (1994). *Where the girls are: Growing up female with the mass media.* New York: Times Books.

Doyle, R. (1993). *Paddy Clarke ha, ha, ha.* London: Seeker and Warburg.

Dyer, C., & Romalov, N. (Eds.). (1995). *Rediscovering Nancy Drew.* Iowa City, IA: University of Iowa Press.

Dyson, A. Haas. (1981). *A case study examination of the role of oral language in the writing processes of kindergartners.* Unpublished doctoral dissertation. University of Texas, Austin, TX: Press.

Dyson, A. Haas. (1984). Learning to write/Learning to do school: Emergent writers' interpretations of school literacy tasks. *Research in the Teaching of English, 18,* 233–264.

Dyson, A. Haas. (1985). Research currents: Writing and the social lives of children. *Language Arts, 62,* 632–639.

Dyson, A. Haas. (1987). The value of "time-off task": Young children's spontaneous talk and deliberate text. *Harvard Educational Review, 57,* 396–420.

Dyson, A. Haas. (1989a). "Once-upon-a-time" reconsidered: The developmental dialectic between function and form. *Written Communication, 6,* 436–462.

Dyson, A. Haas. (1989b). *Multiple worlds of child writers: Friends learning to write.* New York: Teachers College Press.

Dyson, A. Haas. (1993). *The social worlds of children learning to write in an urban primary school.* New York: Teachers College Press.

Dyson, A. Haas. (1994). The ninjas, the X-men, and the ladies: Playing with power and identity in an urban primary school. *Teachers College Record, 96,* 219–239.

Dyson, A. Haas. (1995). Writing children: Reinventing the development of childhood literacy. *Written Communication, 12,* 4–46.

Dyson, A. Haas (with A. Bennett et al.). (1997). *What difference does difference make?: Teacher reflection on diversity, literacy, and the urban primary school.* Urbana, IL: National Council of Teachers of English.

Edelsky, C. (1991). *With literacy and justice for all: Rethinking the social in language and education.* London: Falmer Press.

Fairclough, N. (Ed.). (1992). *Critical language awareness.* New York: Longman.

Feifer, J. (1993). *The man in the ceiling.* New York: Harper Collins.

Fine, M. (1987). Silencing in public schools. *Language Arts, 64,* 157–164.

Finkelstein, N., & Haskins, R. (1983). Kindergarten children prefer same-color peers. *Child Development, 54,* 502–508.

Fishbein, H. (1992). The development of peer prejudice and discrimination in children. In J. Lynch, et al. (Eds.), *Cultural diversity and the schools, Volume Two: Prejudice, polemic or progress?* (pp. 43–47). Washington D.C.: Falmer Press.

Fishbein, H., & Imai, S. (1993). Preschoolers select playmates on the basis of gender and race. *Journal of Applied Developmental Psychology, 14,* 303–316.

Fisherkeller, J. (1995). *Identity work and television: Young adolescents learning within local and mediated cultures.* Unpublished doctoral dissertation, University of California, Berkeley.

Fordham, S. (1994). "Those loud black girls": (Black) women, silence, and gender "passing" in the academy. *Anthropology and Education Quarterly, 24,* 3–32.

Foster, M. (1992). Sociolinguistics and the African-American community: Implications for literacy. *Theory into Practice, 31,* 312–320.

Foucault, M. (1978). *The history of sexuality.* New York: Pantheon.

Foucault, M. (1981). The order of discourse. In R. Young (Ed.), *Untying the text: A poststructuralist reader* (pp. 48–78). Boston: Routledge & Kegan Paul.

Franklin, M. B. (1983). Play as the creation of imaginary situations. In S. Wapner & B. Kaplan (Eds.), *Toward a holistic developmental psychology* (pp. 197–220). Hillsdale, NJ: Erlbaum.

Freire, P. (1970). *Pedagogy of the oppressed.* New York: Continuum.

Gag, W. (1928/1977). *Millions of cats.* New York: Coward, McCann & Geoghegan.

Garnica, O. (1981). Social dominance and conversational interaction: The omega child in the classroom. In J. Green & C. Wallat (Eds.), *Ethnography and language in educational settings* (pp. 229–252). Norwood, NJ: Ablex.

Garvey, C. (1990). *Play* (enl. ed.). Cambridge, MA: Harvard University Press.

Gaskins, S. Miller, P., & Corsaro, W. (1992). Theoretical and methodological perspectives in the interpretive study of children. In W. Corsaro & P. Miller (Eds.), *Interpretive approaches to children's socialization* (pp. 5–24). San Francisco: Jossey-Bass.

Gates, H. L. (1991). Afterword. In Z. N. Hurston (Au.), *Dust tracks on a road* (pp. 257–268). New York: Harper Perennial.

Geertz, C. (1973). *The interpretation of cultures: Selected essays.* New York: Basic Books.

Geertz, C. (1983). *Local knowledge.* New York: Basic Books.

Geertz, C. (1988). *Works and lives: The anthropologist as author.* Stanford, CA: Stanford University Press.

Gilbert, P. (1989). *Writing, schooling, and deconstruction: From voice to text in the classroom.* London: Routledge.

Gilbert, P. (1994). "And they lived happily ever after": Cultural storylines and the construction of gender. In A. H. Dyson & C. Genishi (Eds.), *The need for story: Cultural diversity in classroom and community* (pp. 124–144). Urbana, IL: National Council of Teachers of English.

Giroux, L. (1995, September 1). Analysis AB 170. In *Concurrence in Senate Amendments* [On-line]. Available Internet: http://www.leginfo.ca.gov/bilinfo.html Item: aed/445–9431

Goodwin, M. (1990). *He-said-she-said: Talk as social organization among Black children.* Bloomington, IN: Indiana University Press.

Goodwin, C., & Goodwin, M. H. (1990). Interstitial argument. In Grimshaw, A. (Ed.), *Conflict Talk: Sociolinguistic investigations of arguments in conversations* (pp. 85–117). Cambridge, London: Cambridge University Press.

Graff, H. (1987). *The labyrinths of literacy: Reflections on literacy past and present.* New York: Falmer Press.

Graves, D. H. (1983). *Writing: Teachers and children at work.* Portsmouth, NH: Heinemann Educational Books.

Graves, D., & Hansen, J. (1983). The author's chair. *Language Arts, 60,* 176–183.

Graves, R. (1960). *The Greek myths.* New York: Penguin Books.

Green, B. (1993). Literacy studies and curriculum theorizing; or The insistence of the letter. In B. Green (Ed.), *The insistence of the letter: Literacy studies and curriculum theorizing* (pp. 195–225). New York: Falmer Press.

Greene, M. (1988). *The dialectic of freedom.* New York: Teachers College Press.

Greene, M. (1993). The passions of pluralism: Multiculturalism and the expanding community. In T. Perry & J. W. Fraser (Eds.), *Freedom's plow: Teaching in the multicultural classroom* (pp. 185–196). New York: Routledge.

Greene, M. (1994). Multiculturalism, community, and the arts. In A. H. Dyson & C. Genishi (Eds.), *The need for story: Cultural diversity in classroom and community* (pp. 11–27). Urbana, IL: National Council of Teachers of English.

Greene, M. (1995). *Releasing the imagination: Essays on education, the arts, and social change.* San Francisco: Jossey-Bass Publishers.

Greenfield, E. (1973/1995). *Rosa Parks.* New York: Crowell.

Grider, S. (1981). The media narraform: Symbiosis of mass media and oral tradition. *Arv: Scandinavian Yearbook of Folklore, 37,* 125–131.

Grugeon, E. (1993). Gender implications of children's playground culture. In P. Woods & M. Hammersley (Eds.), *Gender and ethnicity in schools: Ethnographic accounts* (pp. 11–33). London: Routledge in association with The Open University.

Guerrero, E. (1993). *Framing Blackness: The African-American image in film.* Philadelphia: Temple University Press.

Guthrie, W. K. C. (1950). *The Greeks and their gods.* London: Methuen.

Gutierrez, K. (1993). Biliteracy and the language-minority child. In O. Saracho & B. Spodek (Eds.), *Language and literacy in early childhood education* (pp. 82–101). New York: Teachers College Press.

Haberman, M. (1996). The pedagogy of poverty versus good teaching. In W. Ayers & P. Ford (Eds.), *City kids, city teachers: Reports from the front row* (pp. 228–240). New York: The New Press.

Hall, S. (1981). Notes on deconstructing "the popular." In R. Samuel (Ed.), *People's history and socialist theory* (pp. 227–239). London: Routledge & Kegan Paul.

Hallinan, M., & Smith, S. (1985). The effects of classroom racial composition on students' interracial friendliness. *Social Psychology Quarterly, 48,* 3–16.

Hansen, J. & Graves, D. (1983). The author's chair. *Language Arts, 60,* 176–183.

Harris, V. (Ed.). (1992). *Teaching multicultural literature in grades K–8.* Norwood, MA: Christopher-Gordon.

Heath, S. B. (1983). *Ways with words: Language, life and work in communities and classrooms.* Cambridge, London: Cambridge University Press.

Heilbrun, C. G. (1995). Nancy Drew: A moment in feminist history. In C. Dyer & N. Romalov (Eds.), *Rediscovering Nancy Drew* (pp. 11–21). Iowa City, IA: University of Iowa Press.

Henderson, B. (1996). *Voice lessons—On becoming an author: A developmental study of fiction writing in a first-second grade urban classroom.* Unpublished doctoral dissertation, Stanford University, Stanford.

Hodge, R., & Tripp, D. (1986). *Children and television: A semiotic approach.* Stanford, CA: Stanford University Press.

Holmes, R. (1995). *How young children perceive race.* Thousand Oaks, CA.: Sage Publications.

Holquist, M. (1990). *Dialogism: Bakhtin and his world.* London: Routledge.

hooks, b. (1990). Talking back. In R. Ferguson, M. Gever, T. Minh-ha, & C. West (Eds.), *Out there: Marginalization and contemporary cultures* (pp. 437–440). New York: The New Museum of Contemporary Art, and Cambridge, MA: The MIT Press.

hooks, b. (1994). *Outlaw culture.* New York: Routledge.

Hurston, Z. (1942/1991). *Dust tracks on a road.* New York: Harper Perennial.

James, A. (1993). *Childhood identities: Self and social relationships in the experience of the child.* Edinburgh: Edinburgh University Press.

Jacob, E., & Jordon, C. (Eds.). (1993). *Minority education: Anthropological perspectives.* Norwood, NJ: Ablex.

Jenkins, H. (1992). *Textual poachers: Television fans and participatory culture.* New York: Routledge.

Jiichan, C. (1993). *Dragonball Z.* Japan: Culturecom Ltd.

Johnson, B. (1986). Thresholds of difference: Structures of address in Zora Neale Hurston. In H. L. Gates (Ed.), *"Race," writing, and difference* (pp. 317–328). Chicago: The University of Chicago Press.

John-Steiner, V. (1985). *Notebooks of the mind: Explorations of thinking.* Albuquerque, NM: University of New Mexico Press.

Jordan, E., Cowan, A., & Roberts, J. (1995). Knowing the rules-Discursive strategies in young children's power struggles. *Early Childhood Research Quarterly, 10,* 339–358.

Kinder, M. (1991). *Playing with power in movies, television, and video games: From Muppet Babies to Teenage Mutant Ninja Turtles.* Berkeley, CA: University of California Press.

King, M. L., & Rentel, V. M. (1981). *How children learn to write: A longitudinal study*. Columbus, OH: Ohio State University Research Foundation.

King, N. R. (1987). Elementary school play: Theory and research. In J. H. Block & N. R. King (Eds.), *School play: A source book* (pp. 143–166). New York: Teachers College Press.

Kline, S. (1993). *Out of the garden: Toys, TV, and children's culture in the age of marketing*. London: Verso.

Knapp, M. S., & Associates. (1995). *Teaching for meaning in high-poverty classrooms*. New York: Teachers College Press.

Kohl, H. (1994). *Should we burn Babar?: Essays on children's literature and the power of stories*. New York: New York Press.

Laba, M. (1986). Popular culture and folklore: The social dimension. In P. Narvaez & M. Laba (Eds.), *Media sense: The folklore–popular culture continuum* (pp. 9–18). Bowling Green, OH: Bowling Green State University Popular Press.

Labov, W. (1972). *Language in the inner city*. Philadelphia: University of Pennsylvania Press.

Lagemann, E. C. (1994). For the record: Character and community. *Teachers College Record, 96,* 141–147.

Lavie, S., Narayan, K., & Rosaldo, R. (Eds.). (1993). *Creativity/Anthropology*. Ithaca, NY: Cornell University Press.

Lee, P. (1995). *Super Saiyan and the secrets of life: On the role of animation in Asian-American children's social and composing worlds*. Unpublished manuscript, University of California, Berkeley.

Lemert, C. (1993). Introduction, social theory: Its uses and pleasures. In C. Lemert (Ed.), *Social theory: The multicultural and classic readings* (pp. 1–24). Boulder, CO: Westview Press.

Lensmire, T. (1993). Following the child, socioanalysis, and threats to community: Teacher response to children's texts. *Curriculum Inquiry, 23,* 265–299.

Lensmire, T. (1994). *When children write: Critical revisions of the writing workshop*. New York: Teachers College Press.

Levin, D. E., & Carlsson-Paige, N. (1994). Developmentally appropriate television: Putting children first. *Young Children, 49,* 38–61.

Levine, L. (1988). *Highbrow/lowbrow: The emergence of cultural hierarchy in America*. Cambridge, MA: Harvard University Press.

Lewis, C. S. (1950). *The chronicles of Narnia*. New York: Macmillan Company.

Lewis, G. (1991). From common dullness to fleeting wonder: The manipulation of cultural meaning in the Teenage Mutant Ninja Turtles saga. *Journal of Popular Culture, 25,* 31–43.

Lobel, A. (1970). *Frog and Toad were friends*. New York: Harper & Row.

Luke, A. (1994). *The social construction of literacy in the primary school*. South Melbourne, Australia: Macmillan Education.

Luke, A. (1995). Text and discourse in education: An introduction to critical discourse analysis. In M. W. Apple (Ed.), *Review of Research in Education, 21* (pp. 3–48). Washington, DC: American Educational Research Association .

Luke, C., & Roe, K. (1993). Media and popular cultural studies in the classroom. *Australian Journal of Education, 37,* 115–118.

Lunsford, A. A. (1995). *What matters who writes? What matters who responds? Issues of ownership in the writing classroom*. Paper presented at the Annual Convention of the National Council of Teachers of English, San Diego, CA.

Malinowski, B. (1922/1961). *Argonauts of the Western Pacific*. New York: E.P. Dutton.

Martin, D. (1994, August 21). The X-men vanquish America. *The New York Times,* p.1 sec. 2, p. 27, sec. 2.

McDowell, J. (1995). The transmission of children's folklore. In B. Sutton-Smith, J. Mechling, T. W. Johnson, & F. R. McMahon. (Eds.), *Children's folklore: A source book* (pp. 49–62). New York: Garland Publishing.

McMahon, F. R., & Sutton-Smith, B. (1995). The past in the present: Theoretical directions for children's folklore. In B. Sutton-Smith, J. Mechling, T. W. Johnson, & F. R. McMahon (Eds.), *Children's folklore: A source book* (pp. 293–308). New York: Garland Publishing.

McRobbie, A. (1992). Post-Marxism and cultural studies: A post-script. In L. Grossberg, C. Nelson, & P. Treichler (Eds.), *Cultural studies* (pp. 719–730). New York: Routledge.

Meier, D. (1995). *The power of their ideas: Lessons for America from a small school in Harlem.* Boston: Beacon Press.

Miles, J. (1995). *God: A Biography.* New York: Alfred A. Knopf.

Miller, P. (1982). *Amy, Wendy, and Beth: Learning language in South Baltimore.* Austin, TX: University of Texas Press.

Miller, W. (1995, May 22). [Cartoon]. *The New Yorker,* p. 53.

Moll, L., & Whitmore, K. (1993). Vygotsky in classroom practice: Moving from individual transmission to social transaction. In E. Forman, N. Minick, & C. A. Stone (Eds.), *Contexts for learning: Sociocultural dynamics in children's development* (pp. 19–42). New York: Oxford University Press.

Morrison, T. (1992). *Playing in the dark: Whiteness and the literary imagination.* New York: Vintage.

Moss, B. J. (1994). Creating community: Literacy events in African-American churches In B. J. Moss (Ed.), *Literacy across communities* (pp. 147–178). Cresskill, NJ: Hampton Press.

Moss, G. (1989). *Un/Popular Fictions.* London: Virago.

Moss, G. (1993). Children talk horror videos: Reading as a social performance. *Australian Journal of Education, 37,* 169–181.

Mukerji, C., & Schudson, M. (1991). *Rethinking popular culture: Contemporary perspectives in cultural studies.* Berkeley, CA: University of California Press.

Nabhan, G. P. (1994). A child's sense of wildness. In G. P. Nabhan & S. Trimble (Aus.), *The geography of childhood: Why children need wild places.* Boston: Beacon Press.

Narvaez, P., & Laba, M. (1986). The folklore-popular culture continuum. In P. Narvaez, & M. Laba (Eds.), *Media sense: The folklore-popular culture continuum* (pp. 1–8). Bowling Green, OH: Bowling Green State University Popular Press.

Needels, M. C., & Knapp, M. S. (1994). Teaching writing to children who are underserved. *Journal of Educational Psychology, 86,* 339–349.

The New London Group. (1996). A pedagogy of multiliteracies: Designing social futures. *Harvard Educational Review, 61,* 60–92.

Newman, F., & Holzman, L. (1993). *Lev Vygotsky: Revolutionary scientist.* New York: Routledge.

Nicolopoulou, A., Scales, B., & Weintraub, J. (1994). Gender differences and symbolic imagination in the stories of four-year-olds. In A. H. Dyson, & C. Genishi (Eds.), *The need for story: Cultural diversity in classroom and community* (pp. 102–123). Urbana, IL: National Council of Teachers of English.

Ochs, E. (1992). Indexing gender. In A. Duranti, & C. Goodwin (Eds.), *Rethinking context: Language as an interactive phenomenon* (pp. 335–358). Cambridge, London: Cambridge University Press.

Ogbu, J. (1987). Variability in minority school performance: A problem in search of an explanation. *Anthropology and Education Quarterly, 18,* 312–341.

O'Loughlin, M., Bierwiler, B., & Serra, M. (1996). *The possibilities of literacy in an urban school: Report of a field study.* Paper presented at the Annual Meeting of the American Educational Research Association, New York, NY.

Opie, I. (1993). *The people in the playground.* Oxford: Oxford University Press.

Opie, I., & Opie, P. (1959). *The lore and language of school children.* London: Oxford University Press.

Opie, I., & Opie, P. (1985). *The singing game.* Oxford: Oxford University Press.

Orfield, G. (1993). *The growth of segregation in American schools: Changing patterns of segregation and poverty since 1968.* Report of the Harvard Project on School Desegregation to the National School Boards Association. Cambridge, MA: Harvard University. (ERIC Document Reproduction Service No. ED 366 689).

Paley, V. (1980). *Wally's stories.* Cambridge, MA: Harvard University Press.

Paley, V. (1984). *Boys and girls: Superheroes in the dollcorner.* Chicago: University of Chicago Press.

Paley, V. (1987). On listening to what children say. In M. Okazawa-Rey, J. Anderson, & R. Traves (Eds.), *Teaching, teachers, and teacher education* (pp. 77–86). Cambridge, MA: Harvard College.

Palmer, P. (1986). *The lively audience: A study of children around the TV set.* Sydney, Australia: Allen & Unwin.

Perry, T., & Fraser, J. (Eds.). (1993). *Freedom's Plow: Teaching in a multicultural classroom.* New York: Routledge.

Piaget, J., & Inhelder, B. (1969). *The psychology of the child.* New York: Basic Books.

Polakow, V. (1993). *Lives on the edge: Single mothers and their children in the other America.* Chicago: University of Chicago Press.

Pratt, M. L. (1987). Linguistic utopias. In N. Fabb, D. Attridge, A. Durant, & C. MacCabe (Eds.), *The linguistics of writing: Arguements between language and literature* (pp. 48–66). New York: Methuen.

Ramsey, P. (1987). *Teaching and learning in a diverse world: Multicultural education for young children.* New York: Teachers College Press.

Rizzo, T.A., & Corsaro, W. (1991, April). *Social support processes in early childhood friendships.* Paper presented at the biennial meeting of the Society for Research in Child Development, Seattle.

Rogoff, B. (1990). *Apprenticeship in thinking.* New York: Oxford University Press.

Rogoff, B. (1994). Developing understanding of the idea of communities of learners. *Mind, Culture, and Activity: An International Journal, 1,* 209–229.

Rosaldo, R. (1989). *Culture and truth: The remaking of social analysis.* Boston: Beacon Press.

Rosaldo, R., Lavie, S., & Narayan, K. (1993). Introduction: Creativity in anthropology. In S. Lavie, K. Narayan, & R. Rosaldo (Eds.), *Creativity/Anthropology* (pp. 1–10). Ithaca, NY: Cornell University Press.

Rosen, C., & Rosen, H. (1974). *The language of primary school children.* Harmondsworth, Middlesex, England: Penguin.

Russell, H. (with Davey, G., & Factor, J.). (1986). *Play and friendships in a multicultural playground.* Melbourne, Australia: Australian Children's Folklore Publications.

Sachar, L. (1985). *The sideways stories.* New York: Avon Books.

Sahni, U. (1994). *Building circles of mutuality: A socio-cultural analysis of literacy in a rural classroom in India.* Unpublished doctoral dissertation, University of California, Berkeley.

Schieffelin, B., & Cochran-Smith, M. (1984). Learning to read culturally: Literacy before schooling. In H. Goelman, A. A. Oberg, & F. Smith (Eds.), *Awakening to literacy* (pp. 3–23). Exeter, NH: Heinemann.

Schofield, J. W. (1979). The impact of positively structured contact or intergroup behavior: Does it last under adverse conditions? *Social Psychology Quarterly, 42,* 280–284.

Schofield, J. W. (1989). *Black and White in school: Trust, tension or tolerance?* New York: Teachers College Press.

Scott, J. C. (1997). Practice what you preach: Preach what you practice. In A. H. Dyson (Ed.), *What differences does difference make?: Teacher perspectives on diversity, literacy, and the urban primary school* (pp. 172–179). Urbana, IL: National Council of Teachers of English.

Scott, J. W. (1988). Deconstructing equality-versus-difference: Or, The uses of poststructuralist theory for feminism. *Feminist Studies, 14,* 33–50.

Seiter, E. (1993). *Sold separately: Children and parents in consumer culture.* New Brunswick, NJ: Rutgers University Press.

Serreau, C. with Cinea Eniloc Films (Producer), & Serreau, C. (Director). (1989). *Mama, there's a man in your bed* [film]. New York: Miramax films with P. Carcassonne and J. L. Piel.

Sims, R. (1982). *Shadow and substance: Afro-American experience in contemporary children's fiction.* Urbana, IL: National Council of Teachers of English.

Slavin, R. E. (1983). *Cooperative learning.* New York: Longman.

Sleeter, C. (1993). How white teachers construct race. In E. McCarthy, & W. Crichlow (Eds.), *Race, identity, and representation in education* (pp. 157–171). New York: Routledge.

Smith, A. D. (1993). *Fires in the mirror.* New York: Bantam Doubleday.

Smitherman, G. (1977/1986). *Talkin' and testifyin': The language of Black America.* Detroit: Wayne State University Press.

Spickard, P. R. (1989). *Mixed blood: Intermarriage and ethnic identity in twentieth-century America.* Madison, WI: University of Wisconsin Press.

Spigel, L., & Jenkins, H. (1991). Same Bat channel, different Bat times: Mass culture and popular memory. In Pearson, R. & Uricchio, W. (Eds.), *The many lives of the Batman* (pp. 118–144). New York: Routledge Publishing.

Stam, R. (1991). Bakhtin, polyphony and ethnic/racial representation. In L. D. Friedman (Ed.), *Unspeakable images: Ethnicity and the American cinema* (pp. 251–276). Chicago: University of Illinois Press.

Steedman, C. (1992). *Past tenses: Essays on writing, autobiography, and history.* London: Rivers Oram Press.

Stern, S., & Schoenhaus, T. (1990). *Toyland: The high-stakes game of the toy industry.* Chicago: Contemporary Books.

Storey, J. (1993). *An introductory guide to cultural theory and popular culture.* Athens, GA: University of Georgia Press.

Stratemeyer, E. (Creator). (1930). *Nancy Drew Mystery Stories.* New York: Grosset & Dunlap.

Sullivan, C. W. III. (1995). Songs, poems, and rhymes. In B. Sutton-Smith, J. Mechling, T. W. Johnson, & F. R. McMahon (Eds.), *Children's folklore: A source book* (pp. 145–160). New York: Garland Publishing Inc.

Sutton-Smith, B. (1975). The importance of storytaker: An investigation of the imaginative life. *Urban Review, 8,* 82–95.

Sutton-Smith, B. (1989). Play as performance, rhetoric, and metaphor. *Play and Culture, 2,* 189–192.

Sutton-Smith, B. (1990). School playground as festival. *Children's Environmental Quarterly, 7,* 3–7.

Sutton-Smith, B. (1995). The persuasive rhetorics of play. In A. Pellegrini (Ed.), *The future of play theory: A multidisiplinary inquiry into the contributions of Brian Sutton-Smith* (pp. 275–296). Albany, NY: State University of New York Press.

Sutton-Smith, B., Mechling, J., Johnson, T. W., & McMahon, F. R. (Eds.). (1995). *Children's folklore: A source book.* New York: Garland Publishing.

Takaki, R. T. (1993). *A different mirror: A history of multicultural America.* Boston: Little, Brown.

Tatar, M. (1992). *Off with their heads! Fairy tales and the culture of childhood.* Princeton, NJ: Princeton University Press.

Taxel, J. (1992). The politics of children's literature: Reflections on multiculturalism, political correctness, and Christopher Columbus. In V. Harris (Ed.), *Teaching multicultural literature in Grades K–8* (pp. 1–36). Norwood, MA: Christopher-Gordon.

Thomas, L. (1992). *The fragile species.* New York: Maxwell McMillan International.

Thorne, B. (1987). Re-visioning women and social change: where are the children? *Gender & Society, 1,* 85–109.

Thorne, B. (1993). *Gender play: Girls and boys in school.* New Brunswick, NJ: Rutgers University Press.

Tsing, A. L. (1993). "Riding the horse of gaps": A meratus woman's spiritual expression. In S. Lavie, K. Narayan, & R. Rosaldo (Eds.), *Creativity/Anthropology* (pp. 185–196). Ithaca, NY: Cornell University Press.

Tucker, E. (1980). The dramatization of children's narratives. *Western Folklore, 39,* 184–197.

Tucker, E. (1981). Danger and control in children's storytelling. *ARV—The Scandinavian Yearbook of Folklore,* 141–146.

Tucker, E. (1992). Texts, lies and videotape: Can oral tales survive? *Children's Folklore Review, 15,* 25–32.

Tucker, E. (1995). Tales and legends. In B. Sutton-Smith, J. Mechling, T. W. Johnson, & F. R. McMahon. (Eds.), *Children's folklore: A source book* (pp. 193–211). New York: Garland Publishing.

Turnbull, S. (1993). The media: Moral lessons and moral careers. *Australian Journal of Education, 37,* 153–168.

Turner, P. A. (1994). *Ceramic uncles and celluloid mammies: Black images and their influence on culture.* New York: Anchor Books.

Volosinov, V. N. (1973). *Marxism and the philosophy of language* (L. Matejka & I. R. Titunik, Trans.). New York: Seminar Press.

Vygotsky, L. S. (1962). *Thought and language.* Cambridge, MA: MIT Press.

Vygotsky, L. S. (1978). *Mind in society.* Cambridge, MA: Harvard University Press.

Vygotsky, L. S. (1987). *L.S. Vygotsky, collected works: Volume 1, Problems of general psychology.* New York: Plenum Books.

Wagner, B.J. (1991). Imaginative expression. In J. Flood (Ed.), *Handbook of research in teaching the English language arts* (pp. 787–804). New York: Macmillan.

Walkerdine, V. (1985). Someday my prince will come: Young girls and the preparation for adolescent sexuality. In A. McRobbie & M. Nava (Eds.), *Gender and generation* (pp. 162–184). London: Macmillan.

Walkerdine, V. (1986). Video replay: Families, films, and fantasy. In V. Burgin, J. Donald, & C. Kaplan (Eds.), *Formations of fantasy* (pp. 167–199). New York: Routledge.

Walkerdine, V. (1990). *Schoolgirl fictions.* London: Verso.

Wallace, J. (1995). Technologies of "the child": Towards a theory of the child-subject. *Textual Practice, 9,* 285–302.

Walters, D. (1995, October 20). School reform in law, finally. *Sacramento Bee,* p. A3.

Warner, M. (1994). *From the beast to the blonde: On fairy tales and their tellers.* London: Chatto & Windus.

Warner, P. (1990). Fantastic outsiders: Villains and deviants in animated cartoons. In. C. R. Sanders (Ed.), *Marginal conventions: Popular culture, mass media and social deviance* (pp. 117–130). Bowling Green, OH: Bowling Green State University Popular Press.

Watson-Gegeo, K. (1992). Thick explanation in the ethnographic study of child socialization: A longitudinal study of the problem of schooling for Kwara-ae (Solomon Islands) children. In W. Corsaro & P. Miller (Eds.), *Interpretive approaches to children's socialization* (pp. 51–66). San Francisco: Jossey-Bass.

Weber, M. (1978). *Selections in translation* (E. Mathews, Trans.). Cambridge, London: Cambridge University Press. (Original work published 1922).

Wertsch, J. V. (1991). *Voices of the mind: A sociocultural approach to mediated action.* Cambridge, MA: Harvard University Press.

Williams, P. J. (1991). *The alchemy of race and rights.* Cambridge, MA: Harvard University Press.

Williams, P. J. (1995). *The rooster's egg: On the persistence of prejudice.* Cambridge, MA: Harvard University Press.

Williams, R. (1983). *Keywords* (Rev. ed.). New York: Oxford University Press.

Willis, P. (1977). *Learning to labour.* London: Gower.

Willis, P. (1990). *Common culture.* Boulder, CO: Westview Press.

Wolf, M. (1992). *A thrice told tale: Feminism, postmodernism, and ethnographic responsibility.* Stanford, CA: Stanford University Press.

Zelinzer, V. (1985). *Pricing the priceless child: The changing social value of children.* New York: Basic Books.

Zimmerman, B. (1991). *Greek tragedy: An introduction.* Baltimore, MD: Johns Hopkins Press.

Zipes, J. (1993). *The trials and tribulations of Little Red Riding Hood.* South Hadley, MA: Bergin & Gervey.

Zumwalt, R. (1995). The complexity of children's folklore. In B. Sutton-Smith, J. Mechling, T. W. Johnson, & F. R. McMahon (Eds.), *Children's folklore: A source book* (pp. 23–47). New York: Garland Publishing.

Index

▼ ▼ ▼

About the Author

▼ ▼ ▼

Anne Haas Dyson is a former teacher of young children and, currently, Professor of Language, Literacy, and Culture in the School of Education at the University of California at Berkeley. A graduate of the University of Wisconsin–Madison and the University of Texas at Austin, she studies the social lives and literacy learning of schoolchildren. Among her publications are *The Need for Story: Cultural Diversity in Classroom and Community* (coedited with Celia Genishi), *Multiple Worlds of Child Writers: Friends Learning to Write*, and *Social Worlds of Children Learning to Write in an Urban Primary School*, which was awarded NCTE's David Russell Award for Distinguished Research in 1994.